Diversity in Theory and Practice

Diversity in Theory and Practice
News Journalists in Sweden and Germany

Heike Graf (ed.)

NORDICOM

Diversity in Theory and Practice

News Journalists in Sweden and Germany

Heike Graf (ed.)

ISBN 978-91-86523-12-1

Published by:
Nordicom
University of Gothenburg
Box 713
SE 405 30 Göteborg
Sweden

Cover by: Roger Palmqvist
Printed by: Litorapid Media AB, Göteborg, Sweden, 2011
Environmental certification according to ISO 14001

Contents

Foreword

As this book goes to press, Swedish voters have for the first time elected an anti-immigrant party, the Sweden Democrats, to parliament. One of the party's main goals is to have much lower levels of immigration and a return to what it sees as a policy of assimilation. This party is also a "protest party", and appears to have tapped into voter dissatisfaction regarding such issues as how previous governments have handled globalization, immigration, and integration through the years. This current event is one of many indications showing that diversity issues, which are closely connected to globalization processes, have become a burning issue for society, and a highly relevant research issue for scholars.

This book is about immigration, more precisely about diversity and integration of migrant media workers into the labor market; it is about expectations, disappointments, problems, and also solutions. It sheds light on how media workers experience their working conditions according to ethnic diversity. This book is a result of an interdisciplinary research project that brings together work in sociology, journalism, and media studies. Field studies have been carried out in newsrooms located in two countries: Sweden and Germany.

I would like to thank the Baltic Sea Foundation, Sweden for the financing that has made the project and also this book possible. Last but not least I wish to express my immense gratitude to the publisher, Nordicom, and its director professor Ulla Carlsson for their work with the manuscript and their financial support.

Stockholm, January 2011

Heike Graf

Introduction

Heike Graf & Jan Inge Jönhill

The idea behind this project first arose in 2005, as a result of discussions on stereotypes in media reporting on migrants. The following questions inspired our research: Who are the journalists behind these reports, and do they have migrant experiences of their own, or not? How culturally diverse are newsrooms, actually? We then noted the low percentage of migrant journalists in newsrooms (between 2-5 percent), and the lack of statistics and research on this in both Sweden and Germany, and became interested in closing this gap. Some ad-hoc field studies in Germany – undertaken before we applied for funding in 2006 – have indicated that this issue of cultural diversity in newsrooms is seen as a non-issue, and in an interview we received the response that it is also irrelevant: "The only thing that counts is the professionalism, nobody is interested in where a person comes from". Our first impression of this response was that it was a mixture of ignorance and wishful thinking, and was also a defensive lie. We became even more interested in doing research on journalists with migrant backgrounds in the mainstream media.

Since then, the original idea has developed. When we eventually received funding from the Baltic Sea Foundation in January 2007 (until December 2009), we could begin. Our project was titled "Lines of Diversity: Multicultural Perspectives on Journalistic Production in Stockholm and Berlin" and aimed at increasing knowledge about journalistic production processes with a focus on ethnic diversity, based on empirical research in Swedish and German newsrooms. Simply, we wanted to know: How do journalists with migrant backgrounds experience their working conditions, career possibilities, and their possibilities of influencing media coverage? How does ethnic diversity contribute to a changed media coverage? Our method was primarily based on semi-structured interviews with editorial staff working on permanent contracts or/and fixed term contracts, and with freelancers working for Swedish or German newsrooms. The interviews were completed with other forms of material such as reports, policy documents, inquiries and other documents, in order to obtain knowledge about contextual conditions.

In order to address our research questions, a total of 48 persons were interviewed: 35 of them have migrant backgrounds, and work in the press, TV, and radio; and 21 of them (all with migrant backgrounds) live in Germany, the rest in Sweden. We restricted our investigation to journalists working for mainstream news media in the capitals of Stockholm and Berlin. In both cities, multicultural ideals have influenced all sectors, not least of all media (see Hultén & Graf in this volume). Our comparative way of working has helped us to emphasize the similarities and differences between news media in both cities. Our comparative analyses of diversity in newsrooms in Stockholm in relation to newsrooms in Berlin for instance, enable us to shed light upon aspects which were usually taken for granted and therefore 'invisible' in our singular observations.

In general, we can conclude that media organizations in both countries face similar challenges and that journalists talk about similar experiences, but that there are also differences. Sweden has more years of experience in working with diversity issues, while Germany has only recently begun discussing diversity in the media. Some Swedish media organizations have introduced documented diversity plans in order to systematically implement cultural diversity in the organizations. As a result, one can assume that at the beginning the expectations were higher than the results ultimately revealed, and some journalists expressed their disappointments over the lack of progress (see both Hultén and Camauër in this volume). In Germany, the process of implementing diversity is at an initial stage, and many journalists experience positive effects as a result of their migrant backgrounds. Active diversity measures in the form of documented diversity plans, as we know from Sweden, are conspicuous by their absence (with only a few exceptions, including two public service organizations), and are more dependent on single ad-hoc decisions within the specific work places than on systematically documented strategies (see Hultén & Graf in this volume). However, the concept of diversity management that is applied within some German media organizations tries to unite diversity efforts with economic benefits, with the belief that staff members with different ethnic origins are a potential for the company (see Jönhill in this volume). Especially in the case of Germany, most of the interviewed journalists have expressed that a major hindrance to diverse newsrooms is the assumption that a migrant background implies less competence in contrast to adding more and different competences to the newsrooms (see Graf in this volume).

Earlier Research on Media and Diversity

Research on media and diversity in both countries has mainly focused on content analysis, or more precisely, on how immigrants are covered by the mass media (see Horsti 2008 for reviews on Nordic research). In line with research from Germany and other countries such as the USA, immigrants are associated with threats and conflict, which leads to negative attitudes towards immigrants in society, which then tends to reinforce stereotypes of the "other" (e.g. Brune 2004, Campbell 1995, Cottle 2000, Hultén 2001, 2006, Löwander 1997, Ruhrmann & Kollmer 1987, Ruhrmann 1995, Merten & Ruhrmann 1986, Hömberg & Schlemmer 1995, ter Wal 2002, Tufte 2003, van Dijk 1991, 1993).

As early as in the middle years of the sixties, the American Kerner-Commission discredited news coverage on African American residents in the press as biased and "'from the standpoint of the white man's world'" (cit. Cottle 2000: 86). The proposed solution was to train and hire, in the American case, more African American journalists and editors within the mainstream press. More minority newsroom personnel would bring new perspectives to the newsrooms and equitable coverage, the Commission concluded (Cottle 2000: 86). However, research has also shown that there is no causality between more minority media workers and changes in media coverage. For example, it has been found that the increased recruitment of African American journalists did not lead to any remarkable changes in news reporting (Wilson 2000: 87). The same goes for studies on the increased numbers of female media workers (see Eide 1993, Zilliacus-Tikkanen 1997, van Zoonen 1994).

Since the Kerner-Commission, little research has been done on immigrant journalists in mainstream media, but such research has increased in recent years in both countries. On the one hand, we now have statistical information on the representation of journalists with migrant backgrounds in the media – at least in Sweden (see Hultén & Graf in this volume). On the other hand, there were only several studies conducted on these issues. Djerf-Pierre & Levin (2005) have published a small study – on the basis of four interviews – on how journalists with foreign origins experience their careers and how their origins gain importance within the workplace. The authors reveal an ambivalence within Swedish media: On the one hand the media, especially the public service media, want to recruit more immigrant journalists, but on the other hand economic constraints say stop. The ambivalence appears when media criticize discrimination in other fields of society yet discrimination within their own organization, that is, in newsrooms, is not on the agenda (Djerf-Pierre & Levin 2005: 218). Camauër (2006) takes as her starting point within the discrimination discourse an exploration of structural discrimination within Swedish newsrooms. Based on 10 interviews with journalists of foreign origins, the author locates the main fields of discrimination, which take place in connection with recruitment, forms of employment contracts, and treatment by peers and superiors (Camauër 2006: 75).

Whereas the discourse on migrant journalists' representation in the media in recent years in Sweden is mainly focused on discrimination, the discourse in Germany takes a broader approach of exploring integration within society. The first major studies on migrants in newsrooms were published in 2009 (see also Hultén & Graf in this volume). In connection with a research program on media integration of ethnic minorities, a representative quantitative and partly qualitative study on journalists with migrant backgrounds in German newspapers was released (Geissler & Pöttker 2009). The report delivers facts on representation of those journalists in newsrooms and also some brief examples of how they describe their work experiences. Fifty-five journalists filled in a questionnaire, describing their working conditions in different terms, varying between being an asset to their workplace to not being taken seriously (Geissler & Pöttker 2009: 111-112). Another study within the same research project is based on qualitative interviews with 13 journalists with migrant backgrounds and with 10 managers from different media organizations, in order to explore why those journalists are underrepresented in media (Oulios 2009: 123). The author concludes that it is necessary to go beyond the myth of 'it is only job skills that count' to hire a migrant journalist – as articulated by the managers – because most of the interviewed journalists experience the opposite (Oulios 2009: 140).

Applying Normative or Descriptive Approaches?

Research on these issues of coverage of minorities in the media and of migrant journalists' representation in newsrooms mainly makes use of normative theories. It takes its starting point e.g. from postcolonial theories claiming that the domestic media discourse on minorities is grounded in constructing the 'other' in relation to a normative self that is 'better': the other is under-developed and under-civilized in relation to a developed and civilized self. Studies on media have shown, according to these theories, that media display a conscious sense of being above or better than 'the other' (e.g. Löwander 1997, Brune 2004, Hall 1997, Ristilammi 2002).

According to normative theories, media and journalistic practice are both researched from the ideal functions of the media, that is, what the media, and the newsrooms *should* do. Here, the starting points are political theories based on e.g. Charles Taylor (1999) and Jürgen Habermas (1999) stressing the politics of equal recognition of all people and their cultures as a basic human need in a multicultural society, in contrast to a forced assimilation and uprooting. As an example, society *should* integrate Muslim immigrants not by going against their religion, but by incorporating it into Western society (Habermas 2008). In line with these political theories, the media have been ascribed the function of integrating all members of society by a media coverage mirroring the ideal of multicultural societies, and by a staff representing different ethnic cultures within newsrooms. The media are expected to "support the dominant values and moral standards of their own society" (McQuail 2000: 146), that is, the norms of a multicultural society.

Media research is, within this approach, about exploring media's fulfillment of this role or not, and if not, why. In this respect, Anglo-American research pays attention to questions of 'race' by revealing media's participation in racialization, that is, the reproduction of race thinking through media content and within media institutions (e.g. Downing & Husband 2005). In Sweden, the scholarly discourse is very much determined by media's failure to adequately address integration issues. Regarding the representation of media workers with migrant backgrounds in the media, the discourse is focused on discrimination, and partially on structural discrimination (see Nohrstedt & Camauër 2006) in order to find explanations and ways of changing practice. Also in Germany, the academic media and migration discourse is dominated by the normative ideal of integration. As an example, the major research project on media and migration at the University of Siegen explores media's and especially the media worker's role in socially integrating people with migrant backgrounds into society (Geissler & Pöttker 2006: 7). In line with Habermas, the key term of "intercultural integration" is based on the ideal principle of 'unity within diversity' and does not mean assimilation or segregation. In other words, "the right of minorities to be different, limited by the right of the majority to get respect for its laws and core values" (Geissler & Pöttker 2006: 15). According to that approach, an intercultural integration through media means, on the production level, the participation of immigrants in media production, and on the content level, implies a media coverage that supports intercultural integration (Geissler & Pöttker 2006: 23-24).

When researching the relationship between media and (multicultural) society it seems to be difficult to isolate normative or even ideological considerations. However, this normative approach can create problems if we see our study object only through a haze of normative distinctions, that is, good and bad, determining, if the newsroom is acting badly or not according to the norms of a multicultural society. A strictly normative perspective implies looking at phenomena where the media fulfil or do not fulfil the expected role. But if we want to take to account the different realities of a complex world, e.g. of the newsroom's own mode of operation, we observe that these realities are not always in accord with normative theories. Here, instead of looking at *how the media 'ought' to behave*, an alternative way of researching this issue could involve omitting the modal verbs 'ought' or 'should', to allow for an unprejudiced perspective. This perspective only focuses on the question of *how the media behave*.

The above is not only an analytical strategy but is also grounded in theories which are called 'descriptive'. These theories want to explain processes without (only) asking whether they are good or bad, or if they will turn out predictably. They take into consideration a differentiated and complex world that can be explained by a wide range of categories (not only normative categories). If we want to broaden the perspective and want to go beyond normative statements, we can generally make use of observation theories (e.g. Spencer-Brown 1969, von Foerster 1984, Luhmann 1997). Epistemologically, the starting point is basically 'empirical', by noticing the constructive character of our research.

In line with this approach, the interview answers of our informants are understood as constructions or descriptions of an experienced newsroom reality, and not as a blueprint of this reality. These descriptions are the results of observation, and are guided by distinctions that are drawn when describing a newsroom situation. According to observation theories, observing means generally drawing distinctions. It is by noting a difference that we become aware of things (first order observation). In other words: Differences are of relational quality: a thing is different only in relation to some other thing. As applied to our research question: If we want to say something about diversity in newsrooms, we can only say something about the relationship of the observer, the interviewee, to the observed, that is, the relationship of the interviewee to an addressed topic. More precisely, a distinction is not drawn by the world of the newsroom itself and does not describe a phenomenon. It is drawn by the interviewee in an interview situation, and describes a form of the phenomenon from the perspective of the observer, that is, the interviewee (Graf 2010).

This observation-related approach does not mean that we have to refuse normative considerations. Luhmann makes a distinction in the theory of observation between the first and second order observation, or in other words between the 'what' and 'how' level of observation (Luhmann 1997). On the first level, we speak here primarily about cognitive or descriptive differences of *what* is observed. These distinctions can become normative ones if we relate them to normative interpretation premises, that is, the observation of observation as a second order observation, where the *how* of the first observation level becomes visible. During the process of interpreting as an observation of second order, distinctions are coupled to other distinctions, and social structures begin to emerge. Then we can interpret these structures as mechanisms of discrimination in relation to something, but it can also be interpreted in another way. With this approach, we create an opening for other interpretations, but they are not arbitrary since they are related to the empirical outcome and accomplishment of interpreting according to the scientific system's own 'hows'.

We also apply 'scholarly diversity' in this volume, by using both approaches when doing our research. However, each author has to decide which approach s/he wants to use, because they cannot be combined.

Concepts of Ethnic or National Background and Social Identity

To do research on the subject of journalist production and ethnic diversity also raises the demand of discussing what is meant by 'ethnic' and 'ethnic diversity'. In its most general sense, ethnicity is an ascribed part of social relations between persons, who perceive and experience themselves as distinct from members of other groups, and where shared language and cultural traditions are the prominent features. According to a rather common definition, it includes only those with different backgrounds, heredity, or provenance than one's 'own' group. It is in this precise sense of a 'we' that the majority of a population in a given area can perceive, observe, and speak about a minority of others. As Peterson & Ålund argue, the concept of ethnicity has retained this connotation as a term for 'outsider' persons, "culturally alien, groups with minority status, of lower class or just migrants" (Peterson & Ålund 2007: 15). As such a concept, they argue, it is a political concept, a distinction marking political interests of power. We could add that ethnicity in this meaning is also a normative concept in which particular moral values of whatever kind define the 'good or bad' aspects of a certain ethnicity.

From the theory of knowledge we must assume that what we call reality is primarily a social and cognitive construction that is built on pragmatic grounds, i.e. it aims at understanding the world. Our way of constructing the world may but must not at all be normative, e.g. related to issues of political power. Comparative cultural studies, among others in cultural anthropology, suggest that we always tend towards a differentiation of 'we' and 'them', to designate members of other groups of people or other ethnic groups. From the so-called primitive societies some thousands of years ago until today, this has enabled an understanding of persons and groups in our environment, as among others the famous anthropologist Levi-Strauss has shown (Carlbom 2003). But the manner of designating the other or other persons or members of neighbour groups has varied. People around us are never just others and only in some contexts are designated according to what we may term ethnicity. In Eriksen's words:

> Individuals have many statuses and many possible identities, and it is an empirical question when and how ethnic identities become the most relevant ones. (Eriksen 2002: 31)

> There are situations where ethnicity is relatively unimportant and there are other situations where it provides a decisive mechanism for exclusion and inclusion as well as clear guidelines for behaviour. However, there are also contexts where it may be difficult to ascribe a definite ethnic identity to an individual. (Eriksen 2002: 62)

Ethnicity is, in other words, only one marker of the cultural identity of persons, and sometimes also of groups. Other markers of identity relate to our occupation or profession and/or to our role in a family. To conclude thus far, 'ethnic' connotes 'people', but is used as a word to distinguish some people from other people. Ethnicity is at the same time used as a distinguishing characteristic as related to national background.

As Eriksen stresses, it is very essential to distinguish nations from ethnic categories (Eriksen 2002). The nation-state is an invention of modern society. In the social sciences, modern society means the form of society that has been the dominating structure in Europe during a period of at least 150 years, and more or less all over the world since the last century. The emergence of the nation-state, as a typical characteristics of modern society, has had as one effect that it is no any longer 'ethnic' but national, characteristics connected to the nation-state that to a certain extent have shaped its culture. Ethnic background includes first and foremost a mother language, but also includes one's affinity as to religion and/or certain cultural practices, expectations and certain emotions which bind people. According to the definition in the political sciences from 'the classic' Karl Deutsch, a nation has emerged when a group of people come to formulate political and territorial goals (Johansson 1993). In this way, ethnicity connotes nationality, but in the modern history of nation building it is at the same time obvious that nations and ethnic categories must be distinguished.

One main feature of an ethnic group is thus that it encompasses people in a geographic area, which presupposes continuous cultural exchanges or communications among present persons. Another main feature is that ethnic background is inherited, and that persons cannot change their background. National belonging is, however, changeable.

A good reason to use the term ethnicity is that it marks definite differences in some distinct social and cultural contexts in society, and thus it marks the very fact that society is characterized by heterogeneity. During a long period of the 20th century society, at least from a Swedish perspective, society was officially said to be homogenous. During the last decades, the increases in global communication in many respects as well as increased immigration have resulted in a corresponding increase of heterogeneity in society.[1]

In many respects we do not have only a simple differentiation into minorities and an alleged majority. The migrant population itself becomes in the course of a generation differentiated. Some migrants find e.g. spouses within other ethnic or national groups, and then second-generation migrants have blended identities in this sense, as Daun notices (Daun 2001). In the global society of today, many persons and groups are in the situation of having several different ethnic relations. Some persons and groups also discover that they are minorities within minorities (Eisenberg & Spinner-Halev 2004).

In the following chapters in this volume, the authors have taken into account that the concept of ethnic may be problematic. In any case, the word ethnic will be used a bit differently, similar to the concept of culture, which is almost unavoidably defined differently by many authors and as related to different contexts.

The Structure of this Volume

This book is the result of an multidisciplinary project that brings together work in sociology, journalism and media studies drawing on both normative and empirical theories in order to analyze diversity in society and media organizations.

Chapter one by Gunilla Hultén and Heike Graf is a presentation of current contextual societal conditions in both countries, and briefly presents facts on migration, and Swedish and German media organizations within the framework of diversity measures. It begins with a brief description of the respective media landscapes and the composition of the migrant populations in Stockholm and Berlin, and provides examples of initiatives aiming at promoting cultural diversity within journalism. The authors argue that media organizations in both countries are facing similar problems in terms of diversity measures, but are seeking different solutions. Compared to Germany, Sweden seems to be the forerunner, with years of experience regarding media diversity efforts, while Germany has only recently given attention to these questions.

The second chapter by Jan Inge Jönhill takes its starting point from observation theory and systems theory, and provides a theoretical approach to questions of cultural diversity in organizations. By exploring the possibilities and limitations of mass media organizations regarding diversity issues, Jönhill stresses that organizations are highly complex systems that generally, according to Luhmann, treat "'all the same and everyone differently'" (Luhmann cit. on p. 66). In his chapter, he considers how 'locked' the strategic and organizational frames of the mass media organizations are in dealing with these issues. He also examines the organizational conditions for managing diversity issues, as implicated in accordance with common ideas of human rights, equal opportunity, and discrimination laws. He concludes by introducing the concept of diversity management as a new strategy to manage issues of cultural diversity in relation to journalist production and competence in media organizations. This concept implicates that ethnic or national backgrounds are weighed as qualifications.

Chapter three by Gunilla Hultén explores diversity in Swedish newsrooms by interviewing 14 journalists with foreign backgrounds. Starting from the fact that Swedish media organizations have launched a variety of diversity measures to improve diversity over the course of a decade, the author studies the outcome from the viewpoint of the journalists with migrant backgrounds. Hultén examines the "tension between the officially expressed attitudes and the diversity goals of Swedish newsrooms and how journalists who have foreign backgrounds perceive these" (p. 96). According to interviewees' experiences of hiring, advancement, language matters, and leadership issues, the author concludes that the outcome of diversity measures is discouraging, and much work on creating diverse newsrooms remains, e.g. especially within editorial organizations and newsroom cultures.

Chapter four by Heike Graf investigates how journalists with migrant backgrounds observe ethnicity in German newsrooms from a difference-theoretical approach. The study is based on interviews with 21 media workers with migrant backgrounds in German newsrooms of the mainstream media. The author analyzes interviewees' experiences of recruitment, working conditions, and career possibilities by exploring the distinctions the interviewees made in their answers. To interpret the responses, Graf uses the guiding distinction of inclusion/exclusion in order to examine the interdependencies of mechanisms of inclusion and exclusion in newsrooms as related to ethnic background. Graf concludes that a migrant background is seen as both an advantage and a disadvantage, and as part of one's competence as well as indicating a lack of competence. Lasting exclusion mechanisms in newsrooms occur e.g. "when an ethnic background is simply read as being less competent, and this leads to fewer or no job opportunities" (p. 146).

Chapter 5 by Leonor Camaüer sheds light on the impact of the presence of ethnic minority media workers in Swedish newsrooms. Camaüer presents findings from an interview study with 12 media workers of non-migrant backgrounds. The account of these results include the views of Swedish journalists as to the specificity and novelty of the contributions of their minority colleagues, the Swedish journalists' arguments for increased diversity in the newsrooms, and their sense of how professional routines and overarching institutional conditions often hinder the employment of minority media workers as well as their ability to contribute to a more diverse journalistic output. Using the theoretical framework of actual and imagined communities of practice, the study also assesses how Swedish media workers solve tensions between the core values of the latter and the institutional constraints of the former. The main contributions of the minority media workers, as experienced by their Swedish colleagues, were the different range of networks, perspectives, and experiences of the former, as well as the positive impact of their participation in newsroom discussions. Swedish media workers were typically constructed as lacking insight and networks when it came to their experiences and interactions with minority groups. Both are necessary in order to achieve a more diverse output.

Note

1. In a book with the witty title *Is it possible to be both black and Swedish? Texts on racism, anti-Semitism and Nazism* (Jacobsson, I. & Bruchfeld, S. 1999) the authors, among others, present interviews with young immigrants showing how they in their daily life manage the fact of being both 'Swedish' and e.g. black. Being 'Swedish' obviously does not mean ethnic to the interviewed persons.

References

Brune, Y. (2004) *Nyheter från gränsen. Tre studier i journalistik om 'invandrare', flyktingar och rasistiskt våld.* [News from the border. Three studies in journalism on the 'immigrants', refugees and racial violence]. Göteborg: JMG.

Camauër, L. (2006) 'Mediearbetare med utländsk bakgrund och majoritetsmediers diskriminerings-mekanismer' [Media workers of foreign origin and majority media discrimination mechanisms], in Nohrstedt, S.A. & Camauër, L. (ed.) *Mediernas Vi och Dom. Mediernas betydelse för den strukturella diskrimineringen* [Us and them. The media's role in structural discrimination], SOU: 2006: 21. Stockholm: Justitiedepartementet.

Campbell, C. (1995) *Race, myth and the news.* Thousand Oaks, London, New Delhi: Sage Publications.

Carlbom, A. (2003) *The imagined versus the real other. Multiculturalism and the representation of muslims in Sweden.* Lund: Lund University, Lund Monographs in Social Anthropology 12, Dept. of Sociology.

Cottle, S. (2000) *Ethnic minorities and the media.* Buckingham, Philadelphia: Open University Press.

Daun, Å. (2001) Identity transformations in Sweden, in Dacyl, J. (ed.) *Challenges of cultural diversity in Europe.* Stockholm: Stockholm University, Centre for Research in International Migration and Ethnic Relations.

van Dijk, T.A. (1991) *Racism and the press.* London & New York: Routledge.

van Dijk, T.A. (1993) *Elite discourse and racism.* London: Sage.

Djerf-Pierre, M. & Levin, A. (2005) 'Mediefältets janusansikte: medieeliten, journalisterna och mångfalden' [Media's Janus face. Media elites, journalists and diversity], in Göransson, A. (ed.) *Makten och mångfalden. Eliter och etnicitet i Sverige* [Power and diversity. Elites and ethnicity in Sweden], Ds 2005: 12. Stockholm: Justitiedepartementet.

Downing, J. & Husband, C. (2005) *Representing 'race': Racisms, ethnicities and media.* London: Sage.

Eide, A. (1993) *New approaches to minority protection.* London: Minority Rights Group.

Eisenberg, A. & Spinner-Halev, J. (eds) (2004) *Minorities within minorities. Equality, rights and diversity.* Cambridge: Cambridge University Press.

Eriksen, T.H. (2002) *Ethnicity and nationalism: Anthropological perspectives* (2nd ed.). London: Pluto Press.

von Foerster, H. (1984[1960]) *Observing systems.* 2. ed. Seaside, Calif.: Intersystems Publications.

Geissler, R. & Pöttker, H. (eds) (2006) *Integration durch Massenmedien. Mass Media-Integration. Medien und Migration im internationalen Vergleich. Media and Migration: A comparative Perspective.* Bielefeld: transcript-Verlag.

Geissler, R. & Pöttker, H. (eds) (2009) *Massenmedien und die Integration ethnischer Minderheiten in Deutschland* [Mass media and the integration of ethnic minorities in Germany], Bielefeld: transcript-Verlag.

Graf, H. (2010) 'Interviewing media workers', *Mediekultur. Journal of media and communication research,* Denmark, 49: 94-107.

Habermas, J. (1999) 'Kampen för ömsesidigt erkännande i den demokratiska rättsstaten' [The struggle for mutual recognition in the constitutional state], in Taylor, C.: *Det mångkulturella samhället och erkännandets politik* [Multiculturalism and the politics of recognition]. Göteborg: Daidalos.

Habermas, J. (2008) Retrieved March 20, 2010 from http://www.eurozine.com/articles/2008-04-15-habermas-de.html.

Hall, S. (1997) 'The spectacle of the 'Other'', in *Representation: Cultural representations and signifying practices*. London: Sage Publications.

Horsti, K. (2008) 'Overview of Nordic media research on immigration and ethnic relations: From text analysis to the study of production, uses and reception', *Nordicom Review* 29(2): 275-294.

Hömberg, W. & Schlemmer, S. (1995) 'Fremde als Objekt. Asylberichterstattung in deutschen Tageszeitungen', *Media Perspektiven* 1: 11-20.

Hultén, G. (2001) '50 år med främlingen' [50 years of strangers], in Lindblom Hulthén, A. (ed.) *Journalisternas bok 1901-2001*. [The book of the journalists 1901-2001], Stockholm: Journalistförbundet.

Hultén, G. (2006) 'Främlingar i nationens spegel' [The stranger in the mirror of the nation], in Nohrstedt, S.A. & Camauër, L.: *Mediernas Vi och Dom. Mediernas betydelse för den strukturella diskrimineringen* [Us and them. The media's role in the structural discrimination], SOU: 2006: 21 Stockholm: Justitiedepartementet.

Jacobsson, I. & Bruchfeld, S. (1999) *Kan man vara svart och svensk?: texter om rasism, antisemitism och nazism* [Is it possible to be both black and Swedish? Texts on racism, anti-Semitism and Nazism]. Stockholm: Naturochkultur

Johansson, R. (1993) 'Nationer och nationalism: Teoretiska och empiriska aspekter' [Nations and nationalism. Theoretical and empirical aspects], in Tägil, S. (ed.) *Den problematiska etniciteten. Nationalism, migration och samhällsomvandling,* [The problematic ethnicity. Nationalism, migration and change of the society]. Lund: Lund University Press.

Löwander, B. (1997) *Rasism och antirasism på dagordningen – studier av televisionens nyhetsrapportering i början av 1990-talet* [Racism and anti-racism on the agenda. Studies on TV news reporting at the beginning of the 1990s]. Umeå: Sociologiska institutionen, Umeå universitet.

Luhmann, N. (1997) *Die Gesellschaft der Gesellschaft* [The society of the society]. Bd.1, Frankfurt a. Main: Suhrkamp.

McQuail, D. (2000) *Mass communication theory*. London: Sage.

Merten, K. & Ruhrmann, G. (1986) *Das Bild der Ausländer in der deutschen Presse. Ergebnisse einer systematischen Inhaltsanalyse* [The image of the foreigner in the German press. Results of a systematic content analysis]. Frankfurt a. M.: Daǧyeli.

Nohrstedt, S.A. & Camauër, L. (2006) *Mediernas Vi och Dom. Mediernas betydelse för den strukturella diskrimineringen* [Us and them. Media's role of the structural discrimination], SOU: 2006: 21 Stockholm: Justitiedepartementet.

Oulios, M. (2009) 'Weshalb gibt es so wenig Journalisten mit Einwanderungshintergrund in deutschen Massenmedien' [Why are there so few journalists with migrant backgrounds in German mass media], in Geissler, R. & Pöttker, H. (eds) *Massenmedien und die Integration ethnischer Minderheiten in Deutschland* [Mass media and the integration of ethnic minorities in Germany], Bielefeld: transcript-Verlag.

Peterson, A. & Ålund, A. (2007) 'Ras, kön, klass, identitet och kultur' [Race, gender, class, identity, and culture), in Hjerm, M. & Peterson, A. (ed.) *Etnicitet. Perspektiv på samhället* [Ethnicity. Perspectives on society]. Malmö: Gleerups.

Ristilammi, P.- M. et al. (eds) (2002) *Miljonprogram och media. Föreställningar om människor och förorter* [Housing program and media. Representations of people and of suburbs]. Norrköping, Stockholm: Integrationsverket och Riksantikvarieämbetet.

Ruhrmann, G. & Kollmer, J. (1987) *Ausländerberichterstattung in der Kommune.* [Coverage of foreigners in local newspapers]. Opladen: Westdeutscher Verl.

Ruhrmann, G. (ed.) (1995) *Das Bild der Ausländer in der Öffentlichkeit. Eine theoretische und empirische Analyse zur Fremdenfeindlichkeit* [The image of the foreigner in public. A theoretical and empirical analysis of xenophobia]. Opladen: Leske+Budrich.

Spencer-Brown, G. (1969) *Laws of form*. London: George Allen and Unwin Ltd.

Taylor, C. (1999) *Det mångkulturella samhället och erkännandets politik* [Multiculturalism and the politics of recognition]. Göteborg: Daidalos

ter Wal, J. (ed.) (2002) *Racism and cultural diversity in the mass media*. Vienna: The European Monitoring Centre on Racism and Xenophobia.

Tufte, T. (ed.) (2003) *Medierne, minoriteterne og det multikulturelle samfund. Skandinaviske perspektiver* [Media, minorities and the multicultural society. Scandinavian perspectives]. Göteborg: Nordicom.

Wilson II, C. (2000) 'The paradox of African American Journalists', in Cottle, S. (ed.) *Ethnic minorities and the media*. Buckingham, Philadelphia: Open University Press.

Zilliacus-Tikkanen, H. (1997) *Journalistikens essens i ett könsperspektiv* [Journalism's essence from a gender perspective]. Helsingfors: Rundradions jämställdhetskommitté.

van Zoonen, L. (1994) *Feminist Media Studies*. London: Sage.

Exploring Media and Ethnic Diversity in Sweden and Germany

Gunilla Hultén & Heike Graf

The way media are organized in both Sweden and Germany falls under the category of democratic corporatist, according to Hallin and Mancini (2004). The publishing sector is an important part of the democratic corporatist model, and both countries have high levels of newspaper readership with Sweden's being one of the highest in the world. There is a competitive market for print media, but despite this the market is – especially in Sweden – regulated by different measures such as press subsidies. The Swedish and the German media systems are also 'duopolies', where public service broadcasters coexist alongside commercially funded companies, with the public service broadcasters still remaining comparatively strong. Both countries also have a high level of journalistic professionalization, including the sharing of professional standards and a tradition of public-sector involvement in the media landscape (Hallin & Mancini 2004: 145).

Since the beginning of the 21st century the media companies in both countries face economic constraints due to several media crises, including a structural crisis (new possibilities within Internet communication), a cyclical crisis, that is, a downturn in advertising revenue (Weischenberg et al. 2006: 14). As a result, a large number of journalists are facing unemployment, and are forced to work under heightened competition, both of which influence working conditions and the quality of work.

However, there are some important differences in the countries' media systems and media markets. Contrary to the nationally regulated media system of Sweden, Germany is a federal state and the *laender* (federal states) have a strong role in regulating areas such as broadcasting, culture, and education as part of their 'cultural sovereignty'. Germany's media system is still one of the most decentralized in Western Europe. In the area of broadcasting we can find a great number of regional broadcasters and in the area of press, this is reflected in the strength of the regional press, and only a few national newspapers. The populations also differ: Germany has a population of some 82 million people, compared to Sweden's 9.3 million. Berlin has a population of 3.4 million, and the Stockholm region has 2 million inhabitants.

A comparison between these countries is also relevant because of the similarities within public discourse concerning migration and integration. Both countries are migration societies, but have differences within their respective policies. The parliaments in both countries have passed anti-discrimination laws. In 1999 the Swedish "Act on Measures against Discrimination in Working Life on Grounds of Ethnic Origin, Religion or other Belief" entered into force and in Germany seven years later passed "The General Equal Treatment Bill" (Das Allgemeine Gleichbehandlungsgesetz) which prohibits discrimination based on race or ethnic origin, gender, religion, disability, age, or sexual identity. In January 2009 a new Swedish anti-discrimination bill was launched, aiming at promoting equal rights and opportunities regardless of gender, transgender identity or expression, ethnicity, religion or other beliefs, disability, sexual orientation or age. By law, employers are required to take active steps to promote equal rights and opportunities and fight discrimination. These measures are to be goal-oriented and accounted for annually, while in Germany the bill only claims that if employees are discriminated against they will have a right to compensation for damages suffered and can assert their claims before a labour court (see also Jönhill in this volume).

In recent years, the concerns involving the social cohesion and integration of migrants have gained importance in European media debates, focussing on the responsibilities of the news media in contemporary multi-ethnic societies (see e.g. Kevin et al. 2004; Lewis 2008; Sarikakis ed. 2007). On the level of press codes, in 2007 the German Press Council has added an anti-discrimination passage under figure 12 "discrimination", which does not allow discrimination based on sex, disability or ethnic, national, religious or social group affiliations. This also includes reportage on crimes, i.e. not mentioning the ethnic or religious affiliation of a suspect if it is not relevant (Deutscher Presserat 2009: 16). The official code of conduct for Swedish journalists includes similar publicity rules stating that race, gender, nationality, professional, or political affiliation or religious beliefs should not be stressed if irrelevant to the context, or if it is demeaning in nature (Spelregler för press, TV och radio 2007).

Sweden and Germany are in the midst of an intense public debate regarding the need for greater social cohesion and integration, and this is a debate in which media plays a decisive role. In Germany, two nationwide initiatives, the National Integration Plan by the German Government from 2007 and the private initiative of the Charter of Diversity from 2006, have established the discourse in recent years. The first mostly involves the integration discourse, while the second has an economic, that is, profit-oriented approach. The National Integration Plan does not specifically focus on media, but mass media are strongly encouraged to make efforts towards improved integration by e.g.

an active recruitment policy of media workers with migrant backgrounds (Der Nationale Integrationsplan 2007). However, the Charter of Diversity[1] claims that the diversity of a society has an inherent potential and can be put to profitable use by companies. By signing it, organizations pledge to provide a work environment free of prejudice and discrimination, and to create an organizational culture based on the inclusion of people with differing talents and backgrounds (Charter der Vielfalt 2006).

In this chapter, we map the current media conditions in Sweden and Germany, by providing brief presentations of the respective media landscapes and the composition of the migrant populations in Stockholm and Berlin. In addition, we provide examples of initiatives aiming at promoting cultural diversity within journalism. We examine the tensions between officially expressed attitudes and diversity goals, arguing that the media landscapes of the two countries are facing similar problems in terms of diversity measures, but are seeking some different solutions. Compared to Germany, Sweden seems to be the forerunner with years of experience regarding media diversity efforts, while Germany has only recently given attention to these questions.

Media Landscapes[2] in Stockholm and Berlin: Some Facts

Swedish public service television broadcasters face difficulties in maintaining their audiences due to declining shares of viewers, whereas the commercial TV channels have strengthened their positions in the past years. In 2007 the public service television market share was 35 percent in Sweden (Nordicom, Statistik om medier 2010). The two public service television channels, SVT1 and SVT2 taken together, have the highest number of television viewers, followed by the commercial channel TV4. Other major operators are TV3 and Kanal 5. However, the term TV has come to signify a wider range of TV outlets, which also can be consumed via computers and mobile phones. In 2008, the Swedish Radio and Television Authority (that issue licences for broadcasting, that is, other than public service radio and TV) issued 40 licences for TV with national coverage and 14 local and regional licences (Vries ed. 2009: 47).

Sveriges Radio (SR) broadcasts over four nationwide domestic FM channels (P1, P2, P3 and P4), 28 local channels, the Finnish language channel SR Sisuradio and the external service, Radio Sweden. SR Metropol and SR P6 are the two local Stockholm's channels. Additionally the SR website continually streams over 40 radio channels, including four national FM stations and some ten web-only channels.

Swedish commercial broadcasting was introduced in 1993. In 2006 commercial radio reached 33 percent of the audience, with public service radio reaching 49 percent of the audience (TNS Sifo 2009). Local commercial radio here refers to privately owned radio channels, financed by commercials. At present, there are 89 licences on the commercial radio market, and out of these ten operate in Stockholm (Vries ed. 2009: 27). MTG Radio is the largest commercial radio network in Sweden, and operates a total of 46 stations in different locations. MTG Radio AB is owned by Modern Times Group. All radio program production comes out of MTG Radio's headquarters in Stockholm. SBS Radio is the second major commercial radio network. The company is owned by the German media company ProSiebenSat.1, and operates a total of 40 radio stations in various places in Sweden (Vries ed. 2009: 29).

As early as 1984, Germany had a 'dual system' of both public and commercial broadcasting. With 91 channels, Germany is the third largest TV-market in Europe, and out of those, 17 are publicly owned (Färdigh 2008: 17, 19). Because the responsibility for cultural issues such as broadcasting rests with the *laender*, Berlin's public service broadcasting system is a creation of the city-state in co-operation with the bordering state Brandenburg[3] called Rundfunk Berlin-Brandenburg (RBB). It emerged in 2003 from the city broadcaster Sender Freies Berlin (SFB) and from the public service broadcast company of the bordering federal state Brandenburg, Ostdeutscher Rundfunk Brandenburg (ORB). RBB alone produces six radio programs and one TV program, rbb Fernsehen, and together with other public service radio and TV organizations operates two further radio stations and five TV channels (including Das Erste, which is Germany's main public television co-operative network, ARD, made up of the regional public broadcasting services). Out of the public service radio stations, we want to specifically mention the former exceptional radio station Radio Multikulti, which was on the air until late 2008. Sixteen years ago, in 1994, the former public broadcasting service SFB launched a radio station[4] to be the showcase of the 'other' Germany, targeting Berlin residents from different cultures. It broadcasted news and entertainment from and about Berlin's multicultural life, and used world music as a bridge between cultures. Usually the broadcast was in German, but 20 other languages were also used for a few hours each week, for "immigrants and for Berliners and inhabitants of Brandenburg interested in languages" (Radio Multikulti 2007). Funding cut-backs forced this radio station to close in late 2008 because of low ratings.[5] There were protests against the shutdown expressing this decision as being detrimental to integration, but the protests had no effect (Ataman 2008).

There are over 15 commercial radio stations and over 10 TV stations located in Berlin, including SAT.1, N24, VIVA, and FAB. Regarding viewers, taking together ARD, ZDF and the third regional programs, the public service TV channels in Germany have the highest number of viewers, followed by the commercial broadcasters RTL and SAT.1 (Mediendaten 2009). Regarding radio listening, the inhabitants of Berlin-Brandenburg spend more time listening to private radio stations, but the most popular radio station is a public service one, Antenne Brandenburg (RBB Unternehmen 2009).

Germany is the largest newspaper market in Europe, with a circulation of more than 21 million copies per day. But Germany is also the European country where circulation has plummeted the most since 2002. In addition, Germany has the largest European newspaper, Bild, with a circulation of 3.7 million copies. The combined circulation of the Swedish newspaper market is 4.7 million copies per day (Färdigh 2008: 14). Despite this fact, there are more than twice as many dailies per million inhabitants in Sweden than in Germany, 10 and 4.5 respectively (Färdigh 2008: 15, 25). In Sweden, there are about 150 newspapers published at least six days a week. A main character-istic of the Swedish press is the traditionally strong position of local newspa-pers. Even the metropolitan press in Stockholm, which previously aimed at a national distribution, now operate within local markets. The only Swedish newspapers with clear national distribution are the non-subscription evening papers (Sternvik,Wadbring & Weibull eds 2008: 6). The Swedish newspapers with the widest circulation are published in Stockholm, and the major mor-ning newspaper, Dagens Nyheter, and the evening newspaper, Expressen, are both controlled by Bonnier AB, the largest of the Nordic media companies. Their Stockholm competitors, Svenska Dagbladet and Aftonbladet, are owned by the Norwegian media conglomerate Schibsted, which is Sweden's second-largest newspaper publisher after Bonnier AB. The free sheet Metro was first launched in Stockholm in 1995 and has a considerable readership in the region alongside the subscription newspapers. In 2008, Schibsted bought 35 percent of the shares in the company.

The strength of the regional press in Germany is shown by the fact that five Berlin-based publishing houses produce ten subscription and/or paid dailies with a regional focus (Schütz 2007: 582). Berliner Zeitung of the Berliner Verlag is the most subscribed local newspaper, followed by Berliner Morgenpost of Axel Springer Verlag and Der Tagesspiegel of the publisher group Georg von Holtzbrinck. The biggest nationwide newspaper – produced in Berlin – is Die Welt of Springer Verlag, which is a former Hamburg title that moved to Berlin several years ago. Not all dailies are produced by major publishers; there are also the cooperative-owned Die Tageszeitung, and the former GDR title of the communist party Neues Deutschland, owned by a GmbH as a type of a legal entity. Several tabloids such as the local B.Z. and the above-mentioned national tabloid both out of Springer Verlag, as well the local Berliner Kurier of Gruner und Jahr, are produced in Berlin. Berlin's free sheet market differs from Stockholm's insofar as there are only weeklies, Berliner Woche, and Berliner Abendblatt, which belong to the major publishing houses of Springer Verlag and Berliner Verlag. The Swedish-owned and international free sheet Metro has not succeeded in getting a foothold in Berlin or in Germany.

Migration in Stockholm and Berlin: Some Facts

In Sweden, 14 percent of the current population is foreign-born, whereas the percentage for Stockholm is 21. Persons with a migrant background represent 19 percent of the Swedish population, and 28 percent for the Stockholm region population (Statistics Sweden 2009). Foreign or migrant background, as used here, implies a person born abroad, or whose parents were both born abroad. This is the definition used by Statistics Sweden, which differs from German statistics insofar as in Germany, persons with one parent of foreign origin are considered to have a migrant background. This distinction is relevant when comparing ethnic populations of these countries.

There is, however, substantial variation within the different parts of the Stockholm region. In some of the southern suburbs, more than 30 percent of the population is foreign-born. Percentages in the major cities of Göteborg and Malmö are 22 and 30, respectively (Statistics Sweden 2009). In Stockholm the largest immigrant group is from Finland with its 18,500 persons, with the next largest group is from Iraq, with 14,900 persons. The third largest group are the 9,700 from Iran, followed by 9,400 immigrants from Poland and 6,700 from Turkey (USK 2010).

In 2008, the Federal Statistics Office of Germany published for the first time detailed and differentiated statistics on its 'foreign' population by using the term 'migrant background'. The notion of 'migrant background' is a newer one, frequently used since 2006, and has replaced the diffuse term of 'foreigner'. Migrant background as used by this office refers to people with migration experience of their own or that of their parents and/or grandparents (regarding at least one parent, as mentioned above). Having a migrant background means having immigrated to Germany since 1950, or being born in Germany as a foreigner (with foreign citizenship) or being the descendant of one of both groups, that is an immigrant of the second or third generation. In other words: Families with migrant backgrounds are those where at least one of the parents or grandparents is a foreign national or a naturalized German citizen. Those who have direct migration experience are called "Zugewanderte" (in-migrants).

According to the latest statistics published in 2008, 15.1 million people have migrant backgrounds in Germany. That is almost 19 percent of the entire population of Germany, meaning nearly that every fourth family in Germany has a migrant background. The two largest migration groups are the five million late resettlers (Spätaussiedler) from Russia, and the approximately 2.5 million people of Turkish origin. The demographics of Berlin make the city one of the most multicultural cities in Germany, and migration numbers are above average. But in comparison to Stockholm, the city has lower figures (despite the fact that this category includes more possibilities as mentioned above).

Data released in 2007 indicates that 25.7 percent of Berlin's population has migrant background, that is, every fourth inhabitant. In some boroughs, the proportion between a majority without a migrant background and a minority with a migrant background is reversed. In the boroughs of Mitte, Neukoelln and Friedrichshain-Kreuzberg, circa 60 percent of the youngsters are from in-migrated families (Statistik Berlin 2009). In Berlin, the largest ethnic group is Turkish, followed by a group from Poland and Serbia-Montenegro, and then a group from Italy. Turkey, Greece, Spain, Italy, and Yugoslavia are the regions where the so-called guest workers of the 50s and 60s originated. During the 70s, immigrants were mostly from Middle East, Vietnam, and Poland. After the fall of the Berlin wall, most immigrants came from the former Soviet Union.

Journalists with a Migrant Background in Sweden and Germany

There are approximately 25,000 employed journalists in Sweden, out of whom nearly 50 percent work in the Stockholm region (Statistics Sweden, labour market 2008). In Germany, there are circa 48,000 full-time journalists (Weischenberg et al. 2006: 18). We have no exact numbers for Berlin, and know only that journalist associations in Berlin-Brandenburg have approximately 4,000 members (DJV Berlin 2009). But not all freelance or fully employed journalists are members of associations. The official website of the city of Berlin states there are 130,000 media workers in Berlin, but that also includes all types of media work, such as PR. In Sweden about half of all journalists are female (Statistics Sweden, labour market 2007), while in Germany the number of female journalists is only 37 percent (Weischenberg et al. 2006: 45).

When it comes to foreign-born journalists, the numbers are very low in both countries. In Sweden, 5.9 percent of the journalists are foreign-born and only 2 percent were born in a non-European country (Statistics Sweden 2008), in comparison to information from Germany stating that only about 2-3 percent of journalists have a migrant background (Ouaj 1999: 42). The next section will show in detail the country of origin of employed journalists, based on Swedish statistics from 2008.

There are approximately 800 foreign-born journalists in the Stockholm region. The employment rate of journalists who have a non-European background is well below those of doctors (9 percent), and university teachers (7 percent). In 2008, some 1,500 foreign-born journalists were employed in Sweden. Out of those, 31 percent came from other Nordic countries, 33 percent were born in European countries excluding the Nordic countries, 18 percent were born in Asia, and 9 percent were born in North or Central America. All in all, approximately 36 percent had their origins outside Europe (see figure 1) (Statistics

Figure 1.   Number of Foreign-born Journalists by Region of Birth, yr 2008

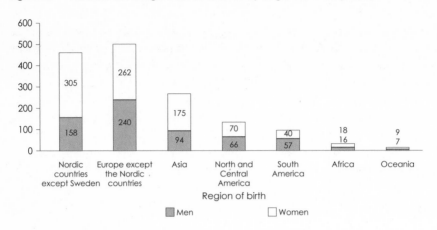

Source: Statistics Sweden 2008.

Sweden 2008). A survey study conducted in 2005 arrived at similar results. The study was based on responses from some 1,000 members of the Swedish Union of Journalists. The overall proportion of foreign-born journalists was 5 percent, and of those working in the metropolitan press, 7 percent. The researchers found that the proportion of foreign-born journalists was the same in 2005 as it was in 1999. This is remarkable, the report concludes, considering the fact that the question of diversity and recruitment had been intensely debated during this period. The study also noted that younger journalists (34 years and younger) are less represented than those who were 55 years and older (Djerf-Pierre 2007: 28-30). Recent figures from Statistics Sweden suggest a slight increase of foreign-born journalists, from 5.4 percent in 2006 to 5.9 in 2008. But definitive conclusions cannot be drawn. These findings place the past years' diversity initiatives in a critical light (see also Hultén in this volume).

A brief overview of the relation between the percentage of all foreign-born persons in Sweden's population and the percentage of foreign-born journalists indicates that Asians are underrepresented among journalists, whereas persons born in the Nordic countries are overrepresented among journalists (see figure 2).

Comparable German statistics do not exist, and we have only a representative survey of 2006 examining all journalists and their working conditions in Germany and a representative survey of 2009, which gathered information on the inclusion of journalists with a migrant background in German dailies. There are no statistics on migrant media workers in broadcasting media. Based on the first mentioned study of 2006 we know that in the years between 1993-2005, the number of permanently employed newspaper journalists decreased by 18 percent, and in the case of public radio and television, the number of

Figure 2.   Percentage of Foreign-born Swedish Population and of Foreign-born
Journalists by Region of Birth, yr 2008 (percent)

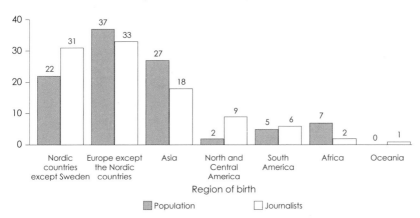

Source: Statistics Sweden 2008.

the freelancers quadrupled. More than 40 percent of the employees in public service broadcasting are freelancers (Weischenberg et al. 2006: 39-40). This comprehensive survey provides many details about German journalists, including demographic and educational backgrounds, working conditions, and the professional and ethical values of print and broadcast journalists at the beginning of the 21st century, but no statistics are given concerning the employment situation of journalists with a migrant background like similar reports in other countries, e.g. in the US (Weaver 2007) and Sweden (Djerf-Pierre 2007). One may speculate as to why this distinction is not drawn. There are arguments saying that ethically, introducing statistics concerning ethnic backgrounds would encourage discrimination (Ouaj 1999: 34), and personnel managers claim that they do not look at the staff's background, because they treat everyone equally, making no distinction between employees' origins (Ouaj 1999: 41). The act of making no distinction is also a distinction, by its avoidance of addressing diversity issues within media organizations. The non-existence of that issue reflects a public and also academic discourse which is characterized by a non-awareness and therefore non-communication about diversity within mainstream media during that time at least until 2006.

A recently published chapter in a book (Geissler & Pöttker 2009) wants to close this gap by publishing the results of a survey conducted in German dailies. The authors find that only 16 percent of all dailies employ journalists with a migrant background, which means that 84 percent of all newsrooms are mono-ethnic (Geissler & Enders et al. 2009: 91). If one makes a projection from this to all employed journalists within newspapers, one can say that only 1.2 percent are journalists with a migrant background and that more than half of them work as freelancers (Geissler & Enders et al. 2009: 92). If we look at their countries of origin, we can state that 44 percent of these journalists come from the former recruiting states (Anwerberstaaaten) of the 60s such as Turkey, Spain, and Italy, and the rest come from Eastern Europe and Western- and Northern Europe, with some from the Middle East, South America, and Africa. That means that most of them have a European background (Geissler & Enders et al. 2009: 95). From the general survey of 2006 we know that the average journalist in Germany is male, just under 41 years old, belongs to the middle class and has a university degree (Weischenberg 2006: 57). The 2009 survey on print media journalists with a migrant background shows, that immigrant journalists are younger (most of them between 26-35), quite often come from working-class families, most of them are female, and like the average media worker have a university degree (Geissler & Enders et al. 2009: 100).

When it comes to broadcasting media, a survey done by the European Institute for the Media in 1999 concludes that only a small number of employees in German mainstream television have a migrant background. They work in foreign language programs, and the size of this group does not exceed 2 or 3 percent, as mentioned above (Ouaj 1999: 42). In general, most migrant journalists are employed within broadcasting, especially radio broadcasting, but there are no exact numbers (Berliner Beiträge 2006: 16). According the latest figures of the public service company ZDF, 18 percent of their employees have a migrant background (Der Nationale Integrationsplan 2008: 86), but exact numbers are not specified and it can be assumed that all aspects of the company's work are included, such as cleaning and catering. The only specified numbers refer to the trainees at the company, and numbers vary between 4.5 and 6 percent (Der Nationale Integrationsplan 2008: 80).

Attitudes Toward Diversity Policies within Media Organizations

Within our project, a telephone survey study was conducted in May and June of 2008 in order to explore attitudes towards diversity in Swedish news media.[6] News organizations of various sizes, comprising newspapers, radio, and TV were called, and 103 participated. Officials in charge of the companies' diversity programs responded to the 13-question survey (see a compilation of this survey at the end of this volume).

The study reveals that the concept of diversity is closely linked to ethnicity and gender and only to a lesser extent to age, religion, and sexual orientation. Of the surveyed companies, 87 percent report that diversity efforts are very important or important to the company. Most companies agree that diversity programs are good for business, have an influence on the journalistic product, and on the good will of the company. However, newspapers lag behind in their diversity programs compared to radio and TV. One explanation is the legal requirements of public service broadcasters to serve all, to support equality, and to reflect all of society. Less than one third of the newspapers report that they have a documented diversity plan, whereas the share is 60 percent in TV and nearly 90 percent in the radio broadcasting institutions. This has consequences for how the organizations view and value diversity efforts. Organizations with diversity plans have significantly more positive assessments of the benefits of diversity. If you consider the "fully agree" responses, there are significant distinctions between newspapers on the one hand and radio and television on the other. The newspapers rate the benefits of diversity less than television and radio newsrooms. The newspapers are much less convinced that diversity creates a better working climate in the workplace, or better reflects the demands of the audience, or improves the good will of the company, or makes the company more attractive as an employer and more competitive, or improves the journalistic product. However, if you add up the ratings of "agree" and "fully agree", differences even out in how the different media organizations perceive and value putting diversity into practice.

Figure 3.   Fully Agree that Diversity Improves/Promotes

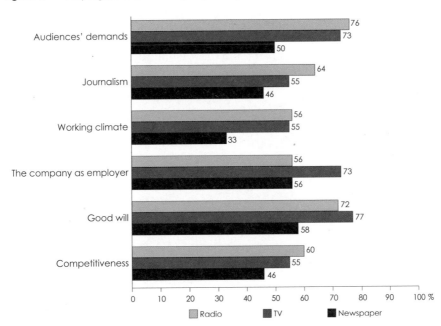

This is in contrast to the actual situation. Half of the respondents stated that 5 percent or less of the news staff had foreign backgrounds – 16 percent responded that they had none. One fourth of the companies rated the percentage between 6 and 10, and 16 percent estimated that more than one tenth of the staff had foreign backgrounds. The rest, or 9 percent, did not know.

It is noteworthy that the largest Swedish public service companies, Sveriges Television (SVT) and Sveriges Radio (SR), do not have any statistics based on their staff's ethnicity. This makes it more complicated to measure progress, or regression for that matter.

How should this discrepancy between ideals and reality be interpreted? When respondents were asked to state what most hampers diversity, the most common replies were:

- Economic reasons. Employment freezes.

- Difficulties of recruitment. Hard to find the right people.

- Older structures, hierarchies and attitudes.

- Key persons lack competence and awareness.

Financial constraints are obviously a hindrance to promoting diversity, but the comments also reveal an inefficiency in managing diversity.

As to attitudes towards diversity policy in German media organizations, we have only a small survey published in 2006. The survey is based on structured telephone interviews with 38 personnel managers of media companies and 24 representatives from training institutions (Berliner Beiträge 2006). Only 30 percent of the requested personnel managers were willing to answer questions on diversity measures within journalism, and therefore the authors claim that the study is not representative. However, that indifference shreds light on practices within media companies. The authors did not openly meet with refusals to cooperate, but did notice a substantial discomfort and also scepticism when speaking about these questions (Berliner Beiträge 2006: 14). The study revealed that German media companies show little or no interest in multicultural hiring practices or in affirmative action policies, and that these mentioned diversity measures are, to a large extent, seen as irrelevant to journalism as such (Berliner Beiträge 2006: 14, 17). When asked about an interest in hiring migrant journalists, only 7 of the 38 personnel managers were positive, which are those media companies producing foreign programs or programs for migrants (Berliner Beiträge 2006: 18-19). Here, specific language and cultural competence is requested for niche programs, not for mainstream programming. Six of them give a 'yes' response to special intercultural measures within the organization, such as recruitment of migrant journalists, special projects with local migrant groups and journalists, and organizing an open channel together with a local Muslim group (Berliner Beiträge 2006: 19). Only two of the local public service Radio and TV companies have documented diversity plans, which we want to discuss further in the following section.

Diversity Policies within Media Organizations
Broadcasting

Sveriges Television (SVT) and Sveriges Radio (SR) are Sweden's largest public service television and radio companies, and are financed by compulsory license fees. The underlying principles of the Swedish broadcasting license are formulated in the Radio and Television Act. The act stipulates some fundamental rules regarding the assertion of democratic values and the principle of all people's equal value. Moreover, SVT's and SR's broadcasting licenses require the companies to provide a diverse array of programming that reflects the various cultures present in Sweden.

SVT and SR must submit an annual report to the Swedish Radio and Television Authority, stating that the content of the programmes conform with the regulations of the Radio and Television Act. The Swedish Broadcasting Commission monitors whether programmes already broadcast are in compliance with the Act as well as with the terms of the licenses the Government have granted. The Commissioners are appointed by the Government for a period of three years. SVT's public service report of 2007 includes an account of the programming in the national minority languages Finnish, Sami, Meänkieli, and Romany. However, ethnic and/or cultural diversity in the programming is not monitored on a regular basis, and is not presented in the annual reports. Nor do the company's diversity policies contain strategies concerning the monitoring of diversity efforts.

Since commercial radio broadcasting channels first began operating in the early 90s, public service radio's share of daily listeners has steadily declined from 70 percent to 48 percent of the population in 2008 (Carlsson & Harrie eds 2010). In 2007 a major reorganization of SR was implemented. The change included staff cuts and reductions in budgets. The shift also had an impact on SR's diversity policy, involving a shift from multicultural programmes to a general diversity within all programming. This shift in the Swedish public service broadcasting context is explicit in how the address of immigrants and minorities was re-defined. Both SR and SVT cancelled their multicultural programmes (i.e. the radio programme Brytpunkten and the television programmes Mosaik, Språka, and Aktuellt för invandrare).[7]

SR's diversity policy states that Sweden is a multicultural society. Therefore, overall programming aims at appealing to all Swedes, wherever they live and regardless of their age, gender, and cultural background. The policy also states that diversity should be a natural part of all of the company's programming. Diversity should be seen as including ethnicity, disability, age, faith, sexuality, class, political affiliation, and regional differences. SR does not support hand-selecting their staff. On the contrary, managers are requested to consider diversity issues in all types of recruitment (Policy – Mångfald på Sveriges Radio). In SVT the diversity issue gained momentum in 2002 when the company denied a woman wearing a Muslim headscarf (hijab) a job as a presenter. The DO (Ombudsman against ethnic discrimination) concluded that SVT's decision was against the law. As a result, SVT reconsidered and rephrased the diversity plan. A new department, the Multicultural Centre, was founded to work with development and diversity issues. The new policy was adopted in 2004, and revised two years later.

From 2006, the Corporate Social Responsibility (CSR) department is responsible for dealing with diversity issues. In April 2008, SVT assumed a new diversity policy that replaced the considerably more detailed previous one. The new document fills less than a page, and states that SVT serves all and that "SVT welcomes and respects differences regarding gender, age, ethnicity, religion or faith, sexual orientation, and disability" (Mångfaldspolicy för SVT 2008). It also declares that in its programming generalizations should be avoided and that the company should prevent all forms of discrimination in the workplace. Diversity aspects should be taken into account in content and as regards program participants. The responsibility of implementing this policy is assigned to all managers at all levels.

In the visionary document Ditt SVT – Strategier mot 2010 (Your SVT – Strategies towards 2010) published in 2008, CEO Eva Hamilton firmly stresses the "serve all principle" of public service broadcasting. The document underlines SVT's democratic mission and states that the programming is "inclusive and welcomes everybody" (p. 13) and that "provisions in minority languages for ethnic minorities should be improved" (p. 15). But the overall programming targeted at ethnic minorities and minority language groups actually decreased during the period 1998-2006, from 4 to just under 3 hours per week (Asp 2007: 60).

In Germany, especially according to the above-mentioned National Integration Plan, the public service corporations have demonstrated numerous voluntary commitments in order to increase diversity. These commitments include concrete measures such as increased recruitment of editors, authors, presenters and actors who are supposed to be role models (or good examples) within specific spots in the programs. But this is a long-term process that calls for further efforts and new interim solutions directed at advancing recruitment and integration, as the first interim report of 2008 states (Der Nationale Integrationsplan 2008: 76). In detail, we can read that the public broadcasting network, ZDF, aims at bringing the editorial staff more in line with the ethnic diversity of the population in general, but on a long-term basis, because of financial limits accompanied by low employee turnovers and few vacancies (Der Nationale Integrationsplan 2008: 80).

The only broadcasting organization in Germany which has developed a diversity strategy is the Association of German Public Service Broadcasting Corporations (ARD). Under the title "Integration and cultural diversity", the strategy is oriented at a mainstream diversity policy under the motto: "Out of the niches" (ARD 2007). The regional broadcasting members WDR and SWR, located in Köln and Stuttgart, are the only broadcasting corporations of ARD (probably the only mass medium in Germany), which have further developed measures in order to implement diversity policy. Both have an Integration Coordinator (Integrationsbeauftragter), that is, a contact person for all issues regarding migration, asylum, and ethnic minorities, and is responsible for implementing integration issues at all levels of the organization, and for systematically recruiting and developing editorial staff with migrant backgrounds. WDR's integration brochure "A picture is more than the sum of its colours. Integration and cultural diversity at WDR" describes integration and cultural diversity as "both a journalistic mandate and a duty for Westdeutscher Rundfunk" (WDR 2007). It applies both to programming and personnel development. Although the public radio broadcaster of Berlin-Brandenburg, RBB, has closed Radio Multikulti, ARD broadcasters WDR and SWR have built up competence centers in radio and television with the help of special programs Funkhaus Europa that has, among others things, taken over the broadcasting of Radio Multikulti, and Cosmo TV, the only integration program on German television. "And in order to not push the topic into a niche, the broadcaster pursues a mainstreaming-strategy: The contents along with the people have to migrate into the main formats" (Bingül 2008). This is termed 'Mainstreaming diversity': migration issues are not topics reserved for the radio program Funkhaus Europa or Cosmo TV, but are direct themes in television and feature films (WDR 2007: 9).

The private broadcasting companies in Germany, however, have argued against positive discrimination on the grounds that people with migrant backgrounds have already been present in all business areas for a long time (Der Nationale Integrationsplan 2007). The implication is, that there are no special diversity plans because diversity results from the 'nature of things', that is, from the market economy. Only the private broadcasting station RTL has stated the need to more strongly integrate young media workers with migrant backgrounds in the program. The private broadcasters claim the signing of the Charter of Diversity as a commitment for diversity (see also Jönhill in this volume). By implementing the Charter of Diversity, it is stated, diversity issues have been placed on the internal agenda (Der Nationale Integrationsplan 2008: 88). The process of discussing diversity has started, but it remains to be seen whether, and how, such changes will be implemented in the media organizations.

Print Media

In Sweden, Dagens Nyheter's mobile newsroom started in 1999 in connection with a project called "low newspaper readership" and ended after four years. The aim was to reach new reader groups that usually do not read the newspaper.

The target audience was 'non-elite': the low-skilled, low-income immigrants living in Stockholm's outlying areas. Petter Beckman was the project manager and editor of the Mobila redaktionen (mobile newsroom), with the purpose of conveying an image of these areas and their inhabitants which was in line with local interpretations (Beckman 2003: 35). Beckman advocates public journalism, and believes that news media need to move away from the traditional ideals of objectivity in order to play a more active role in local community activities. He also believes that news organizations must create a different kind of relationship with the public, one that examines the relationship of journalists to sources and readers. News media need to reformulate the news criteria and change the conventions dominating news work. The consequence is that the journalist is not a 'neutral' observer, but is working from a commitment. Public journalism is oriented towards finding solutions, as opposed to the problem orientation that news journalism usually stands for. Methods of public journalism include organizing town meetings on important local policy issues, and convening reader panels to get feedback and reactions to published articles. Mobila redaktionen ended after four years and had by that time published about 300 articles. Beckman notes that there are no documented measurable outcomes of the project, and writes self-critically that it probably was not possible to identify any social impacts of the experiment, concluding:

> We contributed to place persons with immigrant backgrounds on the newspaper pages, in played-down roles as normal citizens. We merged the voices and perspectives that otherwise seldom met. We showed how to approach difficult integration issues in a fairly decent and constructive manner (2003: 170).

In Malmö the newspaper Rosengård, which circulated in the district with the same name, was in operation for nearly a decade. The newspaper was a free monthly local newspaper with a circulation of 14,000-17,500 copies. The first issue came out in 1993 and the last in 2002. The paper was part of the daily Sydsvenska Dagbladet in Malmö. Nearly 40 percent of the residents of Malmö have foreign backgrounds. In the district Rosengård, the proportion is 60 percent. For this reason, this group was seen as a major potential target audience. The basic idea was that an ad-funded local newspaper in Rosengård would attract more subscribers to the main paper.

The local editorial staff in Rosengård would also produce articles for the main paper with the idea that this would help attract readers of foreign backgrounds throughout the entire distribution area of Sydsvenska Dagbladet. If it worked out well to sell ads in Rosengård, Sydsvenskan would be able to develop more ad-funded neighbourhood newspapers in other parts of Malmö. Hopes for more subscribers and increased advertising revenue did not materialize. There were also economic reasons that determined the closure of the newspaper Rosengård

– the revenues didn't cover the costs for premises, printing, or distribution. The position as editor of the newspaper Rosengård also had low status among Sydsvenskan's editorial staff. Hans Månson, former editor of Sydsvenska Dagbladet states that a major reason for shutting down the newspaper was that it was likely to contribute to the stigmatization of Rosengård by treating the area as something unique (Sandström 2005: 105). Lasse Sandström, former editor of the newspaper Rosengård writes in a critical comment:

> Both projects [Dagens Nyheter's mobile newsroom and the newspaper Rosengård] are similar to some of the well intentioned but unsuccessful efforts by the authorities enforced in suburban areas, projects that residents are genuinely suspicious of. In many inhabitants' eyes, the closure of the mobile newsroom and the newspaper Rosengård confirmed the superficial and temporary interest that established newspapers take in their situation (Sandström 2005: 25).

In comparison to Sweden, the printed press in Germany is more reserved when it comes to diversity efforts. In Berlin, there was only a short-lived print media initiative organized by the left liberal Die Tageszeitung (taz) called Perşembre. Perşembre (engl. Thursday) was a weekly which was bilingually-published in German and Turkish between 2000 and 2002. It was distributed (on Thursdays) as a supplement of the taz but could also be subscribed to, separately.

In general, we can also see from Press' reactions to the National Integration plan of 2007 that diversity measures are not directly on the agenda in print media organizations. The umbrella organization of the German Magazine Publishers (VDZ) has only committed itself to raising the awareness among magazine publishers concerning suitable integration supporting measures (Der Nationale Integrationsplan 2007), and one year later it could only be reported that a project group will investigate diversity plans or policies in the different publishing houses (Der Nationale Integrationsplan 2008: 90).

Media Trainee Programs: More Colour in the Media

Online / More Colour in the Media is a European network involving several transnational projects. The network brings together European radio and television stations, educational institutions, and researchers. It was formed in 1995 to promote the representation of ethnic minorities in broadcasting. In 1998, More Colour in the Media ran a project that Sveriges Radio and German organizations participated in. In Sweden, it was intended, inter alia, to increase the participation of ethnic minorities in radio, both in hiring and in media content. It aimed at for unemployed youths of foreign backgrounds with no previous journalistic experience. During the project they received training in radio production and were trainees on several radio stations in Stockholm, Gothenburg, and Malmö. About 65 young people were trained in the project. Of these, the majority reported that they had found work in the media. The project leader, Dagny Eliasson, described the project as a success, and that it resulted in a marked increase in diversity in terms of both content and scope (Tuning into Diversity 2004: 239).

It is difficult to find documentation on the results of the project. In the general evaluation of the entire project, which involved several European countries, it is described as successful and that it actually affected the work of the radio stations (Ouaj 1999: 71). Swedish journalist Oivvio Polite is, however, critical of the project. He is of the opinion that the project did not aim at ethnic minorities as audiences, or really cared about them. He also thinks that it would have been more efficient to recruit participants for the project among the many trained journalists with foreign backgrounds in Sweden. Of those who were trained in the project, two are now employed by SR, of which one is a project employee, according to Polite (Polite 2005).

In Germany, this Europe-wide project was launched with the same purpose of improving migrant journalists' job opportunities in non-minority media (Ouaj 1999). But the initiative undertaken by Adolf Grimme Institut (AGI) between 1996 and 1998, focused here on gender roles and offered twenty migrant women a seven-month training course in journalism for radio and television, followed up by a year-long work experience placement to facilitate access to the job market. The trainee period was arranged by the Adolf Grimme Institut, and not by broadcasting media, as originally desired. At this time, the broadcasters were not willing to welcome trainees, especially those with migrant background. It was also difficult to find suitable work experience placements. Some of the participants had to switch between different places. Radio Multikulti and the similar radio station within WDR were of great help in offering work experience opportunities. There was no employment guarantee, and therefore no quota arrangement with media organizations. The project was accompanied by conferences on intercultural personnel management in order to create sensitivity to diversity management in media organizations. After the course, six of the 20 participants received permanent or fixed-term employments, and an additional six persons received so-called fixed freelance contracts (Jungk 1999: 220-221). There is no information about the remaining persons. The participants, however, experienced reservations, and concluded that especially the top echelons of the organizations have to heighten their awareness of the opportunities of a multicultural employment policy, and to develop strategies in order to make media organizations more diverse (Jungk 1999: 226).

In the first decade of the twenty-first century, new initiatives were taken, including within Berlin. After the unsuccessful attempt of the AGI, these now offered immigrants trainee opportunities in media organizations. Indeed, projects intended to improve migrant journalists' labour-market opportunities were, and are, continuously launched. A later example is the project "World Wide Voices" started in summer 2005 by Radio Multikulti in co-operation with the newspaper taz. The last call was in April 2008, where eight people had the chance to participate in a four-day workshop at the Electronic Media School in Potsdam-Babelsberg, working on interview management, doing reportage and moderation, and writing broadcast and online-texts. Thereafter the most talented workshop-graduates could prove their skills during a six week-long practical training in a editorial department of the public-service broadcasting network RBB. All of these initiatives have had varying degrees of success, and only a few candidates have received assignments. Now, the situation in Berlin has become worse, as Radio Multikulti has been dismantled as a center for training and working with diversity issues.

Journalist Networks Promoting Diversity in Germany

In 2006, the Berlin journalists of the German Journalist Association established an "intercultural network" as an open network for all journalists, but especially for journalists with migrant backgrounds. The network is seen as strengthening the cohesion among journalist groups, facilitating communication, calling attention to the theme of diversity, and also lobbying. The network works with some success, but cannot address all Berlin journalists with migrant backgrounds. On the one hand, the network is not known for everyone (it is within the Journalist association), and on the other hand the concept of 'intercultural' journalist seems to be off-putting by stigmatizing a group as "disadvantaged", as a journalist expressed it in connection with the study (R 17, see according to the study Graf in this volume). Three years later, in 2009, another network was founded, named "New German Media Workers" (Neue deutsche Medienmacher), avoiding references to ethnicity in its title, and aiming at "bringing the multi-ethnic society into German editorial staff" (Ippolito 2009). The initiative criticizes stereotypes in the media coverage of migrants, such as the Turkish woman with hijab and plastic bags, and the non-presence in the media of integrated immigrants such as the doctor from Iran or the Turkish engineer. It also criticizes the situation within German newsrooms for journalists from migrant families. They do not receive assignments based on their qualifications but on their origins, meaning, they exclusively cover migrant topics. The network wants, with the help of a mentor program, to discover talents, and to support and promote trainees, because journalism as a profession is little acknowledged in families with migrant backgrounds. It also aims at increasing the number of immigrant journalists not only on and off-camera and in front of the microphones but also in executive positions (Neue deutsche Medienmacher 2009). We cannot report on similar (official) networks within Sweden, which probably has to do with the small number of those concerned.

Summing up, the initiatives in both countries are mostly concentrated on public service broadcasting companies as a consequence of the underlying responsibilities of responding to the various cultures in the societies. These companies (some of them in Germany) have developed diversity strategies. The trend is thereby to work for mainstreaming diversity programming, that is, going away from the earlier idea of niche programs to include diversity in all programs. Recruiting journalists with migrant backgrounds is seen as an important step in achieving this, but funding cutbacks are a hindrance to change the situation quickly. Private broadcasters argue for market forces, which naturally would increase diversity when addressing minority groups. This would mean that no special diversity measures are needed. Diversity strategies (e.g. diversity plans) within the press and within most TV and radio organizations are absent in Germany. The survey conducted among Swedish news organizations revealed that most radio and television stations have a documented diversity plan, but only one third of the newspapers possess diversity plans. Whereas radio and TV organizations were convinced that diversity is beneficial to the company, newspapers rated diversity as less beneficial.

In both countries there have been attempts to augment the recruitment of journalists with migrant backgrounds. Other efforts have focused on news coverage and on attracting minority audiences. In Germany, initiatives to improve contacts and career possibilities for these journalists by organizing networks can also be seen as a step forward towards more diverse newsrooms and reporting in mainstream media.

Conclusions

Set in an increasingly commercialized and globalized context, news media are currently challenged by the new contours of the media landscape. They compete within a highly diversified market, including a multitude of media outlets, and these new technologies also involve a change in the nature of journalistic work. This development goes for all news media organizations, whether they are public-service or commercially oriented. Swedish and German news media face difficulties in maintaining their audiences, and have implemented major reorganizations in recent years, including staff cuts and reductions in budgets. The changes in Sweden e.g. also have had an impact on the cultural diversity policies (Horsti & Hultén forthcoming). This is particularly prominent in the policies of the Swedish public service television and radio companies, SVT and SR. Both SVT and SR have cancelled their specific multicultural programmes. Mainstreaming is a key term in the companies' current policies in both countries, and which both state that diversity should permeate all levels of the organization, that is, the content, programming, and staffing.

Although Sweden has a longer tradition of diversity policies within media organizations, we can observe that in Germany in recent years, the number of anchormen and women, journalists, and editors with migrant backgrounds have increased. In general, there is talk of having a 'migration bonus' when applying for a job, as Dunja Hayali, the first co-anchorwoman with a migrant background on German public-service TV, has experienced (Phalnikar 2007, see also Graf in this volume). However, it is also feared, in both countries, that TV journalists with a different skin colour or a foreign name act rather as figureheads or tokens instead of real employees at a senior level. It is necessary to develop mechanisms, not window dressing, as the Integration Coordinator of WDR declares:

> The danger is, however, that one again and again stresses the meaning of diversity without making an real effort. It is important for media organizations to develop structures, strategic goals, and the instruments for putting such goals into action (Zambonini 2008: 123).

Goals in the form of diversity plans or strategies are rarely developed in German media organizations. Private media companies prefer market-oriented goals which are embodied in the organization, as the Charter of Diversity claims it.

Cultural diversity media policies can contribute to newsrooms which are more open to pluralism, but cannot eliminate or resolve the complexity of the challenges of the media industry. As Sarita Malik concludes, most diversity policies are well-meaning and difficult to implement but also easy to dodge (Malik 2002: 184). There are also doubts if e.g. the National Integration Plan of Germany is an effective instrument for implementing diversity measures in organizations or is only "politically wanted wishful thinking – and very difficult to implement because it is very normative and thought from above" (Bingül 2008). But on the other hand "the Summit also had a symbolic function and is therefore important. In this respect, it already has achieved something, it has got the editorial staff moving a little" as a TV editor explains it (Parvand 2009). The overriding normative argument here is that news media have a duty to redefine their role as integrative institutions and in the way they address social cohesion, as well as cultural and ethnic diversity.

Notes

1. Similar Charters were launched in France in 2003, as response to discrimination within workplaces, and in Spain in 2009. Over 600 organizations have publicly declared their commitment to diversity by signing the Charter in Germany, including major media companies.

2. We focus on mainstream media, that is, broadcasting and print media of the majority of the society.
3. Exceptions based on federal legislation or agreements between the *laender* governments only include the Berlin-based Deutsche Welle (DW), a broadcasting service designed to provide information about Germany to foreign countries; and the Cologne- and Berlin-based nationwide radio Deutschlandradio, which is a merger of three different radio broadcasters from when Germany was divided; and the nation-wide public TV provider ZDF located in Mainz.
4. A similar cosmopolitan radio program is Funkhaus Europa, started in 1998 by the largest regional public service broadcaster for North-Rhine Westphalia, WDR.
5. Only 0.8 percent of Berlin's radio listeners, that is, 38,000 persons, have listened daily to Radio Multikulti (Ataman 2008).
6. No comparative study was conducted in Germany.
7. *Mosaik* was cancelled in 2003, *Språka* in 1998, and *Aktuellt för invandrare* was cancelled in 1995 (Anderson 2000). *Brytpunkten* was cancelled in 2007.

References

Andersson, M. (2000) *25 Färgrika TV-år. De mångkulturella programmen från SVT 1975-2000.* [25 years of colourful TV. SVT's multicultural programmes 1975-2000] Stockholm: SVT.

ARD (2007) 'Integration und kulturelle Vielfalt' [Integration and cultural diversity], *Media Perspektiven,* 9: 472-474.

Asp, K. (ed.) (2007) *Den svenska journalistkåren* [The Swedish Journalists]. Göteborg: JMG

Ataman, F. (2008) 'Falsches Signal für die Integration' [The wrong signal for integration], www. spiegel.de, retrieved January 30, 2010.

Beckman, P. (2003) *Riv stängslen: medierna som mötesplats: public journalism i svensk tappning* [Tear down the fences: the media as a meeting place: public journalism in Swedish]. Stockholm: Sellin & partner i samarbete med Institutet för mediestudier.

Berliner Beiträge zur Integration und Migration (2006) *Expertise: Ausbildung von Volontären in den Medien* [Expertise: Education of trainees in media], Berlin: MMB Institut für Medien- und Kompetenzforschung.

Bingül, B. (2008) *Migranten in Medien. Ein Journalist ist ein Journalist ist ein Mensch* [Migrants into the media. A journalist is a journalist is a person], www.migration-boell.de, retrieved January 20, 2009.

Carlsson, U. & Harrie, E. (eds) (2010) *Nordiska public service-medier i den digitala mediekulturen. Pengar, politiken och publiken* [Nordic public service media in the digital media culture. The money, the politics and the audience]. Göteborg: Nordicom.

Charter der Vielfalt [The Charter of diversity] (2006) www.charta-der-vielfalt.de, retrieved October 1, 2009.

Der Nationale Integrationsplan. Neue Wege – neue Chancen [The National Integration Plan. New ways – new chances] (2007) Die Bundesregierung, www.bundesregierung.de, retrieved August 1, 2008.

Der Nationale Integrationsplan. Erster Fortschrittsbericht [The National Integration Plan. The first Progress Report] (2008) Die Bundesregierung: www.bundesregierung.de, retrieved August 1, 2008.

Deutscher Presserat [German Press Council], www.presserat.de, retrieved December 14, 2009.

Ditt SVT – Strategier mot 2010 (2008) [Your SVT – Strategies towards 2010] svt.se/content/1/ c8/01/02/87/87/svt_strat0940.pdf. retrieved November 2010.

Djerf-Pierre, M. (2007) 'Journalisternas sociala bakgrund' [The social background of the journalists], in Asp, K. (ed.) *Den svenska journalistkåren* [The Swedish Journalists]. Göteborg: JMG.

DJV Berlin, www.djv-berlin.de, retrieved October 11, 2009.

Färdigh, M.A. (2008) *Mediesystem i Europa: En studie av de europeiska ländernas mediesystem utifrån ett användarperspektiv* [Media Systems in Europe: A study of the European countries' media systems from a user perspective]. Göteborg: Göteborgs universitet.

Geissler, R. & Pöttker, H. (eds) (2009) *Massenmedien und die Integration ethnischer Minderheiten in Deutschland* [Mass media and the integration of ethnic minorities in Germany]. Bielefeld: transcript-Verlag.

Geissler, R. & Enders, K. et al. (2009) 'Wenig ethnische Diversität in deutschen Zeitungsredaktionen' [Little ethnic diversity in German newspapers], in Geissler, R., Pöttker, H. (eds.) *Massenmedien und die Integration ethnischer Minderheiten in Deutschland*. Bielefeld: transcript-Verlag.

Hallin, D.C. & Mancini, P. (2004) *Comparing media systems: Three models of media and politics.* Cambridge: University of Cambridge Press.

Horsti, K. & Hultén, G. (forthcoming) 'Directing diversity: Managing cultural diversity media policies in Finnish and Swedish public service broadcasting', *International Journal of Cultural Studies.*

Hultén, G. (2006) *Främmande sidor: främlingskap och nationell gemenskap i fyra svenska dagstidningar efter 1945* [On the Strange Side: Estrangement and National Community in Four Swedish Daily Newspapers after 1945]. Stockholm: Stockholms universitet.

Ippolito, E. (2009) 'Türken, die würken' [Turks who act], in *taz*, February, 2.

Jungk, S. (1999) ''Mehr Farbe in den Medien' – ein Modellprojekt zur interkulturellen Öffnung von Rundfunkanstalten' ['More Colour in the Media' – a model for inter-cultural opening of the broadcasters], in Butterwegge, C. & Hentges, G. (eds) *Medien und multikulturelle Gesellschaft.* Opladen: Leske & Budrich.

Kevin, D. et al. (2004) *The information of the citizen in the EU: obligations for the media and the Institutions concerning the citizen's right to be fully and objectively informed* (Final Report). Prepared on behalf of the European Parliament by the European Institute for the Media. Düsseldorf: The European Institute for the Media.

Lewis. P.M. (2008) *Promoting social cohesion: the role of community media.* Report prepared for the Council of Europe's Group of Specialists on Media Diversity (MC-S-MD).

Löfgren Nilsson, M. (2007) 'Journalistiken – ett könsmärkt fält?' [Journalism – a gender marked field?], in Asp, K. (ed.) *Den svenska journalistkåren* [The Swedish Journalists]. Göteborg: JMG.

Malik, S. (2002) *Representing Black Britain. A history of Black and Asian images on British television.* London: Sage.

Mediendaten [Media data] (2009), www.mediendaten.de, retrieved July 28, 2009.

Mångfaldspolicy för SVT 2008 [Diversity Policy for SVT 2008], Unpublished document.

Neue deutsche Medienmacher [The new German media workers] (2009) www.neue-medienmacher. de, retrieved October 1, 2009.

Nordicom, Statistik om medier i Sverige [Statistics about Swedish media], www.nordicom.gu.se, retrieved March 8, 2010.

Ouaj, J. (1999) *More colour in the media. Employment and access of ethnic minorities to the television industry in Germany, the UK, France, the Netherlands and Finland.* The European Institute of the Media.

Parvand, M. (2009) in Wiedemann, K. 'Eine Quote haben wir nicht nötig' [A quota, we do not need], www.vorwaerts.de, retrieved November 10, 2009.

Phalnikar, S. (2007) 'New Face on German TV Highlights Dearth of Minority Presenters', www. dw-world.de, retrieved April 20, 2008.

Polite, O. (2005) 'Mångfald igen' [Again diversity], *Dagens Nyheter,* September 28.

Radio Multikulti (2007) www.multikulti.de, retrieved October 29.

RBB Unternehmen (RBB organization) (2009) www.rbb-online.de, retrieved July 28.

Sandström, L. (2005) *Rosengård i medieskugga: om medier som medel och hinder för integration* [Rosengård in Media Shadow: on media as resource and barrier to integration]. Stockholm: Sellin & partner.

Sarikakis, K. (2007) 'Mediating social cohesion: Media and cultural policy in the European Union and Canada', in Sarikakis, K. (ed.) *Media and cultural policy in the European Union.* Amsterdam: Rodopi.

Schütz, W. (2007) 'Deutsche Tagespresse 2006' [The German print press] *Media Perspektiven* (11): 560-588.

Spelregler för press, TV, radio [Code of conduct for press, TV, radio] 16. uppl. (2007) Stockholm: Pressens samarbetsnämnd.

Statistics Sweden (2008) *Labour market*, www.scb.se, retrieved March 8, 2010.

Statistics Sweden (2009) *Population statistics*, www.scb.se, retrieved March 8, 2010.

Statistik Berlin (2009) www.statistik-berlin.de, retrieved August 28, 2009.

Sternvik, J. Wadbring, I. & Weibull, L. (eds) (2008) *Newspaper in a changing media world: Swedish trends*. Göteborg: Newspaper Research Programme, Department of Journalism and Mass Communication, University of Gothenburg.

TNS Sifo *Radioundersökningar/ Rapport 2009*, in www.tns-sifo.se, retrieved March 8, 2010.

Tuning into Diversity: Immigrants and ethnic minorities in mass media (2002) European Conference on media and minorities, Rome 2002. Project funded by the European Commission, Directorate General Employment and Social Affairs.

USK *Statistik befolkning/ Storstadsjämförelser/Utrikes födda* [Statistics population/ comparison between big cities/ born abroad), www.uskab.se, retrieved March 8, 2010.

Vries, Tove de (ed.) (2009) *Medieutveckling 2009* [Media Development 2009]. Haninge: Radio- och TV-verket.

WDR (2007) *A picture is more than the sum of its colours. Integration and cultural diversity at WDR*, www.wdr.de, retrieved October 20, 2009.

Weaver, D.H. (2007) *The American journalist in the 21st century: U.S. news people at the dawn of a new millennium*. Mahwah, N.J.: L. Erlbaum Associates.

Weischenberg, S. Malik, M., Scholl. A. (2006) *Die SouffleurederMediengesellschaft. Report über die Journalisten in Deutschland* [The prompters of the media society. Report on the journalists in Germany]. Konstanz: UVK.

Zambonini, G. & Erk, S. (2008) 'Kulturelle Vielfalt und Integration: Die Rolle der Medien' [Cultural diversity and integration. The role of the media], *Media Perspektiven*, 3: 120-124.

Interview

R 17 (2008) Respondent interviewed by Heike Graf in Berlin October, 30

Mass Media Organizations and Managing Diversity: Possibilities and Limitations

From a Communicational System Theoretical Perspective

Jan Inge Jönhill

The Matter and the Issue

In this chapter, the main issue concerns the possibilities and limitations of the mass media organization to manage issues of ethnic and national or cultural diversity. In the analysis, the *societal and communicational context* of the issue will be emphasized. A basic assumption is that sociological systems theory is well suited as a framework for this analysis. A brief definition of systems theory is that it is a theory that places the main focus on the very distinction of what belongs and what does not belong to units in society that operate on their own conditions, that is to say, on communication systems and their environments.

What is then meant by communication? According to the German sociologist Niklas Luhmann, communication consists of three components: information, message (or utterance), and understanding. For communication to succeed, information that holds meaning must be made into a message to reach understanding (in a basic sense). The transmission model, involving a message to be transferred to a recipient, which I will come back to later, is too simplistic and ignores the fact that each step in a communication is based on a selection, where the receiver has different choices. The fact that communication is always followed by another communication characterizes communication systems. Systems that produce and reproduce themselves in a continual ongoing process are called self-producing, self-regulating, self-organizing or, in one word, autopoietic systems (Luhmann 1995).

Another basic assumption is that *intercultural communication* is advantageous to communication and cultural development in society. The concept of intercultural communication should be perceived here in a general sense as it is used by Asante and Gudykunst (Asante & Gudykunst 1989). Since communication in our society today, with an immense amount of global interchanges and networks in many situations, must necessarily include intercultural communication, "globalization" should therefore be seen as advantageous to society.

At the same time, it represents a challenge not only for individual persons and groups but also for the organizations of society.

Ethnic and national diversity is important to journalistic production for many reasons. The body of research makes it reasonable to establish as still another assumption that persons on the labour market, among them journalists with a migrant background in many cases have a disadvantageous position in mass media organizations (Berggren & Omarsson 2001; Löfgren & Fägerlind 1999; Lange 1999). Moreover, it is reasonable to assume that such cases of a disadvantageous position may also have a negative impact on journalistic production. In other chapters in this volume, indications and evidence for the latter assumptions (among others from a survey and from interviews made within the framework of this research project) regarding mass media organizations in Sweden and Germany are presented and discussed.

In this introduction, I will proceed with some important distinctions for the further analysis. Firstly, we have to distinguish between what might be a matter for individual persons and what should be regarded as a social issue. To exemplify, when individual persons with migrant backgrounds are regarded as having a disadvantageous position, it may be a matter for the individual person to solve, e.g., if it concerns language difficulties of formal education; although we should presume that there are arrangements in society to assist persons in overcoming such problems. Such shortages may also be a matter of concern for persons without a migrant background. To be regarded as a social issue, the issue has to be a problem for either many persons with, e.g., similar backgrounds, or a kind of typical problem for individual persons and related to a definite social context to be analyzed by the researcher.

Secondly, we always have to clarify and distinguish our point of departure, i.e. if it concerns moral issues or politics, or if it involves a social scientific perspective. If journalists with migrant backgrounds are said to be treated in a way that may be regarded as e.g., discrimination, it can be criticized from a moral or political point of view. However, from a research perspective the task still ought to be to observe, analyze, and describe this issue in order to arrive at an understanding from different observer perspectives; mainly from the point of view of the journalists in question and from the point of view of the mass media organization. The latter point of view, in line with a long tradition in the social sciences from Max Weber onwards, forces us to distance ourselves adequately from the research object (and subject) during our research.

All mass media is organized into companies or institutions. But why emphasize an organizational perspective in this analysis? Let us approach the matter of organization from two angles:

1. Communication is, according to common views in communication theory, not a simple matter of transferring a message from a sender to a receiver. There are a number of obstacles obstructing a single piece of informa-

tion from achieving its goal, this being an understanding of the message by the recipient. The risk alone of misinterpretation of various kinds is considerable. According to Luhmann's sociological communication theory, in principle each individual communication must pass a series of improbability thresholds for a communication to succeed (Luhmann 1995; Jönhill 1997). Furthermore, a significant part of all communication in modern society can only succeed if it occurs inside the framework of or through organizations. All individual mass media – print media, television, etc. – is made up of organizations. Thus, research on organizations is highly relevant to the analysis of how mass media functions and performs or operates regarding diversity issues.

2.   Apart from how to construct reports, journalists, like scientists and all other professionals, always do their job in an organizational context. Organizations are highly complex systems which simultaneously create an immense amount of possibilities and limitations on the communication and actions of the members within the organization. To put it simply, without mass media companies, no reports would be written or broadcast. The mass media organizations create some fundamental possibilities for journalistic production. At the same time these organizations, including their managers, place restrictions on the journalists, select what should be written, or at least decide what is to be published. In this sense, there are fundamental connections between journalistic production and the organizational context.

Thus, the focus in this chapter is on an analysis of possibilities and limitations of the mass media organization in dealing with diversity issues. In other words, I will consider questions such as: How "locked" are the strategic and organizational frameworks of the mass media organizations in dealing with these issues? Or: What are the organizational conditions for managing diversity issues in accordance with common ideas of equal opportunity, as well as with the discrimination laws?

In the next section of this chapter, after some reconsideration of the method and theory approach, the issue of journalistic production and cultural diversity are placed in the context of the highly differentiated global society. In the subsequent sections, I outline the organized context of journalistic production. From the idea of formal organizations to the communicative approach of diversity management, there has been a shift in the modus of observing qualifications and competences in occupational organizations (or organizations of professionals), such as the mass media companies. In observing cultural diversity, one important frame of reference is the increased importance of the idea of culture in organizations during the last decades. When we come to the analysis of issues of possible disadvantages or of discrimination, we face the problem of observing connections between causes and effects, in other words, of how to attribute reasons for the situation at issue. In the penultimate section, I discuss diversity management as an option for managing cultural diversity. I end with some concluding remarks.

Notes on Method and Theory Approach

A main focus in this chapter involves clarifying relations, coherences, and contexts by suggesting relevant concepts or conceptualizations. This is based on a general conviction that one of the main tasks of the social sciences and humanities is to place distinct concepts on events and phenomena which matter or are at issue. It is not seldom that common sense ideas, or commonly used expressions and explications, as seen in the mass media, and also as seen by politicians, are contested by the result of such work.

The main methodology and theory approach, which is used in this chapter, is the methodology of distinctions and systems theory developed by in particular Luhmann. As a methodology and theory, systems theory is used as a tool for the analysis and understanding of the actual reality. By focusing on distinctions, I mean how to distinguish how events and phenomena should relate or be placed on the inside or the outside of the context or system at issue. As scientists we are – according to the methodological assumption from the phenomenologist Alfred Schutz to the cybernetician Heinz von Foerster and to the systems theorist Luhmann (Jönhill 1997) – *observers of second order.* It means that we are *observing observations of others* in order to be able to analyze and describe our research object.

In this chapter the intention is to observe, by the use of policy documents, literature and other sources, how cultural diversity matters in the mass media as organizations by shifting perspectives from those of the organization to those concerned; journalists with migrant backgrounds, and other persons. This includes observing what is meant, experienced, and perceived when being in a disadvantageous position, or by discrimination, cultural diversity, and so on, from one or more chosen perspectives. To give an example: In the introduction to a book on cultural diversity, the authors explicitly express that their perspective is that of the producers. It is about what "producers – companies, organizations, institutions – may gain or lose by increasing the human diversity in their activities, not how these perspectives can appear from the horizon of individuals, groups or the whole of society" (Broomé et al. 2001: 12). The most common emphasis in the literature on cultural diversity is, on the other hand, said to be that of the concerned individuals, or maybe groups. This or any other chosen perspective may, but must not, it should be added, affect the usefulness of such texts as sources in detail. But to perform our analyses, how do we know the reality of those concerned? The point here is that we have to carefully observe the social situation and context of those concerned, in this case journalists with a migrant background.

Such a method also connects to the widespread idea of modern theory of science that we cannot start with so-called empirical facts or data and then try to build concepts, a thesis, and arrive at our conclusions from data. In other words, we have to get rid of the inductive illusion. Instead we have to start with assumptions, a hypothesis grounded in one existing theory or the other, and then test the hypothesis against our data, and thereby discover whether our hypothesis and theory are verified or refuted (Popper 1959). If the latter is the case, we have to start all over again. I will thus, in trying to follow this idea, oscillate between more general observations or concepts, and more concrete observations or concepts applied to the case of cultural diversity in mass media organizations. Luhmann called this method advice *General Theory* (Luhmann 1990).

This idea of general theory is not equal to a holistic approach, but Luhmann's systems theory connects to the idea of multi-disciplinarity. Or as the American economist and philosopher Kenneth E. Boulding phrased it back in the 1950s:

> The more science breaks into sub-groups, and the less communication is possible among the disciplines, however, the greater chance there is that the total growth of knowledge is being slowed down by the loss of relevant communications. The spread of specialized deafness means that someone who ought to know something that someone else knows isn't able to find it out for lack of generalized ears.
>
> It is one of the main objectives of General Systems Theory to develop these generalized ears, and by developing a framework of general theory to enable one specialist to catch relevant communications from others. (Boulding 1968, p. 4)

I will try to follow these ideas in the following analysis of the issue of journalistic production and diversity from the point of view of sociology and organization theory.

Journalistic Production and Cultural Diversity in the Context of the Highly Differentiated Global Society
The Function of the Mass Media and the Acting of Local Media

When we talk about the mass media we presume that together they form a *unit of their own* in modern society. In other words, we suggest that the mass media in their daily work functions independently in relation to the market economy, politics, etc. The plea for a free press indicates the importance of establishing a reasonably clear-cut limit between journalism as a profession and its environment. Sociologically, instead of just repeating the "rhetoric" of a free press, a free market economy, and so on, we can describe the space of freedom more precisely in terms of *contingency*. Contingency means that we have choices, although always a limited number of choices, to communicate and act. Accurate indications as to the contingency of mass media are the codices on the difference, e.g., between the departments of editorship and advertisement, respectively.[1]

Historically, as we know, the mass media did not exist at all in former societies. The same holds for the educational system, social care, medical health, the legal system, politics in the sense of democracy, and the market economy. Prerequisites for the development of modern mass media, and as a becoming system of its own, involve the parallel development of political democracy, the population growth, the industrial revolution, the market economy, the technological revolutions that occurred at the same time, and so on. The result was a number of basically independent systems constituting society. According to the sociological theory of functional differentiation (developed by especially Durkheim, and later Parsons and Luhmann), the function systems define themselves by following the specific function they perform in society (Luhmann 1997; Jönhill 1997). A precise term to denote modern society is thus *the functional differentiated society*.

The transformation from premodern societies to modern or functional differentiated society brought an immense amount of changes to not only the mentioned development of democracy, but also to the technological revolution, and so on, or (to use Max Weber's famous term) the "disenchantment" of the world. This transformation affected in depth also the relation between man and society. In premodern societies, man was tightly coupled to the few subunits of society, whereas in modern society man as a person might only be loosely coupled to the different function systems and the immense amount of organizations characterizing our society. These couplings, which I will come back to, are described in terms of the *distinction between inclusion and exclusion*.

Thus, in a primary sense, modern society is differentiated by function, unlike previous societies which were differentiated hierarchically or, in other words, on the basis of stratification. Put another way, our society is differentiated horizontally, while previous societies were differentiated according to strata, or simply from top to bottom.

Figure 1 illustrates the fact that modern society basically is horizontally differentiated. It is divided into several functional systems, some of which are shown in the figure. In contrast to former societies, society is thus not vertically structured, as a hierarchy from the upper strata to the lower, i.e. from the nobility to the peasants, the slaves, the poor, and so on. In a horizontally

Figure 1.   The mass media as a function system in its societal context. The mass media forms part of modern society, which is characterized by horizontal differentiation.

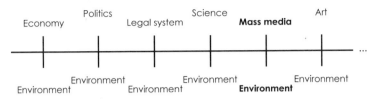

differentiated society, there is no order between the different function systems, which means that the figure could be read from right to left as well. This is the fundamental principle. But since modern society never seems to be "fully modern" (Luhmann 1998) we may, however, observe some hierarchies within different levels of society. In contrast to, e.g., the feudal European societies, these hierarchies are not of primary importance, but are temporary or with limited scope. So is typically the case with organizations, which basically, as long as there are always leaders (chiefs or executives) and employees, will remain hierarchical.

At the same time another non-hierarchical principle, which is more and more often observed both outside and inside organizations, should be mentioned, namely the *network* (White 2007; same 2008). Networks are loosely coupled structures or bonds between persons or organizations. The growing importance of networking during the last decades is obvious. However, for the further analysis in this chapter, networks are not of crucial interest.

Like any function system, the mass media operates on its own conditions. In other words, it is an autopoietic system, i.e. it produces and reproduces itself by communication. Moreover, for communication to operate under the conditions of the function system it must have a specific symbolic communication medium. To determine the characteristics of a function system we must 1) firstly answer the question about the function; 2) secondly answer if it really is about a system of its own; and 3) finally find the specific symbolic communication medium and the binary code for the system at issue (Jönhill 1997).

Talcott Parsons developed the idea that every function system has a symbolic generalized communication medium. The most typical case is money for the economy.[2] This means, in particular, that it stabilizes any communication around the theme of economic transaction on money. In other words, in principle any communication and action in the old market place, today between businessmen and -women, among consumers in shops, etc., are in precisely this context about money and making decisions on whether to pay or not pay. The latter is then the binary code of the economy. Money is not just a medium of exchange, but above all a symbolic medium that simplifies the communication. "Generalized" means that although the medium only has a specific range, it pretends to be generally applicable, i.e. money must be able to apply to all kinds of economic operations. The same goes for power as the symbolic medium of the system of politics, the judicial rights of the legal system, truth – or maybe just the latest research results – of the system of science, and so on. The communication medium and the binary code must be simple in order to make each function system operable.

Luhmann emphasized the function of the mass media in modern society. A bit pointedly, and as a paraphrase of a famous sentence in Shakespeare's' Hamlet, he stressed that:

> What we know about our society, and even of the world we live in, we know it through the mass media. ... On the other hand, we know so much about the mass media that we cannot rely on these sources. (Luhmann 2000b: 9)

From expressions like "all news is good news", we know that the mass media is about news. Thus, the appropriate term for the primary function of the mass media ought to be news. The common term news does not, however, completely cover the function. To be more precise, besides *news and reports* we also have to mention *advertisement*, including publicity, and additionally also *entertainment* as comprising the symbolic generalized communication medium of the mass media.[3] One might argue that science, for example, also has to produce new results and therefore is a kind of news media. Luhmann argues that the three parts, which constitute the communication medium of the system of mass media, as opposed to other systems, specifically have in common the mode of constructing a societal and cultural *memory* (Luhmann 2000b). This means that we normally remember that we received this or that information from the mass media and not from another source, and also that, due to the rapidity of the mass media, we have acquired an ability to forget parts or most of this information.

While the communication medium is about news in a wide sense, the binary code is accordingly about producing news, or just information in the sense of a message that adds something to what is already known. In other words, *the binary code*, which in a primary meaning is directing and steering the operations of the mass media, is *the distinction between information and non-information*. Thus news and reports, advertisements, and entertainment must continuously contain something that has not been reported, broadcast, cabled or published before. The companies or departments within companies and the journalists, who have nothing to inform their readers, listeners and viewers, will rapidly lose their attention.

Of course, being an autopoietic system does not mean that the mass media floats freely in space independent of other parts of society and its environment. But it does mean that the mass media operates independently of other systems. At the same time there are a lot of structurally conditioned connections to other systems, or *structural couplings* (Luhmann 1997). The mass media has structural couplings not only to, e.g., the economy, the legal system and the system of politics, but also to science and to the system of education. As such these couplings, however, do not affect the daily operations.

I have already mentioned second order observation as a methodological tool for this analysis. This is to say that second order observation is a tool in the system of science. However, as Luhmann has shown, second order observation is basic in any communication system in modern society and thus also for every function system. To the mass media this means, among other things, that all journalistic production is relentlessly exposed to demands on observations of observations and reflection. These observations of observations are not just about demands for verifying sources, and so on, but a more or less constant observing of all aspects of the journalistic doings.

In accordance with the picture of the mass media, which I have briefly given here, the mass media does not just "passively" convey information. Like any communication, it is constructed actively anew, whether it is about news on cultural diversity or any other theme. This view is in accordance with, e.g., Janina Dacyl's principal observations on the media and contemporary societal discourses on cultural diversity (Dacyl 2001). But this fact does not guarantee any pluralism of the mass media, and Dacyl's critical assessment that the "globalization" may standardize and make the media even more homogenous all over the world also seems appropriate, although Dacyl, contrary to my thesis, also argues for the media's "fostering" role in society and thus uses normative arguments here (Dacyl 2001). According to systems theory, no social system, and thus no function system, could be said to have any normative function in society. Anyone may put claim on politicians, on managers of companies, on teachers, on priests, on journalists or the mass media companies, and so on, but no system in modern society has any kind of normative function for society as such. If this would be the case, as it is said from a normative position, it would be a deficiency of society. As Luhmann has shown in his extensive analyses of the function of norms, values and moral, in connection with the development of his theory of society, so is reality, i.e. so is the construction of society. Furthermore, moral communication in fact implies an increased risk of conflicts and violence in society (Luhmann 1997; Jönhill 1997). Thus, it seems reasonable to assume that modern global and multicultural society would not survive if the mass media, and as well as other function systems, would have a "fostering" role in society.

It should, however, be pointed out that such an assumption is made from a general perspective on precisely the function of the mass media. It does not mean, for example, that the actions of a local newspaper or television company in a certain situation cannot be said to have any possible effect as part of the communication in society, i.e., acting either in a favouring or disadvantageous manner concerning issues of xenophobia and discrimination of immigrants. As the mass media in general, any local media must be assumed to be important in the communication of news, and they may of course contribute in one direction or the other in the political contested immigrant issues. This has been the case of a local paper in a suburb of Stockholm and a radio channel in Berlin, respectively, focusing on the living conditions for persons with migrant backgrounds (see in this volume Hultén and Graf, respectively). Likewise, Lasse Sandström (Sandström 2004) argues that a local newspaper edition in Rosengård, a suburb of Malmö in the south of Sweden, for some years had an impact in favouring communication and "integration" (integration in a rather concrete and common sense use of the word). Thus a local media may be a means to favour or, on the contrary, to disfavour improvements in the communication between immigrants and the local population. This is, however, not to say that we, from a social scientific point of view, should argue that the mass media positions itself in this or that (political or moral) orientation in issues on this political agenda, which, like any such issue, never can be about a simple "either or" position, and that also always are changing.

The Paradox of Cultural Diversity in the One Global Society

The actual concept of cultural diversity is in a sense new. The concept of diversity ought to be understood in relation to the concurrent and paradoxical concept of the world as unity, the world as one global society common to all human beings (Jönhill 1997). The idea of such a global unity is in its turn also rather new. "Globalization" in the past 25 years has become a key word in descriptions of today's society (e.g. Eriksen 2007; Clegg et al. 2008). As a concept, this key word is literally and from a sociological point of view vague. A phenomenological definition is that "the world has become in important respects a single social system" (Giddens 1989: 519). From the point of view of a theory of society, we can add that modern society as a single global system is *based on communication* (Luhmann 1997).

Although poverty and uneven distribution of material and communicational resources in different parts of the world have been well-known facts for a long time, the idea of the world or the earth in terms of one global unity is rather new. One reason, which actualized the increased dependencies of all regions of the world, was the oil crisis (of Europe and the USA), which was connected to a political and economic conflict in the beginning of the 1970s. To describe these increased dependencies and connections, the American sociologist Immanuel Wallerstein substituted the earlier term "the international system" with "the modern world-system" (Wallerstein 1974). This world-system designated, according to Wallerstein, however, only an economic unity and it thus renewed the concept of a *world economy* as used by Karl Marx. At the same time, Luhmann argued that observations of the phenomenon of "globalization" should be complemented by the theoretical analysis of society as one unity. Otherwise we cannot understand its evolution and differentiation, he argues (Luhmann 1971, Luhmann 1997; Jönhill 1997). What is important in this context is that *we cannot understand the meaning of diversity without relating it to the concept of unity.*

In systems theory, modern society is, thus, described as a communication system and as *one* global system or the world society. Although it implies one global unity, one of the obvious central characteristics of the global society is its *complexity and diversity*. The concept of complexity affects most analyses, not least the fact that society is an internally highly differentiated system. Society is characterized by *diversity,* especially as regards culture. Culture cannot be referred to in the singular, but is, and always has been, characterized by differences or diversity. According to a traditional line of thought, while society articulates universality, culture stands for particularity and thus that which is diverse (Jönhill 1997). Human diversity enables an immense variety and richness, but at the same time, as the Swedish ethnographer Åke Daun shows, the transformations of a person's identities challenge in many instances cultural values and norms in different regions or parts of this global unity (Daun 2001).

One implication is that global communication is equal to communication, involving an immense number of cultures. Hence we could speak about cross-cultural or *intercultural communication* (Allwood 1985; Asante & Gudykunst 1989).

Ethnic or National Background and Social Identity

Another current and frequently used term for that which is culturally distinguishing is *ethnicity*. We elaborate on the term in the introduction of this volume. Here I will add a few points. Why a focus on ethnicity when discussing diversity issues? The answer, as the cultural anthropologist Hylland Eriksen (Eriksen 2002) puts it, is that

1. Conflicts and civil wars with an ethnic ascribed character have increased during the last 25 years;

2. Migration, especially due to conflicts or wars, has grown;

3. "Globalization" as part of the modernization process paradoxically accentuates the particular or uniqueness of human cultural differences; and

4. The fall of the Soviet Union and the so-called real socialist states had as one effect that formerly concealed cultural differences manifested themselves in political conflicts which rose to the surface.

The concept of ethnicity has been used in the humanities and the social sciences only since the 1980s (Björklund 1983; Tägil 1993). As indicated in the introduction, the concept of ethnicity is problematic due to the mixed, and therefore sometimes confusing, meaning of the term (Daun 2001; Eriksen 2002; Rönnqvist 2008).

Ethnicity is one marker of the cultural identity of persons, and also sometimes groups. But it is only *one of many markers of the identity of an individual person*. We could therefore say that we have many identities. More common markers of identity relate to our occupation or profession and/or our role in a family. Thus, the most important identity of a human being in most cultures and forms of society has focused on one's role as peasant, fisherman, artisans of different kinds, and so on, or on one's family role as a father or mother, and so on. During the last two hundred years, drastic changes affecting most persons' daily lives have occurred. The identity of a person refers to how a person constructs, interprets, understands and perceives herself or himself, and others. The identity of one's self is thus not about a true or authentic "me", but is first and foremost formed as distinct from the identity of others.

Migration or resettlement, economic and technological changes and differentiation, professionalization of the working life and the process of modern individualization, etc. have all led to an increased focus upon personal identity. When one searches for a job, i.e. tries to become included in an occupational organization, the normal focus is on qualifications, and not on background. In the building of personal relations and a family the typical focus is, correspondingly, not on heredity but on the individual person emotionally, and, as Fredrik Barth has shown, on diverse interests, cultural elements, mixed religion, etc., or idiosyncrasies (cf. Eriksen 2002; Daun 2001).

As we also discuss in the introduction of this volume, we must distinguish between ethnic and national background. At first, like the concept of ethnic identity, the concept of national identity is also rather vague. As Daun shows, on the one hand we can observe

an increase in the strength and importance of national identity which concerns both nationalism as a normative position and nationalism as a general sense of national uniqueness. (Daun 2001: 295)

On the other hand

national identities tend to become less important for individuals. The national "we" becomes more complex and problematic. (Daun 2001 ibid.).

Daun argues that these contradictory processes are implied by the same phenomenon, namely cultural differentiation through internationalization (Daun ibid.) or, as I would prefer to put it, differentiation through increased global communication. Today numerous persons all over the world experience the matter of fact that both ethnic and national identity denote rather undistinguished clichés.[4]

In most cases nationality is, I will add, a more relevant marker of a person's identity than ethnicity. When the nation-states in Europe, and later in most parts of the world, were built, it was done without regard to cultural or ethnic differences. One result, as is well-known, has been an increased number of conflicts and wars, genocide, and so on. As far as Europe is concerned regarding the situation today, insofar as we could still talk about ethnic groups, we could say that the nation-state includes several ethnic groups. So, for instance, approximately nine million persons have a Swedish national background. But as a Swede, one can simultaneously be a "Stockholmer", and then be from city districts like Östermalm or the South of Stockholm, and so on. "Swedish" is, and precisely in this case contrary to Ericsen's somewhat ambiguous definition of the term, a designation that above all marks nationality. To be "Swedish", if we accept this term as not just being confusing (cf. Daun 2001), is thus not equal to "ethnic Swedish", but addresses national identity. If we were to talk about ethnicity here it would refer to persons' reminiscences of heredity from definite parts of landscapes, etc. To use the concept of ethnicity in Sweden in designating minorities seems adequate foremost for the nationally recognized minorities, like Samis (or Laplanders) and Romans. Likewise being a German designates nationality, while at least reminiscences of ethnic belonging in certain everyday contexts still is designated in terms of Bavarian, Swabian, etc.

In general, the same conditions are apparent in modern society for all parts of the world. Ethnic groups are in most cases not bound to national borders. Thus Nigerian designates nationality, whereas, e.g., Yorubian designates one of many ethnic groups inherited in, among others, Nigeria; Kenyan designates nationality, but, e.g., Masai ethnic group; Afghani designates nationality, but, e.g., Pashtuns ethnic group; and Chinese designates nationality, while The Republic of China officially recognizes 56 distinct ethnic groups. To summarize, it is important to understand the complex conditions of migration issues, including the context of minority backgrounds. Above all, we are never dealing with simple questions of minorities, on the one side, and the majority in a certain region or a nation-state on the other.

From Integration and Homogeneity to Diversity and Heterogeneity

The reasons for the fact that society today more than ever is a multicultural society are, as is well known, several. The phenomenon of "globalization" is usually described in terms of not only phenomena typical for modern society during the last centuries, such as increased world trade and international travel, but it is also increasingly related to more intense and intertwined global communication supported by different technical means, networking, and, as is also well known, global exchanges and communication medias, such as internet-based media. The growth of migration during the last decades has to do with wars and political conflicts, which in many cases have ethnic overtones. Another reason for the growth of migration involves the new possibilities of the world labour market. In summary, modern society faces demographic changes more than ever before.

In modern European political history, there has been in a broad sense, I will argue, *a development from social and cultural diversity and heterogeneity towards homogeneity and integration, with a switch back to diversity and heterogeneity*. The multicultural sides of Swedish history have for a long time largely been denied, at least in the rhetoric of politicians. To exemplify, in addition to Swedish, Finnish was the language that was spoken in the old Swedish parliament in the 19th century, and German was the language spoken for centuries in many of the council cottages in the cities on the Swedish east coast. But as in other European nation-states, ideas of national unification, and thus constructions of homogeneity, have characterized the typical nation building. So, e.g., according to the historiography that permeated 20th century Swedish schooling, the teaching of history was strongly marked by national trends (Abrahamsson et. al. 1999).

Until about the 1970s, the migration policy in Sweden was dominated by ideas of integration in the sense of *assimilation* (Abrahamsson et al. 1999). This idea of integration was in principle the Durkheimian idea of the necessity of a homogeneous population as to norms and values. A main argument from Durkheim and followers for justifying the idea of integration and homogeneity was that society would fall apart without common norms and values.

Durkheim was, however, as Luhmann has showed in detail, wrong in his judgment of the consequences of the growing differentiation of society. While too many demands on integration and homogeneity may result in conflicts and disintegration, heterogeneity and diversity instead open up for possibilities of managing contradictions, disagreements and conflicts, and thus allowing modern society to survive (Luhmann 1997).

Furthermore, if one argues in favour of integration, someone must have the power to define those norms which everyone ought to be integrated into. This is of course the case regardless of whichever nation state it concerns. To quote from a critical report of Swedish integration policy:

> While immigrant integration and participation is well covered, there appears to be very little research on the 'integration' of Swedes into a multicultural society. An extension of this would include research on cultural relations between ethnic groups, including the Swedes. (Vasta et al. 2003: 38)

Integration policies in most EU nation states have, however, changed a lot since the increase in migration during the last decades. In Sweden we can observe a policy change towards fewer expectations as to homogeneity and more insight into the value of cultural plurality. The praxis of the immigrant policy in Sweden has thus been changed from the simplified idea of assimilation in the 1960s, towards the ideas of a more slow and "accepting" integration in the 1970s, and to the currently pragmatic ideas of introductory programmes aimed at newcomers (Ds 2000: 43; SOU 2004: 48; SOU 2010: 16).

Equality and Inequality as a Structuring Principle in Society

During the last decades, claims for equal rights or equal treatment have been voiced in the mass media from the political arena on issues connected to ethnic and other minorities. Equality can, however, only mean something as a distinction from inequality. If not, equality would signify indifference, that is to say, something without meaning.[5] Claims for equality are, on the one hand, usually observed as part of the "modernization" process, and on the other hand as "the right to be different", i.e. in a sense unequal. To be respected as such has been strongly argued for by both individuals and minority groups during the last decades all over the world. How is this paradox to be understood? Recognizing other cultures means respecting other persons and groups on the basis of different values, and thus recognizing something diverse or unequal in one culture by distinguishing it from others. Then how can the multicultural global society manage cultural differences making differences?

The distinction between equality and inequality is a main feature that differs when comparing different forms of societies (Luhmann 1997). This distinction is important as a structuring principle, both from the side of society and from individual persons, respectively. It is connected to the issue of social affiliation and thus the distinction between inclusion and exclusion. At the same time, equality must not be confused with inclusion. Following ideas in modern political philosophy is, however, confusing since, on the one hand, from the French revolution onwards equality has been said to be the ideal while, on the other hand, critical theories have successfully argued that inequality often seems to prevail. As Luhmann has formulated it, *functional differentiation means that the principle of equality as well as that of inequality is basic to the function systems*. It is about the heterogeneous, or, in other words, that "function systems are equal in their inequality" (Luhmann 1997: 613).

Thus, equality is crucial not as an abstract principle, but with respect to an individual person's access to function systems. The concept of equality only has an information value if it differs from inequality. This is obvious in modern society. To exemplify: The judicial contract is based on inequality. Each kind of contract supplies one with a right, which cannot be provided to everyone.

If in the educational system one person has better grades than another, then it may not mean that the former is allowed to vote in political elections, but not the latter. Or if one person gets credit but not another, then it should be reflected on in an economic and rational way and it must not determine e.g. whether one is accepted to a school or not. In modern society all kinds of inequality must be seen as temporary. In any case, it cannot be passed on to the next generation, which was the case in stratified societies. In a general sense, inequality means *unequal distribution of communication chances* (Luhmann 1997; Jönhill 1997). *Equality*, in its turn, *means equal opportunity*, and obviously it cannot designate equality of results.

The matter of fact that modern society is non-hierarchical and also that it lacks a centre is, I will argue, one reason why in principle it is well-suited to manage cultural differences precisely when it comes to providing equal opportunities to persons regardless of cultural background. However, as a differentiated system society consists of other forms of systems that may operate to counteract the principle of equal opportunity. This is a characteristic of organizations.

Mass Media as Organizations

In addition to editorial aspects, the very organization should be considered as most essential to journalistic production, stresses Lars Hultén in a discussion on changes in the newsroom and how to understand who determines such changes (Hultén 1996). Elaborate observations of organizational aspects of mass media are, however, rather rare. In an article from the beginning of the 1970s, the American editor and journalist Ben Bagdikian sketched some of the changes within American mass media companies that had taken place after World War II. The readers and the audience changed rapidly, especially during the 1960s, and so did the ownership of the companies, he states. From being small companies, often family-owned, they became large corporations (Bagdikian 1973). Bagdikian stresses the importance of the organizational structure in the shaping of media content. The working conditions for the journalist, the relations between media companies and the political establishment, as well as the status of minorities and of women in the media staff, are all dependent on the organizational structure of the mass media. Typical for the time period, Bagdikian concludes with some optimistic impressions: firstly he assumes that social scientific media research will increase in importance, and secondly:

> Also, the new breed of professional journalists – those more knowledgeable in social science techniques, less ingrained with inherited xenophobia when their own institution is involved, and more concerned with challenging tra-

ditional assumptions – are increasingly reaching positions of editorial power and can be expected to understand and sympathize with serious research into the dynamics and structures that control our news and public information. (Bagdikian 1973: 578)

Apart from Bagdikian's naivety in his optimistic assessment, his awareness of the importance of the growing professionalization of journalism as a kind of immunity against xenophobia, as well as his awareness of the organizational constraints, is nevertheless apparent. This brings us to a more in-depth analysis of mass media as organizations.

As Weick puts it regarding organizations, a primary focus ought not to be on the organization as a formal structure, but on organizing as communication and action (Weick 1969). As a result of decision-making, every organization is then established as an autonomous entity which cannot be governed or controlled from the outside. In other words, we can talk about organizations as operationally closed, self-producing or, in other words, auto-poietic systems (Luhmann 2000a; Morgan 1997; Seidl 2005). Organizations are closed systems insofar that they operate on their own terms and shape their own goals or programs. They respond to their environment, but can only do so by actively acquiring knowledge of it. This means that even if a company is obliged to comply with new laws, this will not happen automatically, but requires an active effort by the company. One consequence of organizations' closeness is that events in the outside world often have a limited or, using a "classical" sociological term, non-intended impact. Thus, the requirement of mass media organizations from legal or political authorities to communicate and act according to specific standards or rules of law, such as in issues of discrimination and cultural diversity, may have difficulties in being realized.

The Organized Context of the Journalist

Modern society brought about the advancement of the goal-oriented organization, and the corporation became the forerunner in its further development. Between 1850 and 1950 an organizational revolution took place (Boulding 1953). In our daily life, everyone can rather easily see that the use of organized communications and actions is a distinctive feature of our society. The American sociologist Warren Breed was one of the pioneers in studying mass media organizations in this sense. In his article "Social Control in the Newsroom: A Functional Analysis", he outlines the organizational prerequisites of the American newsroom of the 1950s (Breed 1955).

The article is based partly on the sociological theory of organization and management at that time, and partly on data collected by the author some years earlier. He starts from some basic presumptions distinguishing, among others, between executives and the staff or the "staffers", i.e. reporters, re-write men, copyreaders, etc. Like every other organization, the newspaper company has a goal. This is the policy. The principal areas of policy are, according to Breed, politics, business, and labour. The policy is, however, often not clearly stated, especially if it is about politics. Breed's main point is to analyze some features of how social control or power relations are upheld (Breed 1955). Since the 1950s, newsrooms have of course undergone drastic changes, but the main features of the media, as organizations with relations between executives or managers and the staff, remain roughly the same. This analysis on control in the organization as maintained by conforming norms and values also concerns what we today refer to as organizational culture, which I will come back to.

Breed's analysis of the media organization is well in accordance with "classi-cal" and in some respects modern organization theory. Organizations in modern society are basically defined by a few fundamental distinctions:

1. Membership; one can always, and empirically, decide if a person does or does not belong to a definite organization.

2. Goal or program; organizations always have definite delimited goals, conditioning a person's behaviour and acting on the basis of role func-tions.

3. Places and staff (including executives); to realize their programs, organiza-tions have efficacious persons at specified positions. Hence the emergence of role positions and professions.

4. Decisions; the function of the organization is to make and implement decisions.[6]

Another characteristic of the organization as system is the relation between organization and its environment. In terms of institutional (and neo-institutional) theory, organizations have been regarded as institutions with constraints from the inside while at the same time relating to an outside world, a setting. Ac-cording to Meyer & Rowan they also try to adapt to their environment (Meyer & Rowan 1977). The latter hypothesis follows from the assumption of organiza-tions as, in a basic meaning, rational entities. In other words, if an organization does not adapt to its environment, it will run the risk of getting into trouble, collapsing or, as a company, going bankrupt. According to the "classic" ap-proach in organization theory from Weber and others, it will not happen as organizations are, it was argued, basically rational actors.

However, as we know from an amount of empirical evidence today, all kinds of organizations are now and then going bankrupt, which means that there is obviously no such adapting mechanism as is presumed. From, among others, James March and Luhmann we must assume that organizations cannot basically be described as rational units, yet to communicate and act rationally is one of the frequent issues organizations need to manage (Luhmann 2000a). The latter assumption means in this context that we can observe media organizations acting quite differently when it comes to diversity issues. Organizations are expected to regard and be influenced by the outside world, i.e. their environment, while they themselves also influence the outside world. But they have the possibility to choose not to care about what is happening in the outside world as to, e.g., staff or personnel issues. Due to the specific function of the mass media, the media organizations have obviously a special relation to environments of audiences, advertisement customers, etc. But the same goes for many other types of organizations.

How Inclusion Occurs in Occupational Organizations

A main assumption in systems theory is that society is an all-encompassing communication system that consists solely of communication, including actions – but excluding humans in the sense of flesh and blood, as psychic beings, and also excluding all kinds of artefacts. Inclusion simply means that we as persons, i.e. humans as communicating beings, are relevant to the system at issue. As "complete" individuals, or as human bio-psycho-social beings, we are then, logically, always on the outside of society.

Modern society is *socially open* in the sense that the inclusion of all persons is in general anticipated. In other words, modern society as an overall communication system is *primarily including*. It is socially open in the sense that inclusion is in general anticipated due to contingency. The same goes for interactions (social meetings) and also for the function systems of society. Among the latter are the systems of family, of economy, of education, of religion, and so on. Everyone is, so to speak, welcomed, though not to every meeting, but to many potential meetings, and also to the sharing of potential family bonds, to economic relations, to education of many kinds, to adhere to a religion, and so on. However, to obtain money for survival, to apply for a job position or perhaps to start a business, to be admitted to an education, to adhere to a religion and thus a church, and so on, we also have to be a *member of an organization*. We are all therefore dependant on organizations (Luhmann 1997; Jönhill 2011).

Viewed as social beings, i.e. as persons, we are always included in society as long as we are able to communicate, but at the same time we are, paradoxically, excluded from most subsystems in society, i.e. organizations, groups, networks and interactions, as we have no access to them. On the whole, we may only be included as persons and within our roles, or to be more precise *role functions*, in a few organizations, such as a work organization, and at the same time in several function systems, e.g., the economy, the system of family, the system of politics as a citizen in a nation state (i.e. in an organization), etc.

The role as manager, trader, teacher, etc. could, as we know, be performed differently, for better or worse, e.g., simply qualified/insufficiently qualified, or acting according to the law/unlawful or illicit acting. The same goes for journalists or researchers in the social sciences and the humanities, and so on. The inclusion in an organization thus relates to the role function of the position and we can denote this as *membership role* (Luhmann 1964) or *inclusion role* (Stichweh 2005).

To an individual person both inclusion and exclusion, in every single case, are obviously about a process. To obtain a "permanent" job and thus become included in a work organization may have been the result of a process including basic education, professional education, part-time jobs, time limited jobs, networking, job-seeking and recruitment processes, etc., with the risk of failure at each step. For a migrant, there are in many cases additional steps to take. To become excluded from a social system is the result of a corresponding process. In different ways, persons have to go through a process of moving either towards inclusion or towards exclusion as regards citizenship (being a migrant), permanent residence, and also perhaps regarding family, membership in a union, a church, etc. However, the processes involving the move from exclusion to inclusion, or the other way round, have to *pass a limit* in order to proceed from the one side to the other. Focusing on these concepts *as distinctions,* and not just as a "more or less", i.e. as a variable, means paying attention to this very fact and its implications (Jönhill 2011).

Thus, *a hallmark of organizations* is that, contrary to society, which certainly is unexpected for many of us, *they are primarily excluding* (Luhmann 1995, Luhmann 1997; Luhmann 2000; Stichweh 2005). Organizations are able to decide how to recruit their staff, how to manage the organization and its staff, and they also have the capacity of discriminating the staff. That is to say, *every person is* outside of or *excluded from almost every organization in the world*, i.e. except those few organizations to which s/he has been included. We normally have to gain admission to a school or a university, i.e. an organization, to acquire the education we need for a possible future job, or for acquiring the knowledge we would like to have, and thus to then be included in the education system. We have to be employed in a company or an institution, i.e. an organization, to be included in the economy, etc. And admissions and appointments are decided within organizations. As Luhmann explicitly has pointed out:

> Society is equipped with capacity of discrimination through its organizations. They treat all the same and everyone differently (Luhmann 2000a: 393).

From this perspective, exclusion as a result of discrimination of persons and groups with a migrant background ought to be understood in a more complex way than is the usual case within social sciences and social policy studies.

Exclusion is always about being excluded from specific relations or systems, and we cannot generalize about "outsider-ship". The distinction between being inside and outside always has to do with communication opportunities, or lack of communication opportunities, within the actual system. While organizations are able to discriminate they can also, however, relinquish this on different grounds; be it due to the labour market situation, customers or other competition reasons.

There are, however, several reasons for certain individual persons encountering a disadvantageous position regarding inclusion in organizations. Discrimination is one. Discrimination due to ethnic or national background can be observed everywhere in society. However, if we are to speak about "structural discrimination" this may, from the view of systems theory, be relevant only to organizations. This also holds for organized measurements, regulations, etc. of nation states, i.e. of the organizations of the system of politics. Organizations can make decisions about whatever they want, and thus they can decide to treat individuals or groups differently, "correctly" or "incorrectly"; in the latter case, e.g., unfavourably or with disadvantages to persons based on ethnic or national background. Society can, via its law system, create and invoke laws that forbid discrimination, but organizations can nevertheless in their practice, via informal organized measurements, non-decisions, etc., decide not to act on such issues.

Figure 2.

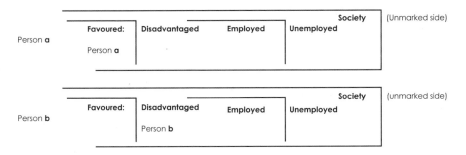

In systems theory form analysis can be used as a tool to indicate how guiding distinctions operate. In figure 2, I show the distinction between inclusion and exclusion as related to society and as a partially operating distinction. Form analysis (Spencer Brown 1969. Cf. Baecker 2007; and Simon 2007) is used as a tool to trace traits of identity- and role-building. Instead of a circle distinguishing an inside from an outside, an angle is used to show the same kind of limit. The limit marks in each case the distinction of being included or excluded. As long as we as human beings are able to communicate, we are always included in a general sense. Let us assume that person a has a job as a journalist in a media company and thus is, as employed, included in the organization. S/

he is also included as to teamwork; s/he might expect to have at least equal opportunity to career chances in the company, etc. Person b has also a job as a journalist and is thus included, but s/he is excluded as to teamwork, to expected career chances, etc. The reason for person b to be excluded may be a disadvantageous position due to shortcomings, e.g., as to language or discrimination due to ethnic background, etc. Although simplified, while my aim here is to demonstrate the principle, the figure indicates that inclusion and exclusion is never a simple distinction. The "value" of being placed on the one side or the other is in this context not about a metaphor, but equal the values in Wittgenstein's so called truth tables, which are the forerunner to Spencer Brown's form analysis (Spencer Brown 1969; cf. Becker 1997).

Inclusion, Social Identities and the Changes of Demands of Qualifications

The mass media organization of the 1950s in the USA, which Breed regarded (Breed 1955), was, as I have shown above, in basic respects still the same as it is today. But besides the immense technical changes, we can observe a lot of changes, among others, in the very organizing of the job. Some of these changes affect the way we are affiliated with the organization. In other words, they affect the form of inclusion in the organization.

One such remarkable change during the last decades is the introduction of group production or teamwork and self-steering groups. One example originally developed for the industrial production but spread to many branches, are the so called quality circles. Quality circles are teams which meet regularly in order to communicate on and solve production problems. As is well shown by Nygren and others, this kind of team and other kinds of teamwork characterize the daily work situation in the newsroom today. At the same time demands of multi-skilling (writing articles, making TV programs, taking photos, and so on) are put on journalists (Nygren ed. 2008).

The employment situation for most journalists has also changed a lot during the last decades. This is of course due to changes in the market situation for all kinds of mass media, as well as to technical changes, and so on. The way or modus of how employees relate to or are included in organizations has, however, changed for most persons during the last decades. In many branches we can, e.g., observe tendencies from permanent employments towards time-limited positions, and thus a more unsecure employment relation (Allwin et al. 2006). This may have negative effects for persons with only a few and weak connections in the labour market, like migrants in general. However, with regard to journalists with migrant backgrounds it seems that in this case, as is shown in other chapters in this volume, it is not possible to draw any unambiguous conclusions.

Being included in modern society means, as I have discussed above, becoming relevant to a certain system. As a professional or an applicant for a position as a professional, a person may try to demonstrate his or her competencies as, e.g., a journalist. Whether a person likes or dislikes this situation, in order to understand what it is about the point of departure should be the organization and not the individual person. We are principally not of interest as human beings to the organization, as men or women, "Swedes" or migrants to any organization. But we are presumed to be of importance as professionals in a specific *role function* in an occupational organization.

At the same time, we are presumed to be included in a role as citizens of a nation state (i.e. in the system of politics). And at the same time, we are presumed similarly to be included in a family in a role as partner, mother, father, and so on. Obviously, however, neither a job nor membership in a family can be taken for granted, and thus in this sense exclusion is so to speak the point of departure for all of us. Most persons take citizenship for granted, while those who are migrants have to obtain a citizenship to become included in this respect.

Furthermore, as I also elaborated on above, we form different social identities in our different role functions. This is especially apparent in working life. The personal identities that we emphasize in one social context may be very different from those that we emphasize in another. Thus, identities are both multiple and changeable (Stichweh 2005; Clegg et al. 2008).

To the "classics" of the social sciences, one of the huge advancements of modern society was the rationale and rationality of its organizations. In pre-modern societies a prerequisite for getting a position, irrespective of eventual education, skills, etc. for the position at issue, was typically the expected or "right" heredity, and personal bonds, i.e. status and rank, as well as age and (in most cases) male sex. According to the formal or "classical" theory of organization and profession research, expectations of the employee should solely be related to qualifications related to the role function, such as skills, education, and so on. It implies that personal characteristics like gender, heredity, or age should not be considered.

Insofar as changes concerning patterns of individuality affect motivation and thus performance, the personality of the employee becomes even more relevant for the organization than his or her special skills. This is apparent from a communicative approach.

During the last decades the production process in all kinds of work organizations has undergone thoroughgoing changes. These changes have to do with both internal changes in the organization and changes in the environment of the organization affecting both the human being and society. Among these changes are those societal changes where "globalization", as regards the work force and the customers, is one key word.

Other changes include the changes in the patterns of individuality, which are often called the "modern individualization process". Such a change affects the mode of performance in occupations in many ways. The very modes of organizing daily work – which have shifted towards team work, internal and external networking, and so on – place focus again on the personality aspects of the employee.

One important trait in management during the second part of the last century is that Taylorism has been replaced by ideas that emphasize communicative competences. In addition to the formal and occupational prerequisites on the role function in its narrow sense, the general *communicative competences* of the employee are viewed as crucial or even more relevant to the organization than the former demands. The latter includes what is commonly meant by "social and cultural competences". In addition to the body, the psyche and one's communicative ability are all becoming more and more important dimensions of the individual person for the organization (Baecker 2003). These changes also include what is called performative learning ability, i.e. the ability to learn that learning is useful in practice and that there is continually something new to learn. For journalists, as for many other professionals, it is, e.g., important to be continually prepared to learn new techniques and new ways of organizing one's job.

The meaning of communicative ability or competences is interpreted differently. In most cases, it does not mean the mastery of grammar or pronunciation. Exceptions might be found in, e.g., the mass media, where a correct handling of language should be rather important.

The question is how to assess what is observed to be relevant to the organization regarding a person's identity, including one's background and the demands of qualifications, which are required by the organization and which affect the demands of qualification. In this context, I find it adequate to distinguish between two main traits within managing diversity issues. Among the most widespread management strategies there are, in part, Human Resource Management (HRM), and in part diversity management.

Within the management strategies of HRM the evaluation of communicative ability or competences is interpreted in a very personalizing manner[7]. HRM can be described as the management of personality in all of its aspects (Åkerstrøm Andersen 2007; Åkerstrøm Andersen & Born 2008). However, as Barbara Czarniawska has argued critically, the employee is not a "resource" for the organization in terms of his or her entire human body and soul, which is assumed following the advocators of HRM (Czarniawska 2005). As an employee, a person remains in a definite position and function in the organization. According to the concept of role function and social identity used here, a person's entire personality should not be viewed as useful within an organization.

In difference to HRM, advocators of diversity management argue that what is deemed as communicative competence is not the entire human being, but only the specified qualifications for the position at issue. However, in contrast to the old manner of evaluation, social and cultural competences, and especially what is diverse, may well also be relevant. I will return to diversity management.

Organization as Culture

Like everything else, the relationships between different departments of a mass media company undergo changes. The staffs of the editorial office and the sales department have developed different cultures, as Lars Hultén notices (Hultén 1996). Nowadays, editors-in-chief place demands on closer cooperation between these departments. Such demands were, however, much more difficult to communicate some decades ago, due to a widespread idea of contradicting interests between "commercialism" and "the mission of the mass media". Today these interests are said to be compatible (Hultén 1996). Hultén speaks about two different cultures in the mass media company: on the one hand a "culture of the editors", and on the other hand a "corporation culture".

Although Hultén's distinctions from the point of view of organization theory are rather vague, his observations capture some important points as to the mass media organization as culture. The word *culture* is often confusing and difficult to define, but it cannot be avoided. From a communicational view, culture could be defined as *a way of thematizing communication in society* (Luhmann 1997). The idea of culture was introduced into organization and management theory in the beginning of the 1980s by, among others, Gareth Morgan (Morgan 1986). Since then it has been crucial in the analysis of how norms, values, and patterns of behaviour stabilize the organization and allow it to function, yet at the same time tends to hinder changes in an ever-changing environment. As it is essential to the understanding of diversity, the concept of organizational culture should also be highlighted here.

The term culture has many different meanings. In his book, *Organizational Culture and Leadership,* Edgar Schein initially revolves around the concept of culture. Schein's brief definition of culture as related to organizations is that it concerns the forming of unstructured behaviour and actions into more structured behaviour and actions, and "culture formation is always, by definition, a striving towards patterning and integration" (Schein 2004: 17). He lists eleven elements which in the earlier and present literature have been used to describe culture: 1) observed behavioural regularities when people interact; 2) group norms; 3) espoused values; 4) formal philosophy (broad policies and ideological principles); 5) rules of the game (implicit unwritten rules); 6) climate; 7) embedded skills; 8) habits of thinking, mental models, and linguistic paradigms; 9) shared meanings; 10) "root metaphors" or integrating symbols; and 11) formal rituals and celebrations (Schein 2004: 12-13).

Thus, organizations develop their own culture, i.e. norms and patterns of employee behaviour and conduct, shared values, and so on. Within large organizations, different groups of employees or different departments can develop their own cultures. Here we can talk about subcultures of the organization (Schein 2004). Hultén's above-mentioned distinction between a "culture of the editors" in the editorial office and of a "corporation culture" in the sales department respectively is an example of subcultures in this sense. The concept of culture, Schein argues, helps in the understanding of subcultural phenomena in organizations and cultural analysis, which is necessary for management today. Defining a definite organizational culture is a complex matter due to the "hidden rules" designating the concept. Organizational culture and management are closely connected, and management is in a sense a management of culture (Schein 2004). The on-going process of managing and the forming of the organizational culture are parts of the same dynamic processes.

Although organizations are changing all the time, in an ever-changing environment, organizational culture is a slow-moving phenomenon (Hofstede et al. 1990). In other words, due to the organizational culture, changes may have difficulties in breaking through.

The success for the concept of branding is one of many expressions for the importance of organizational culture. So e.g. television companies like TV4 or SVT in Sweden and ARD and RTL in Germany communicate and advertise themselves as brands, i.e. not only as trademarks (companies in a judicial meaning) but as "personal" identities which are symbolized in diverse respects. The brands of these companies includes TV-programmes which in turn, to put it simple, are brand names themselves with logos of their own and so on. At the same time they are, as TV-programmes with their staff and other resources, part of the brand (or extended brand) of the television company. The phenomenon of branding is, besides, not related to the form of ownership. From the view of organizational culture brand is a form of self-description of the success of the company. We can say, as Dirk Baecker puts it, that while the brand of these companies designate a self-description of their success, the concept of organizational culture (of which brand is a part) designates the self-description of the self-description of the company (Baecker 2003).

All in all, these are reasons for the emphasis of the organizational culture of companies today. Thus, the intangible term of organizational culture stands for a reflected idea of the organization. As to the mass media companies, explicit studies of organizational culture, however, seem to be rare.

Management as Communication and Organizational Culture

During the last decades, the intensity in many kinds of global communication and networking has accelerated. This communication is, in different ways, bound to organizations and networks. At the same time, management of organizations has been more and more focused upon. It is observable not only in organizational practices, but also in the mass media, by politicians and in the social sciences. Against the backdrop of such changes it seems obvious that management first and foremost should be described as communication. As management is about making decisions we could, to be more precise, describe management as the performing of decisions via communication (Baecker 2003).

To view the mass media organization as culture leads us close to the issue of how to manage cultural diversity in the mass media organization. The strategy of diversity management during the last decades has had a vast impact all over the world. I will return to this theme after a discussion on how we should interpret the most frequent explanations for the fact that persons with a migrant background run a risk of falling into a disadvantageous position within media organizations or, as applicants for a position, in relation to media organizations.

Causalities – Attributing Reasons for Disadvantages in Relation to Organizations

Journalists with migrant backgrounds with a position in Sweden are estimated to be about 5% of all employed journalists (see a survey as an appendix to this volume), while the percentage of the population with migrant backgrounds is about 20 %. If we take for granted that without any hindrances every occupation should mirror the population as to gender, ethnic or national background, normal age in the work force, and so on, this figure should be evidence for stating that journalists with a migrant background are disadvantaged when they apply for a position as a journalist. Indications for discrimination as one reason are presented in other chapters in this volume. We cannot, however, assume discrimination being the reason in this case by just comparing these two figures.

Generally the labour market, either in Sweden or elsewhere, does not resemble any kind of mirroring of the population, for several reasons (Allwood, et al. 2006; Nekby & Rödin 2007). One simple reason has to do with the history of the modern industrial society and the heritage of, e.g., the "patriarchal" family structures from former societies. Thus, occupations are not equally distributed in any respect. To understand this matter of fact and issue

regarding migrants in order to try to contribute to some possible solutions
or resolutions, we have to carefully analyze different possibilities, evidence,
and reasons. Otherwise eventual efforts might not become appropriate. From
the point of view of modern theory of science, we know that the *relation
between cause and effect* as to every social issue is complex (Jönhill 1997). In
other words, in the normal case there are several causes behind any effect,
which causes social problems for persons, groups or parts of society. Thus,
we have to provide evidence for certain causes that could be *attributed* to
the effects. The evidence presented in other chapters in this volume does not
make it possible to draw any general conclusions. Here I will briefly discuss
the issue in a general sense.

In the case of journalists, at first we can notice that there are biases between,
on the one hand, different selections or samples of the population and, on the
other hand, many relatively small professions. To demonstrate with a reasonable degree of certainty that a migrant background or a culturally diverse background might be decisive for a person's disadvantageous situation or position
further presumes that applicants for a journalist job are registered according to
their background and secondly that "migrant background" is clearly defined in
individual cases. If, e.g., a person born in Sweden or Germany with parents
being migrants from a neighbouring country is grouped together with persons
who are migrants themselves with a non-European background, we have to
do with a rather broad definition compared to a definition which only includes
persons of the latter category.[8] This brings us back to our research issue, and
to the need to nuance or reformulate our question.

In a number of studies applying the economic model of human capital,
it is shown that the reasons that persons with a migrant background have a
disadvantageous situation and position in the labour market can be of several
different kinds. Such reasons include language deficiency, incomparable formal education, differences in the supply and demand situation within different
branches, matching problems, reasons due to structural changes in definite
branches, recessions, and so on (Sjögren & Zenou 2007; Rönnqvist 2008). As
to journalists, in certain positions language deficiency or lack of enough language proficiency may be an important issue, while at the same time there are
other journalist positions where some language deficiencies are not decisive
if balanced against other competencies (cf. Graf 2008).

Discrimination as a Social Issue

One of many reasons for finding oneself in a disadvantageous situation or position is obviously discrimination. Discrimination occurs in diverse situations and
systems of society but is, when it occurs, most evident in organizations. In the
latter case, it is more often possible to find an actor to be legally attributed. It

is a social issue when it concerns daily social relations. From a societal context, since discrimination is about breaking and violating norms and justice, it is an issue for the legal system.

Discrimination due to ethnic or national background has become a social and political issue in many parts of the global society during the last decades. How is discrimination possible? To discriminate means, literally, to treat similar cases differently (NE; Nilsson 2002). Discrimination in such a literal sense is in most cases in fact not experienced as problematic, e.g., in a judicial sense where every contract means something different and unequal and thus discriminates everyone except the contract holder. Nor does discrimination need to be problematic. When e.g., disabled persons receive the right to technical aid, special transport means and tools, etc., such different and special treatment is normally not seen as a social problem.

A case where it is difficult to talk about discrimination is when a migrant receives a position for the very reason that he or she has a migrant background, and not because of competence. In its turn, the reason for such a decision may, on the part of an organization, be a consideration as to demands from customers, politicians, and so on. Hence, as Graf has shown, to become the "token Turk" as a journalist in Germany may be an ambivalent, or even a type of unwanted, positive discrimination (Graf 2008).

Discrimination occurs when the disadvantageous or unfavourable position, put in a social and political context, could be attributed to a person's cultural heredity, gender, sexual preferences, age, etc. Otherwise, we are not dealing with discrimination as such but with other cases of disrespect, humiliation, etc., or acts which are perceived and experienced as morally and/or politically reprehensible. Furthermore, discrimination, socially and individually, is also a matter of the *perception and experience* of the concerned person.

Discrimination thus becomes a social problem when similar cases are managed differently and are also perceived by those committed, or others, as an offence and as an unjust or prejudicial distinction in the treatment of other persons, especially on the mentioned grounds. Obvious discrimination may be intentional as well as unintentional. That discrimination always is a matter of perception can be shown by two examples: Pensioners' discounts on entrance-fees to some public institutions are thought of by most people as part of the efforts of the welfare state to assist old-age pensioners. But there is a lot of evidence from mass media that, e.g., wealthy old-age pensioners perceive such discounts as an insult and as discrimination. Another example can be when a person with a (typical) Swedish national background encounters a person with a non-European background and the former tries to be helpful in the situation by speaking English. This action could also be perceived as discriminating, if the person with the non-European background has been an inhabitant of Sweden for many years and speaks Swedish.

Apart from such situations of communicative misunderstandings, discrimination as a social or legal issue involves a shift in connotation, which involves power.[9] It is difficult for society to solve issues of discrimination due to the fact that discriminating actions occur as events and behaviour among persons and groups in all kinds of situations. Discriminating actions within the organizations of society are, however, different. Due to procedural connections, in most cases it is easier to observe from inside rather than outside of organizations. In professional organizations, the issue of discriminating actions, whether intentional or non-intentional, is mainly an issue for the management.

Discrimination as an Issue of the Legal System

The actual social issues and discussions on discrimination due to ethnic or national background could be traced at least as far back as the American legislation against discrimination based on ethnic background ("race" in the American sense) in the USA from the early 1960s onwards.

In Sweden, a new law against discrimination was introduced in 2009. As it states, discrimination is intended to signify:

> direct discrimination: that someone is disadvantaged by being treated worse than any other has been or would be treated in a comparable situation, if this disadvantage is related to gender, transgender identity or expression, ethnic belonging, religion or other belief, disabilities (both mental and physical), sexual orientation, or age. (SFS 2008: 567, 4 §)

The law thus sets seven legal grounds for discrimination. To prohibit discrimination, the law also requires an equality plan for workplaces (over a minimum size of 25 employees (SFS 2008: 567)). In practice, as to the possibilities of sanctions, these are demands which are to be interpreted as strong recommendations. A "diversity plan" is not explicitly required by law, but is recommended by the Swedish Discrimination ombudsman (DO 2010).

In the European Union, as well as in most EU states, the legislation against discrimination is more or less identical to Swedish law. Thus, the German Allgemeines Gleichbehandlungsgesetz (AGG 2006) is comparable to the Swedish law. The six or seven legal grounds in the legal statues are in their turn almost identical to the characteristics of diversity described in the literature of diversity management from the early 1990s. Hence, in 1994 Loden & Rosener mentioned six primary dimensions of diversity – age, sex, race, ethnicity, physical ability, and sexual orientation (Broomé et al. 2001).

Quota

If we assume that disadvantages are caused by discrimination, it can be argued that positive discrimination or quotas might be a possible means to change praxis in order to achieve some kind of equality in opportunity. Since the American anti-"racism" legislation in the 1960s, quotas have belonged to one of the leading arguments in the hitherto political agenda of measures to prohibit discrimination. In Europe, quotas have mostly been used concerning underrepresented gender. EU law permits such positive discrimination in recruitment processes if the merits of two applicants can be defined as "essentially equal".

Via organizational frameworks and programming, quotas have been applied as politically induced measurements intended to prohibit discrimination in Sweden. The social and political intention, it has been argued, is to avoid overt discrimination and have an impact on biased attitudes (Reich, Michailakis & Jönhill 2005).

Using quotas in a recruitment process for a position involves comparing and assessing applicants in two steps. Firstly, the qualifying criteria of competences, i.e. formal merits such as education, skills, experiences, and nowadays also communicative abilities, and so on, are all assessed. Then in a second step, fixed aspects of human diversity, i.e. either gender or ethnic or national background, or age, or sexual preferences, or disabilities, are weighed in. It is reasonable to assume that the latter step in many cases will be contrary to or conflicting with the first. The latter step may in practice occur in the form of a negotiation (Reich, Michailakis & Jönhill 2005).

However, in recruitment processes within public organizations and authorities in Sweden, in several cases quotas have been ruled as illegal. This has been the case when the judicially proven effects of positive discrimination are shown to have resulted in negative discrimination of others when, e.g., gender is set against migrant background or vice versa. Quotas are thus shown to be illegal in some cases and generally, at least judicially, problematic.[10]

Another problem with quotas is that they revive the idea of representativeness, may it be on the grounds of cultural heredity, gender or of age, etc. in a workplace, a company, and so forth. As Baecker notices in the case of gender, the idea of representativeness is paradoxical, as it is not the gender as such that matters to any organization (Baecker 2003).

In modern political theory, the idea of democracy is, analogously, not understood as a matter of representation. The class structure of early modern society indeed allowed for the idea of representation, whereas the political party formation was more or less based on classes, above all by a constellation of bourgeois parties against the working class parties. Today, this does not hold for the system of politics anymore and thus the entire idea of representation falls short. According to e.g. Robert A. Dahl's pluralist principle of democracy,

democracy can be regarded as a form of governance where several elites are competing for people's votes (Dahl 1989).

In the selection of, e.g., boards of companies, the idea of representativeness may still be regarded as essential by researchers promoting quotas. But it is important to differentiate between quotas as a principle, when applied to different kinds of inclusions of professionals in organizations, from quotas in political contexts. Conclusions on the effect of quotas in the former cases, however, do not affect the idea of using quotas within election processes for boards of companies, institutions, and authorities or in political elections of a different kind (Dahlerup 2008; Dahlerup & Freidenvall 2008).

The Management Strategy of Diversity Management as an Option
Defining Diversity Management

As I have indicated above, management is always about communication, and also about culture. Since the beginning of the 1990s, diversity management has spread globally and become one of the leading management strategies today. The impact of diversity management in Germany, Sweden, and other countries in the EU is impressive. At least from a practitioner's perspective it seems relevant to speak of *a new paradigm for management* (Gilbert, et al. 1999; cf. Frohnen 2005; Rönnqvist 2008; Wingborg 1999). Diversity management, or managing diversity, was developed in the American organizational theory and praxis in the early 1990s (Cox 1993; cf. Fägerlind 1999; Weber 2006). Taylor Cox, who has formulated much of the idea in a model, gives us this definition:

> By *managing diversity* I mean planning and implementing organizational systems and practices to manage people so that the potential advantages of diversity are maximized while its potential disadvantages are minimized. Further I view the goal of managing diversity as maximizing the ability of all employees to contribute to organizational goals and to achieve their full potential unhindered by group identities such as gender, race, nationality, age, and departmental affiliation. (Cox 1993: 11)

This thought of arguing in favour of maximizing what is said to be advantageous for the organization as well as for individual persons and minimizing what is said to be disadvantageous may not be disputable. Nonetheless, we can always ask if this or that communication and action could be done better in relation to the goal at issue. This implies that we are dealing with a *normative* definition; like any other management strategy, Cox's definition of diversity management is normative.

For a social scientific analysis it is, however, necessary to observe the phenomenon of diversity management to enable us to ask critical questions. In other words, we should observe the observation of diversity management and thereby shift the perspective to a non-normative one. In this case, and to be concrete, we must ask: How does diversity management work? And *what are the possibilities and the limitations of* diversity management in managing issues of cultural diversity? And how far can diversity management ensure that the organization operates in favour of a person's diverse abilities regarding their cultural background in their role functions as journalists, yet at the same time prohibit discrimination?

Background

Although the concept of diversity management may have somewhat different meanings in practice, these differences are not of importance for my analysis. The development of diversity management started in the USA and therefore it has, from the beginning, been influenced by the American situation. During the last decade it has undergone changes as it has spread more globally. From a sociological point of view, I will give the background in a few points:

1. A primary explanation for the success and its background is that diversity management is a business impetus based on economic calculations in the market economy. As a management strategy it started around 1990 in the USA with reports on expected scarcity of the skilled work force in the USA in the near future. In the USA, these reports were about estimations that the majority of the whole population, the educated population, and of the entire workforce, would be non-white in 2000 (Cox 1993). These reports had a great impact on the spread of diversity management in the USA and comparable reports in the EU had a similar importance in Europe (Merx & Vassilopoulou 2006). In a way, diversity management could be seen as an extension of the rationale for competition in the marked economy known by the motto that "Diversity is the company's best friend". Or, to connect to a wide spread scientific concept, it relates to the notion of requisite variety (Ashby 1956).

2. Another important factor, closely connected to the first mentioned, is the increased importance of global markets and multinational business operations (Cox 1993) or, in short, the phenomenon of the "globalization" of the world economy. The dependency on foreign markets, i.e. foreign customers and business partners, has grown immensely during the last decades.

3. Another point is that disastrous wars and political conflicts during the last decades have led to moving and migration of the work force all over the world (Sassen 2000). The dissolution of the former Soviet Union and the

so called real socialist states in Eastern Europe created migration patterns of importance especially to the EU states.

4. Furthermore, the anti-discrimination legislation in the USA, from the 1960s (especially the Affirmative Act) and onwards, impelled some managers in professional organizations to handle issues of "race" (in the Anglo-American use of the term) or ethnic and national background in accordance with changes in the legislation. According to Cox, this seems to be the least important point. As to legislation he only (in this context) mentions the American Disabilities Act from the 1990s (Cox 1993). Thus, I argue that Cox somewhat underestimates this point. Today, and not least from a European perspective, the legislation and the politically promoted policies stress the importance of legislation as one driving factor for the carrying out of the principle of equality in opportunity (EQUAL 2010). The political and judicial side of diversity management can be observed in different laws, regulations, and codices.[11]

5. As Cox clearly states the importance of cross-functional teams has grown in organizations (Cox 1993). However, already the concept of team, at least from a European organizational perspective, usually denotes a workgroup that consists of professionals with different occupational backgrounds. As different professional backgrounds imply differences as related to organizational culture, the issue of how to manage cultural diversity appears in this sense.

6. My last point is that the idea of and the practice of diversity management is interconnected to the development of the concept of and the practice of organizational culture as seen from the 1980s onwards.

Diversity management is thus a prominent example where cultural diversity is viewed foremost as a resource, as an asset to the organization (Abrahamsson et al. 1999). Within common management literature, diversity management is presented as "best practice" or a way for adjusting the organization to the market situation. But from the view of organizational theory, it is apparent that for a company to apply any kind of management strategy, it first needs to decide whether to choose to apply this as a strategy in its operations. Like any other system, organizations cannot just adjust themselves to the market situation as if the environment functions as a kind of self-regulator. We can nevertheless state that during the last decades a dominant amount of managers have found, and thus decided, that diversity management is a "winning strategy" in relation to employees, customers, clients, audience, viewers, and so on.

In addition, laws and regulations are in a sense obstacles for organizations, which as far as possible ought to be transformed into positive measures. Thus, the anti-discrimination laws and regulations are transformed into market economic possibilities. We can then observe a shift from "anti-discrimination" to diversity (Merx 2006).

From the literature it is apparent that diversity management presupposes in a way a new reflection on how to select and place stronger focus on qualifications and competence. In this respect it may be seen as an adoption of the actual managing of personnel issues in many types of organizations (Ortlieb et al. 2008). This is especially clear in recruitment processes, but also in the following up of careers in organizations, in different kinds of internal selections, negotiations and bargaining (for salary raises, etc.). Following this idea of recruitment processes for different professions, factors such as ethnic or national background – and also especially gender, family status, sexual preferences, and age – should be observed without distinction, i.e. without relevance alongside "ordinary" criteria of qualifications. The literature on diversity management is immense, but as regards mass media organizations, the references are relatively few and I limit myself to some specific points in this section.

Within Mass Media Organizations and Elsewhere

In a policy brief from the European Social Fund, it is stated:

> In most EU countries, the mainstream media are considered to be the most appropriate channels for information and communication for all groups in society. However, they do not, as yet, reflect the diverse nature of our societies in an adequate way. This is true both for the composition of the staff of media companies and the issue of fair portrayal, meaning how programming is made and how selection of programming is done. These two perspectives are closely connected since the issue of fair portrayal is directly affected by, for example, recruitment policy, who is visible on the screen, how are programmes selected etc. (EQUAL 2010)

As a result, diversity management is believed to improve the working climate and the journalistic product, thus contributing to the competitiveness and reputation amongst media consumers. This may be the case simply because mass media organizations operate in a social and cultural context influenced by actual diversity matters. Inspired by initiatives from the EU and EQUAL, a number of diversity projects in the mass media in many European countries aim at promoting journalists with a migrant background, as seen in the slogan aiming at "More Colour in the Media" (More colour in the media 2010). Evaluations of these projects are not yet done.[12]

Surveys have shown that most mass media companies in Sweden apply some kind of diversity management and evaluate it as a "winning" strategy (see

Hultén in this volume). The public television company in Sweden has a rather well documented diversity policy. To quote from a policy document:

> SVT's HR unit and its Sustainable Development Department are tasked to operate and monitor the issues found in SVT's policy of ethnic and cultural diversity. The intention is to increase the ethnic and cultural diversity both in the personnel area as in all programming genres. Here these issues are operated with a broader perspective on diversity, at the same time as other areas of discrimination also are dealt with. Assessments of goals in the action plans that SVT's various regions have established are implemented, and diversity issues in the SVT, both as to personnel and program issues, are run. (Swedish Television 2008: 66)

Although the leading private television company, TV4, does not have a comparable amount of policy documents, their policy is about the same. All in all, a majority of the mass media companies adhere to diversity management as a policy (see the survey in the appendix of this volume). Although the situation in Germany as compared to Sweden is, for many reasons, a bit different for journalists with a migrant background, as Hultén and Graf show (see this volume), there are no significant differences when it comes to management policy. The German public television company has a rather well documented diversity policy (WDR Integrationsbroschuere 2010).

As regards organizations in general, diversity management has been successful in Sweden, as in most EU countries (Fägerlind et al. 2005; Fägerlind & Ekelöf 2001; Persson 2005; Rönnqvist 2008). In Germany, diversity management during the last years has been initiated by major companies as a codex, the "Charter of Diversity", and after some support from the government it has spread to most branches (The Charter of Diversity of German Companies 2010) so that several hundred of the most important companies and other organizations have publicly declared their commitment to a "Diversity charter" stating that:

> We can only succeed in business if we embrace and harness diversity – in our workforce and in the varying needs of our customers and business associates. (The Charter of Diversity of German Companies, 2010)

The statement indicates that this management strategy is not an accidental phenomenon, since it also seems to have remained rather stable throughout the last recession as well:

> Since foundation of the diversity charter more than 700 companies have dealt with diversity issues. Despite all prophecies of doom diversity management has not fallen victim to the 2009 crisis. Whereas budgets for Diversity activities

were reduced in some companies, in others they but increased. Companies in Germany have realized the potential of diversity. It was as well recognized that diversity and inclusion are no short-term projects which can be driven up and down, but which need stable bases and honest commitment in order to be successful at last. (The Charter of Diversity of German Companies, 2010)

Diversity as an Opportunity
The 'Charter for Diversity' of Companies in Germany

The diversity of modern society, influenced by globalisation and demographic change, has a strong effect on economic activity in Germany. We can be economically successful only if we recognise and utilise the diversity that exists in our society. This applies to the diversity not only in our workforce but also in the variety of needs of our customers and business partners. Diversity among employees, with their varying abilities and talents, presents opportunities for innovative and creative solutions.

The aim of implementing the 'Charter for Diversity' within our company is to create a working environment that is free of prejudice. All of our employees should experience appreciation – regardless of gender, race, nationality, ethnicity, religion or philosophy of life, disability, age, sexual orientation and identity. Recognising and promoting this diverse potential creates economic advantages for our company.

We are creating a climate of acceptance and mutual trust. This has positive consequences for the recognition we receive from our partners and customers, both here in Germany and in other countries throughout the world.

Within the framework of this Charter, we will

1. Cultivate a corporate culture characterised by mutual respect and recognition for each and every individual. We are creating conditions under which superiors and employees alike will recognise, share and live these values. This objective requires full commitment of the executives and team leaders in particular.

2. Review our human resources processes and ensure that these support the varying abilities and talents of all employees, and our standards of performance accordingly.

3. Appreciate the diversity of our society, both within and outside the company and recognise its potential for the company when it is successfully put into action.

4. Make the implementation of the Charter a topic for internal and external dialogue.

5. Provide annual public reporting in regard to our activities and progress in promoting diversity.

6. Inform our employees about diversity and involve them in the implementation of the Charter.

We are convinced that practising diversity and valuing the difference will have positive effects on German society.

(The Charter of Diversity of German Companies, 2010)

As mentioned diversity management is, like any management strategy, primarily a market economic impetus. How then, one may ask, does diversity management relate to moral values or "social responsibility"? Like other management strategies, diversity management might also pertain to ideas and images of ethics and ethical codes. Although it may seem that business ethics could e.g. from the view of the mass media be good for companies, companies who have invested their reputation in e.g., the management idea of corporate social responsibility (CSR), cannot be certain of receiving any economic benefit from this kind of action (Morsing & Vallentin 2005). Furthermore, the risk of negative goodwill and negative publicity in the mass media in the event of problems due to unfulfilled promises and expectations, must be taken into consideration at all times. Such findings fit well with Luhmann's conclusion from several analyses, that ethics, and thus moral values, have very little impact on most parts of society (Luhmann 1997).

Changes take time, and the ideas of benchmarking or "best practice" are used in the market economy to state whether the company at issue belongs to the former or the latter in a kind of imagined game in the market competition. Both comparative and competitive arguments are used in politics. Thus some companies can always be observed to be "lagging behind" (Köppel et al. 2007) in applying diversity management. In Sweden it has been argued in a similar way that time might be "lost" if the changes are evaluated to have been too slow or not fast enough (Integrationsverket 2007).

How, then, do diversity criteria operate in practice in a recruitment process? Diversity criteria are included in the criteria of qualifications in a recruitment process in two different ways:

1. Although they were once thrown out as qualification criteria in the modern formal organization, diversity factors are now re-introduced. But they are placed in a new context, as employee communication competences.

2. Diversity factors are also re-introduced as employee communication competences as related to the team, or as balance in the team. So it is argued that a person with a migrant background may add something or be a benefit to a group of typical "Swedes" or "Germans", and that a woman will be a benefit to a group of male employees, and so on.

In the first sense, the focus is on the new employee with a diverse background and on him or her as beneficial to the organization. The second sense also includes an intention about benefits for the organization, but in this case the focus is on the personnel of the team altogether, and thereby diversity as a benefit for the team, and subsequently for the whole organization.

Observing Qualifications and the Differences Between Quota and Diversity Management

As I have shown above, in a number of cases of migrants' disadvantageous positions in the labour market in general, and among journalists in particular, we find different grounds. It has been argued that positive discrimination or quotas, i.e. favouring disadvantaged persons so that they may have equal opportunities within the labour market, could and should be one solution in prohibiting discrimination. As I indicated above, there are crucial problems with quotas as a principle, and therefore also for persons with a migrant background. I will limit myself to giving a short account of some important arguments against the use of quotas in work organizations:

Firstly, the use of quotas in application and recruitment processes, as well as in, e.g., internal promotion of persons' careers, means using two different and paradoxical ways of assessing a person's qualifications. The result may easily be that persons recruited via quota may experience themselves as a kind of secondary work force.

Secondly, as is indicated from empirical studies (among others in this volume) there is evidence of discrimination among journalists with a migrant background in the labour market. However, there are, as is also well documented, several other reasons besides discrimination that could explain the less favourable position of migrants in the labour market, such as language, differences in formal education, difficulties in matching due to differences in formal exams, and so on (Sjögren & Zenou 2007; Rönnqvist 2008). If then quotas were applied in the latter cases, it could result in a confusion of effect and cause with effects that are likely to be negative for both the migrant and the organization.

Thirdly, as studies of the use of quotas have shown, there may be arguments in favour of quotas in political elections, but the application of quotas in work organizations in general has been observed as problematic (Dahlerup & Freidenvall 2008).

Finally, to argue for the use of quotas, and especially a more frequent use of quotas – and in spite of the mentioned complex reasons concerning the problematic situation of many migrants in the labour market – means arguing in favour of a strong conflict-oriented perspective. This might probably run the risk of increasing conflicts of an ethnical or national character in society.

Applying diversity management implies differing in one's presumptions and point of view from those who are assumed with the proposal of quotas. To sum up the arguments in favour of diversity management:

1. First and foremost diversity management presumes a more dynamic view on how to manage the issue of diversity in the multicultural society.

Thereby it is also less conflict-oriented, as Broomé et al.. stress (Broomé et al. 2001).

2. Moreover, as Broomé et al. argue, the striving for diversity must not lead to the kind of stigmatization or doubts about one's own capabilities, which may be a result of people obtaining an education or position through group affiliation rather than on their own merits. This may be contrary to quotas, where this risk at least seems obvious (Broomé et al. 2001).

3. By applying diversity management, ethnic or national background, gender, age, sexual preferences, disability, and so on, are in fact judged as qualifying. However, they are not qualifying as categories in themselves, but as part of a person's individuality in the sense that individuality includes everything that is communicative, and has to do with communicative ability, and is relevant as to one's expectations, pretentions, and idiosyncrasies (Baecker 2003).

4. The above-mentioned points concern communicative competences. Communicative competences, that is to say, communicative ability – or in more common words "social and cultural competences" – imply also a performative learning ability (via prolonged general education), which is today a precondition for many professions. When diversity management is applied, then, it is in line with the increasing focus on communication in society. As a consequence, the employee's communicative competences are valued as more relevant to the organization than the formal and occupational prerequisites for the role function in a position in its narrow sense.

Concluding Remarks

The main research question in this chapter has concerned the possibilities and limitations of the mass media organization on how to manage issues of cultural diversity in relation to journalistic production. In the last section I have shown how diversity management can be viewed as an option for solving at least some of the problems which migrants, in this case journalists with a migrant background, may face in Swedish or German mass media organizations. Diversity management is widely applied within mass media organizations. It implicates that ethnic or national background – and as well as gender, family status, sexual preferences, age, etc. – are weighed in as qualifications.

In a certain sense, cultural diversity has always existed. Cultural diversity in the actual sense is, however, to be understood as a concept, which is used to describe matters and issues of society, and in particular occupational organizations of today. We can distinguish at least four different but connected reasons and backgrounds for the development of diversity management: 1) the phenomenon of "globalization"; 2) the American anti-racism legislation from the 1960s onwards; 3) the concept of cultural diversity; and 4) incentives of the market economy as to expected scarcity of the skilled work force and also preferences of customers, clients, etc. with a "multi-cultural" background.

In order to give an understanding of the issue, the analysis has placed an emphasis on its context. As I have argued, systems theory is well suited for this kind of analysis. By giving an overview of the mass media as a function system in the global modern society, journalistic production was placed in its societal and communicational context. From this macro perspective the analysis turned to the issue of how social identity is constructed in modern society. It is argued that we as persons have multiple identities in order to fit into the complex highly functionally differentiated society. In this context it should not be surprising that a common language term such as ethnicity should be used cautiously.

The ongoing transformation of modern society affects most professions in work organizations and involves the individual person in many respects. The focus on mass media as organizations demands an analysis of the function of organizations and on how persons are related to or included in organizations. The distinctiveness of organized communications implies that most of us are included in a few organizations, yet are excluded from most other organizations to which we do not belong.

The introduction of diversity criteria as criteria of qualifications can be described as a mode of introducing diversity as part of a person's "social and cultural competences", or more precisely communicative competences in professional organizations, such as the mass media organizations. The media as organization is always able to discriminate simply, as Luhmann has shown, due to the fact that the organizations of society function in this way. That is to say that organizations can make decisions in favour of or disadvantageous to equal opportunity.

As a market economic impetus diversity management aims not only at avoiding discrimination but also at using diversity to advance the organization. However, as it is a management strategy, it of course does not imply, e.g., that relatively more persons should be included, i.e. become members of a certain organization, i.e. be employed, be appointed to schools, etc., as a result. As social scientists, we know that any solution to societal issues may also bring about new risks. Diversity management should in this respect be observed as part of the management's communication advances, but the result, which we can never be sure of, may for different complex reasons become quite another.

A general conclusion is that equal opportunity, on the one hand, is a structuring principle of modern society, where the individual's access to functions is in principle equal. On the other hand organizations are, and paradoxically also as a principle, able to discriminate and make other decisions, which are unfavourable to individual persons or groups.

Managing cultural diversity in a positive sense is not to say that everything that has to do with culture is "good" or should be seen as relevant. The observations in this chapter are not that diversity management is the only solution to this issue. One argument, however, is that there is evidence that diversity management is more adequate than other modes of managing this issue. This includes the idea of quotas and also a high confidence as to legal regulations.

A limitation of this study is that the documentary sources too often refer to diversity management as policy and too little is based on empirical material. This is to some extent due to the matter of fact that the applications of diversity management are still rather new. Further research, especially on the mass media organizations, may give more evidence of the positive results of diversity management, and also on the shortcomings of this mode of managing cultural diversity as regards journalists with a migrant background.

Notes

1. Such codices are typical for the professional bodies of the mass media as well as for individual mass media companies. See the German Pressekodex, 2007, and the Swedish "Spelregler för press, radio och TV", 2010, respectively.
2. In fact, Parsons used the term generalized symbolic media of interchange and not the term communication, since he was an action theorist. In order to simplify it I will here translate his theory into Luhmann's vocabulary. Luhmann's term is symbolic generalized communication media (Luhmann 1997; Jönhill 1997).
3. Already this "classical" Parsonian and Luhmannian concept of the symbolic generalized communication medium of the mass media responds to a large extent to the Bourdieuan question, which Nick Couldry raises, on "how to understand the media both as an internal production process and as a general frame for categorizing the social world" (Couldry 2003). The symbolic generalized communication media simply functions to manage both processes. Any individual news is produced internally in the function system of the mass media, and in the mass media companies it also pretends to inform us about this news as being essential for coping with the social world. See also Görke & Scholl's short review of Luhmann's theory on this point (Görke & Scholl 2006).
4. Cf. Kevin Robin's arguments of the limitations of the national frame (e.g. Robins 2006). Or in the words of a person with a truly multi-cultural background, the music producer Lucy Duran: "I am very comfortable in Spain, I love Spain, … but I am not really Spanish, because I didn't grow up here. I feel very comfortable in London, but I am not English. … I love Greece, …. Put me into Mali, I'm totally at home…. – I am comfortable in many different places, but I don't belong to any of them. …" (Interview by Giorgos Markakis, Swedish Radio, programme 2 "Klingan", 18. June 2010. Thanks to the producer Lennart Wretlind for making the interview available.)
5. Cf. "Equality" in Stanford Encyclopaedia of Philosophy.
6. Max Weber developed the concept of membership, goal, places and staff, and, most notably, James G. March and Luhmann later added the concept and the theory of decision (Weber 1968 (orig. 1919); Luhmann 2000a).
7. HRM is often viewed as just a management practice concerning personnel matters in an organization, but sociologically and from the point of view of its founding fathers, it is obviously also a theory approach. I use the term in the latter sense here. Cf. e.g. a textbook like Clegg, Kornberger & Pitsis 2008.

8. See further the definition and discussion of migrant background in the introduction and above in this chapter.
9. I follow Max Weber's classical definition of power as the possibility of conditioning the actions of others (Jönhill 1997).
10. See documentations from the Swedish Centrum för rättvisa(Centre for Justice).
11. See anti-discrimination laws in Germany and Sweden, respectively: BGB 2006; SFS 2008:567. See further Löfgren & Wadstein 1999; Merx 2006.
12. A network called Online/More Colour in the Media gives a good overview of an amount of ongoing projects of this kind all over the world. See *More colour in the media* 2010. See also Hultén and Graf in this volume.

References

Literature

Abrahamsson, K., et al. (eds) 1999) *Olika som bär – om etnisk diskriminering och mångfald i arbetslivet* [As different as two peas in a pod – on ethnic discrimination and diversity in the workplace]. Stockholm: Rådet för arbetslivsforskning, Institutet för framtidsstudier.

Allwin, M., et al. (2006) *Gränslöst arbete – socialpsykologiska perspektiv på det nya arbetslivet* [Boundless work – social psychological perspectives on the new working life]. Malmö: Liber.

Allwood, J. (1985) *Intercultural communication*, in Papers in Anthropological Linguistics 12. Göteborg University: Department of Lingustic.

Allwood, J., Edebäck, C. & Myhre, R. (2006) 'Analysis of immigration to Sweden in the framework of the European intercultural workplace project', in Aalto, N. & Reuter, E.: *Aspects of intercultural dialogue*. Köln: Saxa Verlag.

Asante, M.K. & Gudykunst, W.B. (eds) (1989) *Handbook of international and intercultural communication*. Thousand Oaks, London, New Delhi: Sage Publications.

Ashby, W.R. (1956) *An introduction to cybernetics*. London: Chapman & Hall.

Bagdikian, B.H. (1973) 'Shaping media content: Professional personnel and organizational structure', *The Public Opinion Quarterly*, Vol. 37, No. 4: 569-579.

Baecker, D. (2003) *Organization und Management* [Organization and management]. Frankfurt a M: Suhrkamp.

Baecker, D. (2007) *Form und Formen der Kommunikation* [Form, and forms of communication]. Frankfurt a M: Suhrkamp.

Berggren, K. & Omarsson, A. (2001) *Rätt man på fel plats – en studie av arbetsmarknaden för utlandsfödda akademiker som invandrat under 1990-talet* [The right man in the wrong place – a study of the labour market for foreign-born academics who immigrated in the 1990s]. Stockholm: Arbetsmarknadsstyrelsen, Utredningsenheten 2001: 5.

Björklund, U. (1983) *Etnicitet – en antropologisk översikt* [Ethnicity – an anthropological overview]. Stockholms Universitet, Socialantropologiska inst.

Boulding, K. (1953) *The organizational revolution: A study in the ethics of economic organization*. New York: Harper & Brothers.

Boulding, K.E. (1968 (1956)) 'General systems theory – The skeleton of science', in Buckley W. (ed.) *Modern systems research for the behavioral scientist*. Chicago: Aldine Publ.

Breed, W. (1955) 'Social control in the newsroom: A functional analysis', *Social Forces*, vol. 22, No. 4: 326-335.

Broomé, P., Carlson, B., Ohlsson, R. (2001) *Bäddat för mångfald* [Paved for diversity]. Stockholm: SNS förlag.

Bruchfeld, S. & Jacobsson, I. (1999) *Kan man vara svart och svensk? Texter om rasism, anti-Semitism och nazism* [Is it possible to be both black and Swedish? Texts on racism, anti-semitism and nazism]. Stockholm: Natur och kultur.

Clegg, S., Kornberger, M. & Pitsis, T. (2008) *Managing and organizations*. Thousand Oaks, London, New Delhi: Sage Publ.

Couldry, N. (2003) 'Media meta-capital: Extending the range of Bourdieu's field theory', *Theory and Society* 32: 653-677.

Cox, T. (1993) *Cultural diversity in organizations. Theory, research & practice.* San Francisco: Berrett-Koehler Publ.

Czarniawska, B. (2005) *En teori om organisering* [A theory of organizing]. Lund: Studentlittteratur.

Dacyl, J. (2001) 'An assessment: Media and contemporary societal discourses', in Dacyl, J. & Westin, C. (eds) *Cultural diversity and the media.* Stockholm: Stockholm University, CEIFO.

Dahl, R.A.. (1989) *Democracy and its critics.* New Haven & London: Yale University Press.

Dahlerup, D. & Freidenvall, L. (2008) *Kvotering,* [Quota]. Stockholm: SNS förlag.

Dahlerup, D. (2008) 'Gender quotas – Controversial but trendy', *International Feminist Journal of Politics,* 10: 3, 322-328.

Daun, Å. (2001) 'Identity transformations in Sweden', in Dacyl, J. (ed.) *Challenges of cultural diversity in Europe.* Stockholm: Stockholm university, Centre for Research in International Migration and Ethnic Relations.

Eriksen, T.H. (2002) *Ethnicity and nationalism: Anthropological perspectives* (2nd ed.). London: Pluto Press.

Eriksen, T.H. (2007) *Globalization. The key concepts.* Oxford: Berg & Oxford International Publishers Ltd.

Frohnen, A. (2005) *Diversity in action. Mulitnationalität in globalen Unternehmen am Beispiel Ford* [Diversity in actionmultinationality in global enterprises using the example Ford] Bielefeld: transcript Verlag.

Fägerlind, G. (1999) *Managing Diversity – strategier för mångfald i USA* [Managing diversity – strategies for diversity in the U.S.]. Stockholm: Sveriges Tekniska attachéer.

Fägerlind, G. et al. (2005) *Olikhet som drivkraft – en idéskrift kring vinnande mångfald* [Difference as a driving force – An essay about diversity as a winning concept]. Stockholm: ISA, NUTEK, Vinnova, Visanu, Visanu 2004: 3.

Fägerlind, G. & Ekelöf, E. (2001) *Mångfald i svenskt arbetsliv – idéer, aktiviteter och aktörer* [Diversity in Swedish working life – Ideas, activities and actors]. Stockholm: Svenska ESF-Rådet, Vinnova, FAS, Integrationsverket.

Giddens, A. (1989) *Sociology.* Cambridge: Polity Press.

Gilbert, Jacqueline A., et al. (1999) 'Diversity management: A new organizational paradigm', *Journal of Business Ethics,* Volume 21, Nr. 1. Holland: Springer.

Görke, A. & Scholl, A. (2006) 'Niklas Luhmann's theory of social systems and journalism research' (theory review), *Journalism Studies,* Vol. 7, No 4. London: Routledge.

Graf, H. (2008) "'I am the token Turk': Experiences of journalists with migrant backgrounds in German newsrooms", conference paper, presented at: International Association for Media and Communication (IAMCR), 26th World Congress, July 20-25, 2008, Stockholm, Working Group for Media Production Analyses.

Hofstede, G. et al. (1990) 'Measuring organizational cultures: A qualitative and quantitative study across twenty cases', *Administrative Science Quarterly* 35: 286-316.

Hultén, L.J. (1996) 'Nyhetsrummet i förändring: om journalistik som kollektivt berättande' [The changing newsroom: on journalism as a collective narrative], in Carlsson, U. (ed.) *Medierna i samhället. Kontinuitet och förändring. Professorer i journalistik och medie- & kommunikationsvetenskap reflekterar.* Göteborg: Nordicom.

Jönhill, J.I. (1997) *Samhället som system och dess ekologiska omvärld. En studie i Niklas Luhmanns sociologiska systemteori.* [Society as system and its ecological environment. A study of Niklas Luhmann's sociological systems theory]. Lund: Lund University, Dept. of Sociology.

Jönhill, J.I. (forthcoming 2011) *Inklusion och exklusion – en distinktion som gör skillnad i det mångkulturella samhället* [Inclusion and exclusion – A distinction that makes a difference in the multicultural society]. Malmö: Liber förlag (forthcoming).

Lange, A. (1999) *Invandrare om diskriminering IV. en enkät- och intervjuundersökning om etnisk diskriminering* [Immigrants on discrimination IV. A questionnaire and an interview survey on ethnic discrimination]. Stockholm: Stockholm university, CEIFO.

Luhmann, N. (1971) 'Die Weltgesellschaft' [World society], in Luhmann, *Soziologische Aufklärung, 2: Aufsätze zur Theorie der Gesellschaft.* Opladen: Westdeutscher Verlag.

Luhmann, N. (1990) 'General theory and American sociology', in Gans, H.J. (ed.), *Sociology in America.* Newbury Park, California: Sage Publ.

Luhmann, N. (1995) *Social systems.* Stanford: Stanford University Press.

Luhmann, N. (1997) *Die Gesellschaft der Gesellschaft* [The society of society] Vol. 1-2. Frankfurt am Main: Suhrkamp.

Luhmann, N. (1998) *Observations on modernity.* Stanford: Stanford University Press.

Luhmann, N. (2000a) *Organization und Entscheidung* [Organization and decision]. Opladen: Westdeutscher Verlag.

Luhmann, N. (2000b) *The reality of the mass media.* Stanford: Stanford University Press.

Löfgren, E. & Wadstein, M. (1999) *Aktiva åtgärder för att främja etnisk mångfald i arbetslivet* [Active measures to promote ethnic diversity in the workplace]. Stockholm: Ombudsmannen mot etnisk diskriminering.

Löfgren, E. & Fägerlind, G. (2000) *Att se med andra ögon – bilder från svenskt arbetsliv förmedlade av invandrade ingenjörer* [To see with different eyes – pictures from Swedish working life mediated by immigrant engineers]. Stockholm: Rådet för arbetslivsforskning m.fl.

Merx, A. (2006) *Von Antidiskriminierung zu Diversity* [From anti-discrimination to diversity]. Online Dossier der Heinrich-Böll-Stiftung: Das Allgemeine Gleichbehandlungsgesetz: Ansätze in der Praxis, http://www.migrationboell.de/web/diversity/48_825.asp (retrieved 2009-03-22).

Merx, A. & Vassilopoulou, J. (2006) *Das arbeitsrechtliche AGG und Diversity-Perspektiven* [The labour legislation AGG and diversity perspectives], http://www.idm-diversity.org/files/Merx-Vassilopoulou-AGG_Diversity.pdf (retrieved 2009-03-22).

Meyer, J.W. & Rowan, B. (1977) 'Institutionalized organisations: Formal structure as myth and ceremony', *American Journal of Sociology*, Vol. 83, No. 2.

Morgan, G. (1986) *Images of organization.* London: Sage Publ.

Morsing, M. & Vallentin, S. (2005) 'CSR and stakeholder involvement: The challenge of organizational integration'. Copenhagen: Copenhagen Business School (unpublished paper).

Nekby, L. & Rödin, M. (2007) *Kulturell identitet och arbetsmarknaden* [Cultural identity and the labour market]. Norrköping: Integrationsverket.

Nilsson, A. (2002) *Rekrytering – ett vapen för framtiden* [Recruitment – a weapon for the future]. Stockholm: Stockholms universitet, CEIFO.

Nygren, G. (ed.) (2008) *Nyhetsfabriken: journalistiska yrkesroller i en förändrad medievärld* [The news factory: journalistic professional roles in a changed media world]. Lund: Studentlitteratur.

Ortlieb, R., et al. (2008) *Diversity und Diversity Management in Berliner Unternehmen. Im Fokus: Personen mit Migrationshintergrund* [Diversity and diversity management in Berlin companies: A focus on people with migration background]. Berlin: Freie Universität.

Persson, T. (2005) *Diversity management – Affärsnytta med mångfald* [Diversity management – business benefits with diversity]. Sydsvenska Industri- och Handelskammaren, http://www.handelskammaren.com (retrieved 2009-09-09).

Popper, K. (1959) *The logic of scientific discovery.* London: Hutchinson & Co.

Reich, W., Michailakis, D. & Jönhill, J.I. (2005) *Claims to gender equality. The conflict between individual qualifications and social equality in academic recruitment*, research project application. Stockholm: The Swedish Research Council.

Robins K. (2006) *The Challenge of Transcultural Diversities. Cultural policy and cultural diversity*, Strasbourg: Council of Europe Publishing.

Rönnqvist, S. (2008) *Från Diversity Management till mångfaldsplaner? Om mångfaldsidéns spridning i Sverige och Malmö stad* [From diversity management to diversity management plans? On the spread of the idea of diversity in Sweden and Malmö City]. Malmö: Lunds universitet, Lund Studies in Economic History 48.

Sandström, L. (2004) *Rosengård i medieskugga. Om medier som medel och hinder för integration* [Rosengard in the media shadow. On the media as resources and barriers to integration]. Stockholm: Stiftelsen Institutet för mediestudier.

Sassen, S. (2000) *Guests and aliens*. New York: New Press, 2000.

Schein E.H. (2004) *Organizational culture and leadership*. San Francisco: Jossey-Bass Publ.

Seidl, D. (2005) *Organizational identity and self-transformation. An autopoietic perspective*. Alderhot: Ashgate Publ.

Simon, F.B. (2007) *Einführung in die systemische Organisationstheorie* [Introduction to systems based organization theory]. Heidelberg: Carl-Auer Verlag.

Sjögren, A. & Zenou, Y. (2007) *Vad förklarar invandrares integration på arbetsmarknaden? En teoriöversikt* [What does the integration of immigrants in the labour market explain? A theoretical overview]. Stockholm: Integrationsverket.

Spencer Brown, G. (1969) *Laws of Form*. London: G Allen and Unwin Ltd.

Stichweh, R. (2005) *Inklusion und Exklusion. Studien zur Gesellschaftstheorie* [Inclusion and exclusion. Studies on the theory of the society]. Bielefeld: transcript.

Tägil, S. (1993) 'Den problematiska etniciteten. Nationalism, migration och samhällsomvandling' [The problematic ethnicity. Nationalism, migration and social transformation], in Tägil (ed.) (1993) *Den problematiska etniciteten. Nationalism, migration och samhällsomvandling* [The problematic ethnicity. Nationalism, migration and social transformation], Lund: Lund University Press (CESIC studies in international conflict, 10).

Vasta, E., et al. (2003) An evaluation of Swedish international migration and ethnic relations (IMER) Research 1995-2002. Forskningsrådet för arbetsliv och socialvetenskap [Swedish Council for Working Life and Social Research].

Wallerstein, I. (1974) *The modern world-system. Capitalist agriculture and the origins of the European world-Economy in the sixteenth century*. New York: Academic Press.

Weber, G. (2006) *Making differences matter. Managing cultural diversity with a global mindset, a comparative study on various approaches to diversity management*. Örebro University (master thesis).

Weber, M. (1968) *Economy and society, vol. I*. New York: Bedminster Press (orig. 1919).

Weick, K.E. (1969) *The social psychology of organizing*. Reading: Addison-Wesley Publishing Co.

Wingborg, M. (1999) 'Argument för etnisk mångfald i arbetslivet' [Arguments for ethnic diversity in working life], in Abrahamsson, et al. (ed.) 1999.

Åkerstrøm Andersen N. (2007) 'The self-infantalized adult and the management of personality', *Critical Discourse Studies*, 4: 3, 331-352, http://dx.doi.org/10.1080/17405900701656932 (retrieved 2009-09-09).

Åkerstrøm Andersen, N. & Born, A. (2008) 'The employee in the sign of love', *Culture and Organization*, Vol. 14, No. 4, 325-343. London: Routledge, http://www.informaworld.com (retrieved 2009-09-09).

Policy documents, etc.

AGG 2006 (Allgemeines Gleichbehandlungsgesetz). http://www.gesetze-im-internet.de/agg/index.html (retrived 2010-07-26).

BGB (2006) Bundesgesetzblatt Teil 1 Nr. 39. Allgemeines Glechbehandlungsgesetz (AGG), [German general law of equal rights].

Centrum för rättvisa (Centre for Justice) http://www.centrumforrattvisa.se/fall#Likabehandling (retrieved 2010-07-16).

The Charter of Diversity of German Companies (2010) (English version of Charter der Vielfalt). Berlin: Die Beauftragte der Bundesregierung für Migration, Flüchtlinge und Integration, http://www.vielfalt-als-chance.de/index.php?id=14 (retrieved 2010-07-15).

DO (Diskrimineringsombudsmannen) (2010) http://www.do.se/ (retrieved 2010-07-26).

EQUAL (2010) *Policy Briefs. Reflecting the colours of the world. Media, diversity and discrimination*, http://ec.europa.eu/employment_social/equal/policy-briefs/etg1-reflecting-color-world_en.cfm Equal database, Brussels: EU, European Commission, Employment, Social Affairs and Equal Opportunities (retrieved 2010-03-07).

Köppel, P., Yan, J. & Lüdicke, J. (2007) *Cultural diversity management in Deutschland hinkt hinterher* [Cultural diversity management in Germany is lagging behind; Report) Kompetenzzentrum Unternehmenskultur/ Führung. Gütersloh: Bertelsmann Stiftung.

More color in the media 2010. Media Diversity Institute, London, http://www.media-diversity.org/en/index.php?option=com_content&view=article&id=429&Itemid=44 (retrieved 2010-07-14).

NE (Nationalencyklopedin) [Swedish National Encyclopedia]. http://www.ne.se/ (retrieved 2010-07-26).

Pressekodex 2007. http://www.initiative-qualitaet.de/index.php?id=1364 (retrieved 2010-07-14) (German press codex).

SFS 2008:567. (Swedish) Discrimination Act, http://www.sweden.gov.se/sb/d/108/a/115903 (retrieved 2010-07-14).

Ds 2000:43. *Begreppet invandrare: användningen i myndigheters verksamhet* [The concept "immigrant": the use in authorities' activities] (Ds, Departementserien [Ministry Series] Stockholm, http://www.sweden.gov.se/sb/d/108/a/1878 (retrieved 2010-07-19).

SOU:2004:48. Statens offentliga utredningar [Swedish Government Inquiries, Swedish Government Official Reports), Stockholm, http://www.regeringen.se/ (retrieved 2010-07-19).

SOU 2010:16. Sverige för nyanlända. Värden, välfärdsstat, vardagsliv [Sweden for newcomers. Values, welfare state, daily life), Delbetänkande av Utredningen om samhälls- orientering för nyanlända invandrare, [Swedish Government Inquiries, Swedish Government Official Reports] http://www.regeringen.se/ (retrieved 2010-07-19).

Spelregler för press, radio och TV (2010) Pressens Samarbetsnämnd, Stockholm, http://www.sjf.se/portal/page?_pageid=53,38437&_dad=portal&_schema=PORTAL (retrieved 2010-07-18).

Swedish Television (2008) Sveriges Televisions public service-redovisning 2007. Stockholm, http://svt.se/content/1/c6/69/84/42/PSR%202008.pdf (retrieved 2010-08-15).

WDR Integrationsbroschuere (2010) http://www.wdr.de/unternehmen/service/infomaterial/ (retrieved 2010-07-14).

Diversity Disorders
Ethnicity and Newsroom Cultures[1]

Gunilla Hultén

Sweden, like many other European countries, has been engaged in the debate concerning media's role in a multi-ethnic context. Diversity in Swedish newsrooms and in media content has been a topic of discussion for more than a decade. A variety of initiatives to promote media diversity have been put into practice, including strategies to improve the representation of minorities and to increase the recruitment of journalists with minority backgrounds in mainstream media (see also Hultén & Graf in this volume).

Despite these efforts, the outcome is discouraging. It is evident that Swedish media organizations have difficulties in developing an effective means of promoting and implementing diversity in the newsroom processes. Similar situations, that is, lack of change and progress, can also be found in, for instance, the Netherlands, UK and the U.S. (Deuze 2002; Journalists at Work 2002; American Society of Newspaper Editors 2009).

Numerous studies over the years have concluded that mainstream media is characterized by the underrepresentation and misrepresentation of immigrant and minority groups, as well as by difficulties for ethnic minority journalists in gaining access to the media. Since the 1960s and the civil rights movement, various initiatives to promote diversity and diversity policies have been developed. In the 1960s and 1970s, these were mainly based on the ideas of assimilation and integration. In the 1980s multicultural and anti-racist policies replaced the previous paradigm (Cottle 1997: 3-4; Malik 2002: 183). Simon Cottle also claims that efforts concerning cultural representation have become increasingly an issue of the politics of difference and diversity. This change also implicates shifts of institutional arrangements and production regimes. Among the shaping forces that he identifies are the intensified commercial imperatives and the changing politics of multiculturalism (Cottle 1997: 6-8, see also Cottle 2000). Sarita Malik observes that these changes amalgamated in what she calls "the commercialization of multiculturalism" (Malik 2002: 183). Currently in Sweden there has been a discursive shift from multiculturalist media policies to more vague policies of

mainstreaming cultural diversity. Concurrent with this change, commercial interests and competition have increased (Horsti & Hultén, forthcoming). I understand
diversity as an ambiguous and elastic concept (cf. Freedman 2008; Lentin & Titley
2008). Media diversity policy generally refers to two interrelated notions. The
first is based on the liberal idea of media freedom, and concerns pluralism in
the marketplace aiming at a variety of opinions and outlets. The second centres
on the representation and participation of ethnic minorities to enhance diversity
in media content and staffing. Des Freedman observes a shift in the discourse of
diversity, from looking at diversity as a public good towards an understanding
of diversity in terms of efficiency in the marketplace (2008: 77).

Katharine Sarikakis remarks that the concept of social cohesion has become
the antonym of "social exclusion" and is vague and problematic to use. She
contends that social cohesion, media, and cultural policy are all connected to
the changing notions of citizenship and the citizens' relationship to institutions
as shaped through policy (Sarikakis 2007: 68-69). News organizations are operating in a commercial media environment, and therefore the needs to attract
large audiences, including minority communities, are crucial for legitimacy
and the institution's survival. Given the changing demographics of Sweden,
ethnic diversity efforts have become more important to media organizations
if they want to stay in business. But, as Isabel Awad argues, business-driven
media policies do not necessarily respond to the democratic needs of a multicultural society (Awad 2008). Instead, she explains that a laissez-fair approach
to cultural diversity in the media, relying on commercial instead of normative
justifications, reduces diversity to a business asset but does not secure a wider
diversity of voices and social perspectives in the media. News media also face
competition within a highly diversified market with a multitude of media outlets.
The new technologies also involve a change of the nature of journalistic work.
Sonja Kretzschmar notes a twofold media development. On the one hand, she
observes that competitive media markets enhance mainstream content, which
mostly reflects ethnic majority opinions. On the other, she sees the increasing problems of the disintegration of ethnic minorities in Western European
countries (Kretzschmar 2007: 230-231).

This chapter is concerned with the responsiveness of Swedish media organizations to an increasingly diverse society. I examine the tension between
the officially expressed attitudes and the diversity goals of Swedish newsrooms
and how journalists who have foreign backgrounds perceive these. As earlier
stated (see Hultén & Graf in this volume), nine out of ten Swedish media organizations agree that diversity in the workplace is valuable and has positive
effects on the company. In contrast, the interviewed journalists often expressed
disappointment with their company's efforts to improve diversity in hiring and
in content. The journalists drew attention to the need to change editorial organization patterns, reporting practices, and newsroom cultures as well as the

need to redefine journalistic missions regarding ethnic diversity. This chapter concerns the market focus of news production, and argues that the present tendency towards mainstreaming cultural diversity in media content may lead to the exclusion of minority voices and the undermining of diversity efforts. The discussion finally argues that social cohesion in media policies based on the idea of national unity among citizens, clashes with the claims for recognition and communicative rights in multi-ethnic societies.

The chapter starts by presenting interviews with journalists who have migrant backgrounds in the Stockholm region. A majority of the interviewed journalists point to the dissonance between the goals expressed in diversity programs and their practical implementations. Several tend to believe that adaptation to the organizational culture is required if you want to succeed, and point to the difficulties in transforming standardized professional practices. The last section of the chapter introduces the views of three media managers of different types of Swedish news organizations operating in the Stockholm region. Journalistic improvements and financial necessity seem to be the twin motives behind efforts at enhancing diversity. Specifically, this section focuses on the criticism of reporting conventions and of news values, thus touching upon the core values of the professional ideology of journalism.

In a positive understanding, diversity is about equal rights and opportunities. In a more negative interpretation it is also about exclusion and discrimination. The Swedish Discrimination Act requires employers to take active measures to promote equal rights and opportunities in the workplace regardless of sex, transgender identity or expression, ethnicity, religion or other belief, disability, sexual orientation or age. Such measures are to be goal-oriented and accounted for annually (Discrimination Act 2008: 567).

The term diversity is generally applied to a variety of aspects based on gender, ethnicity, sexuality, religion etc. Diversity in the newsrooms most often refers to hiring people from different backgrounds and on bringing new perspectives to reporting. Diversity can also be addressed in terms of news coverage, i.e. how stories on migration-related issues are reported in the news organization. Until the late 1980s, a majority of all Swedish journalists were men (Löfgren Nilsson 2007: 46). But as mentioned above, today every other journalist in Sweden is a woman. In the context of gender equality, the ideal of a 50/50 percent distribution is generally accepted. But in the field of ethnic or cultural diversity, the issues of possible and desirable distribution are complicated. As mentioned in chapter one, 14 percent of Sweden's population is foreign-born, whereas the proportion seen in Stockholm is 21 percent. But there is great variation within the different parts of the Stockholm area. In well-off municipalities like Vallentuna and Danderyd, the percentages of foreign-born inhabitants are 11 and 14 respectively, while the share in Botkyrka is 37 percent, and in Södertälje 30 percent (Statistics Sweden 2009). But 95 percent of the news workers employed by Swedish media organizations are of Swedish origin. Should the distribution in the newsroom reflect the national, regional, or local situation? Are quotas at all applicable?

The American Society of Newspaper Editors (ASNE) has calculated the number of minority participants in the newsrooms since 1978. The goal expressed by ASNE is to have the percentage of minorities working in newsrooms nationwide equal to the percentage of minorities in the nation's population by 2025. Currently, minorities make up 33 percent of the U.S. population, but only 13 percent of the journalists working in the newsrooms (ASNE, 2009). This type of census is not used in Sweden. The distribution of women in the newsrooms is systematically measured, but when it comes to ethnic diversity statistics are sparse.

In the report *Mångfald som vision och praktik* [Diversity in theory and practice] the diversity management and diversity implementation of six companies and organizations were evaluated (Westin 2001). Charles Westin, former professor of International Migration and Ethnic Relations, points out that diversity initiatives tend to be viewed as a means to deal with the consequences of what is considered a problematic immigration rather than a goal in itself (Westin 2001: 13). The researchers report that various officials working with diversity issues are highly critical of categorizing people in terms of ethnicity or culture. As I prepared of this research project, I met similar arguments in my contacts with the Human Resource departments of some media companies. "We don't use the concept of ethnicity. It is qualifications and skills that count", one HR consultant said. One of the respondents in my interview study raised the question of how relevant ethnic background was in relation to the scope of this research project.

> How can you single out ethnicity as an explanatory aspect from the facts that
> I am female and was brought up in a small society in the north of Sweden
> by middle-class parents? (R 6)

It is not possible or desirable to study how ethnicity as an isolated factor explains the respondents' positions and conditions in the workplace. But that does not reduce the importance or the necessity of paying attention to how certain phenomena are understood and construed as ethnic issues by the respondents and by their workplaces.

In the news industry, ethnic diversity is taken into account in the formulation of new media strategies to attain new markets and audiences. Efforts to increase diversity include both mission and market justifications. Diversity is part of the democratic mission of the news media, and of its moral obligation to deliver adequate reporting to the citizens. In addition, diversity efforts are important to media organizations for financial reasons. Those who ignore the demographic shift may not survive in the marketplace.

The Interviews

In this section I will discuss some of the key themes appearing in fourteen interviews with journalists who have foreign backgrounds working in the Stockholm region.[2] Ten of the respondents are women and four of them men. The selection of interviewees was based on prior knowledge, identification through newspapers, radio and TV, and recommendations. The sampling aimed at reflecting different types of media experiences. The youngest was 24 years and the oldest 61 years. Nine are foreign-born and five have foreign-born parents. They or their parents come from the Nordic countries, Europe, Asia, and Central America. The respondents work for newspapers, public service and commercial TV or radio broadcasting companies in the Stockholm region, or are freelancers. Eight of the respondents hold journalist qualifications. The remaining six had other professional training before entering journalism. Among the younger journalists the most common entry into their first job in journalism was as a trainee.

Six of the interviews were conducted in the respondents' workplace, four were carried out in my office, two took place in the homes of the interviewees, and one person was interviewed in a café. The interviews were conducted between October 2007 and October 2008. The method used was the semi-structured individual interview. The interviews were between 40 and 60 minutes long, and were digitally recorded and transcribed in their entirety. Since my interest is the informational content of the interviews, I have used a denaturalized transcription method, which has not taken into account vocalizations and nonverbal interactions, such as laughing, coughing, hand-waving, or smiling. In the transcriptions the interviews have been slightly edited for repetitions, stuttering et cetera.

The method used for constructing the questionnaire and for analyzing the data has been inspired by Mc Cracken (1988). The interviews focused on the following overarching themes: the general background of the respondent, working conditions, news production, organization of the news room, responsibility and influence, career potentials, and prospects. In writing up the results, the analyzing process aimed at discerning and organizing the emerging patterns and themes in the respondents' answers.

Most of them are critical of the job their company is doing to improve diversity in hiring and in content, and some are not convinced that they have equal opportunities for advancement. The journalists tend to believe that adaptation to the organizational culture is required if you want to succeed, and point to the difficulties in transforming standardized professional practices. At the same time, several are aware of expectations of introducing alternative news beats and sources. Others still oppose the role as the caretakers of migration issues.

Hiring and Advancement

Having an immigrant background can be both an asset and a drawback. All of the respondents are in favour of an increased hiring of foreign-born journalists, but point to the multifaceted features of diversity in the newsrooms. They identified the dilemma of implementing diversity programs in a climate of economic decline and budgetary constraints. In the past years, several Swedish media companies have cut newsroom jobs or have put a hiring freeze into place. The interviewed journalists also recognized the classic problem of the "last-hired-first-fired" as an obstacle to achieving more diverse newsrooms.

There seems to be something of a generation gap between the journalists who entered the profession in the 1970s and 80s and those who were taken on more recently. The more experienced professionals had to fight their way to the newsroom, while some of the younger ones were partly recruited because of their ethnic background. Especially the newly hired journalists express insecurity about the grounds on which they were employed. This can cause personal and professional dilemmas. Respondent # 5 was not very experienced when she was hired, and she commented:

> Still, they choose to take me on. Personal qualities that I really can't help counted. And that is that I have a different origin, which I am sure weighed in because I know they need people with different backgrounds on the editorial staff. /.../ So the combination of being young and immigrant explains to a large extent why they hired me. You can call it quotas, if you wish. /.../
>
> Nobody says it aloud: she's got the job because she is an immigrant. But I know it is a quality that is needed in the newsroom. /.../ I find it really hard. It's something you don't know how to handle. /.../ It's ambiguous. If I declare that they took me on because I'm an immigrant, I feel as if I reduced myself to my origin, to something less valued. (R 5)

To respondent # 11 it has been expressed openly that she has been of interest to recruit because of her background, and gave the following example.

> I got a call some weeks ago: "Hello, I am from [name of media company]. We have a free position this fall and now we are looking for someone with a non-European background. When I called the HR department at [name of media company] they tipped me about you. So I asked: "What is it that I have reported and written about that you think is good?" There was a complete silence. It was quite obvious that the person who called had never read an article that I had written. They had not even taken the trouble to check what I had done before, they just went after the name. I felt quite offended and insulted. More than anything I was dejected by the lack of progress.

Newsrooms still believe that if you take on an immigrant it's a cure-all that will solve everything.

Respondent # 4 applied for a vast number of jobs before she eventually was hired. She described her way into journalism as a discouraging experience and a battle: "It was really, really hard." When she finally got a position she felt that it was her personal qualifications in combination with her foreign background that were decisive. After her training as a journalist, she did her internship at a radio station.

I didn't really want to work with radio because you can't hide your accent. But since they were actively looking for someone who had a migrant background I dared to take the step.

Some respondents mentioned the intrinsic pressures and isolation in being a "token" or "panic" hire. They indicated the dilemma in having none or just one single foreign-born colleague in the workplace. Respondent # 5 said:

Most of the time I don't think about the fact that I have different ethnic background than my colleagues, but lately I have felt that it would be nice to have someone to seek support from.

And continued:

There are some tricky situations. For instance when you attend a morning meeting and an EU proposal on marriages is up for discussion and the only focus is on the extreme Sharia laws and Muslims. And then we are perhaps two Muslims in the room and the rest are Christians. I do not mean that editors are biased, but the attitude can be very generalizing. You want to open your mouth and say: Hey hey, stop it, you can't define Muslims in that way. Then I feel that I would have needed someone to back me up.

Respondent # 1 recently quit her company because she refused to take on a token role. Her presence in the newsroom was just a way to uphold the diversity of the editorial staff, she remarked. Respondent # 7 described herself as different from the rest of the staff group:

We look at things in totally different ways – not always but often. /.../ I have experiences that most journalists don't have. I have grown up in two cultures, which most [journalists] have not. The average journalist was brought up in a white, Swedish middle class family. I was not. I have a working class background, my parents are foreigners and I grew up in "bad" neighbourhoods.

Another (R 6) responded in a similar vein:

> I represent a completely different part of Sweden, not only because of my ethnic background but also because I'm a woman. My way of thinking is different /.../

Some of the interviewed journalists are not convinced that they have equal opportunities for advancement, or that they are being judged by the same evaluative criteria as the journalists of Swedish origin. The journalists underline the importance of supportive managers who promote diversity. The message from eight of the respondents is that they do not feel adequately supported in their ambitions to advance in the organization.

> There is so much hypocrisy! They cry: Do you know someone, do you know someone [with a migrant background] to hire? What about me? I am here. Why don't they employ me? It doesn't matter how much I struggle. /.../ I have tried to figure out why. Is it because of my ethnic background, is it culturally conditioned, is it because I am a woman, or is it a question of my lacking the required skills? (R 6)

And added:

> I have several journalist friends with foreign backgrounds. They are surpassed by their colleagues even though they are more competent and have been in the company for a longer time.

Respondent # 7 has also experienced the difficulty of being considered for job openings.

> If [name of the company] is serious in their efforts, well then, hire me – a woman of the "right" age and with the "right" ethnic background. But it [the diversity policy] doesn't mean a thing. (R 7)

The journalists often feel that much of the company's diversity efforts are mere window dressing. Diversity policies are frequently regarded as empty words, and many express a disappointment with their companies' performance regarding diversity issues and an impatience with the slow pace of change.

> There are so few journalists with immigrant backgrounds. /.../ People might think it's an advantage to have a foreign background, but that's not the case. The newsrooms could be much more active in the recruitment process. The search could be much more effective. For instance, there are also a number of foreign-born journalists working for regional papers and there are jour-

nalism students who could be recruited. But today there a few newsrooms that hire people. (R 8)

Respondent # 13 pointed to the hardships of entering the media business if you don't have any contacts:

> The nepotism and the importance of connections in the industry are prob-
> lematic, especially if you want to come to terms with the fact that practically
> all journalists have the same ethnic background and the same class and
> educational backgrounds – completely Swedish, middle class, and university
> background. When you consider that practically all recruiting takes place
> through contacts, it is easy to cynically ask oneself how can it ever become
> any different?

Another concern of the respondent was how employers value different competences:

> What I think is really important, it is not first and foremost to look for strange
> names, but to consider what the newsroom needs. There will be a lot going
> on in Iran and in Turkey in the near future. Would it be a good idea for the
> newsroom to have journalists who speak Persian or Turkish? Yes, it would. We
> have no equivalent here of candidates to choose from. If it were possible to
> choose someone who has this additional qualification, it would be beneficial
> for the newspaper and make really good coverage possible.

To respondent # 12, it is self-evident that her background is part of her professional skills.

> It is easier for me to contact my fellow countrymen. Of course they are more
> at ease talking to me. There is nothing strange about that. I have knowledge
> of certain things. Just like Swedes know that Swedes think and behave in
> certain ways, I know how my fellow countrymen are reasoning and I know
> how to find my way among them.

Her background was also taken into consideration when she was offered a
job.

> I was not enormously qualified. I had never worked in a big newsroom.
> But I love this job. I don't know if that was what did it. /.../ I have taken
> the long route to show that this is what I want to do. But I also believe
> that my background is partly an explanation. I think the newsrooms today
> want to demonstrate that they consider diversity. That is something that I

have noticed. I think in a different way. I can think of angles that the other reporters don't.

One respondent was recently promoted, and had a very hard time to begin with. She felt that some of her colleagues both questioned and disregarded her.

> At the beginning I really hated it /.../ I think that they [the colleagues] felt that I couldn't do the job. I don't think the reason was that I'm an immigrant, but because I'm a woman and that I look young to them. Ok, maybe a bit because I'm not Swedish, after all I don't speak perfect Swedish. /.../ Initially I was kind, and then I actually became angry. (R 4)

She believed that one reason why she was promoted was that she is hard working, determined to pursue a career as a journalist, and that her editor recognized that. She described the support she received from her editor as crucial:

> She has been really good and encouraging. She has given me more power. To begin with I was a little powerless. I felt like a puppet, if you wish. She saw the potential in me. /.../ I really appreciate that, because if I had not had that power they [the colleagues] would have continued to tread on me. (R 4)

Openness, a willingness to listen, and the capacity to give good advice are some of the aspects that the journalists felt characterized a committed leadership. Far from all, however, have experienced the encouragement they would have desired. There "is not any support whatsoever", one briefly stated (R 7). Instead, she and others have turned to parents and families for support.

Language Matters

What level of Swedish fluency is required for acceptance into a journalism position? Not having Swedish proficiency was one common response editors gave when asked which factors most restrict ethnic diversity in their workplace (Berggren 2002). However, in the telephone survey (see survey in this volume), only one official mentioned insufficient language skills as a hindrance to diversity. The interviewed journalists placed less emphasis on language skills as a requirement to enter journalism, and remarked that it was more a question of attitude than a genuine barrier. The respondents who came to Sweden as adults commented that the difficulties they faced in mastering the language made them lose professional confidence. Respondent # 2 looked forward to reporting in Swedish:

I believed it would be fun, but when I listened to myself speaking Swedish with an accent I didn't feel happy. More than anything I felt shy. I thought: ugh, now I have said something wrong. I embarrassed myself in front of the Swedish people.

One respondent (R 1) experienced difficulties when she began as a journalist, and had to face strong opposition because of her accent. One of her supervisors told her straight out that she was better off if her voice was not heard on radio, and she had to fight for the right to speak with an accent.

To tell you the truth, I had to struggle. But finally I was accepted as the one with an accent. I am a [nationality] woman, but my voice is very nice, very lyrical, and I am great /.../ I tried to compensate the accent with other things that I am good at /.../

Nowadays I don't think about it. I know that I never can make it [the accent] disappear. I can't even speak correctly. I know that, but I can't do anything about it. So I just don't care.

To respondent # 4, language issues have been more of a social than professional impediment in interactions with the staff:

I become silent and am afraid of saying something stupid, or that everyone is going to think that I am an idiot because they can't understand my Swedish. In certain discussions I have been totally ignored.

Respondent # 6 noted that an English accent is more readily accepted than an Arabic one, and raised the question as to why one type of pronunciation is considered more prestigious than the other:

In radio or television you rarely hear people speaking Swedish with an accent. /.../ [T]he progress is very slow. /.../ I realize that people must grasp what is being said /.../ but you don't have to speak with a perfect Swedish accent to be understood. (R 5)

Still respondent # 10 saw some progress:

A few years ago a news anchor was expected to sound a certain way to be perceived as a professional. Today you can hear different dialects and even newscasters with an accent. So something is happening.

Respondent # 12 felt that too much emphasis is put on language skills, and brought attention to the assistance you can get from spellcheck on the computer and from colleagues. Her opinion was that you don't have to be one hundred percent correct:

> I will never perform as well as a native Swedish speaker. That is a fact. But that's not why I'm here. One can find someone who writes grammatically perfect Swedish, not a single spelling error, but the texts are crappy and uninteresting. There are too many hang-ups about language skills in journalism schools and newsrooms. You have to let it go.

Practices and Leadership

Diversity is not only about numbers; it is also about reporting practices and attitudes. It is not clear that increasing the number of foreign-born persons in the newsroom results in an improved coverage of migration-related issues. There are a number of barriers facing better diversity coverage, including tight deadlines, a newsroom culture that sticks to established reporting patterns, and inaccurate stereotypes. These production practices are hard to transform. Hiring more journalists with foreign backgrounds may not be the answer. "It doesn't make you a good journalist just because you are an immigrant", respondent # 3 noted. He was very critical of existing practices, especially those of "objective" mainstream journalism. In his view, it is necessary to establish other working methods in order to bring about better coverage. Respondent # 9 also drew attention to the role newsroom managers have in finding and building new practices:

> As a reporter you learn and are aware of what the editor appreciates, what gets you a pat on the back when you have done a good job. And the opposite.

Many of the respondents are aware of the expectations placed on them to introduce alternative topics and news sources just because of their migrant background. A diverse take on stories and news events is sought after, and was often one reason why they were hired, but this issue is seldom discussed openly. However, respondent # 14 raised the question straight away when he was employed.

> When you're an immigrant you think: do I get this gig just because I'm an immigrant and am expected to write about the suburbs and all that crap? So when I got this job I asked him [name of the editor]: did I get this gig just because you need a *blatte* [someone with immigrant background]?

This ambiguity helps to encourage guesses and assumptions. One journalist stated:

But you have to realize that just because I have a different background it doesn't mean that I have more immigrant friends than you do. I don't come from Rosengård or Södertälje or Akalla, you see.[3] I don't have those contacts. /.../ And that scares me sometimes. What is expected of me? (R 5)

One (R 7) added:

You shouldn't just concentrate on the colour of someone's hair or a strange name. Each newsroom has to ask the question: what do we lack in order to /.../ obtain our objectives. In a democratic perspective the aim is hopefully to reflect society as adequately as possible in a variety of aspects.

Reporters with foreign backgrounds often oppose the role of caretakers of migrant issues.

Maybe I have consciously avoided issues concerning refugee policies. /.../ [I] can feel like a traitor, because you can't disregard who you are, but I hate to do things just because they are expected of me. (R 5)

Respondent # 12 also used to avoid covering issues regarding asylum seekers and cultural diversity:

I just wanted to be an ordinary journalist. I did not want to be accused of taking advantage of my background and I didn't want anyone to even consider that I had got the job because of that. But when you realize that you have a particular skill, and when there are a number of jobs that can prove that to yourself – not for other people – then it doesn't matter. It's a fact that I was a refugee, that I have lived in refugee camps, I know the problems that exist, I know the difficulties my parents faced in their daily lives. And that is the way that we journalists should work. Write what you can, write what you know!

A homogenous editorial staff is not the only factor that hampers diversity and different news beats. The participants also identified the attitude of newsroom managers as essential to promoting diversity. The editors must place pressure on the reporters, respondent # 9 said:

Editorial guidelines are necessary: this is what we consider good journalism in this field. It is of vital importance as to how they are formulated. If they consist of general advice like "we need to have more immigrants in the paper", they are useless. You can't follow those.

Therefore, editorial rules need to be specific and precise, he remarked and gave an example of a recent newsroom discussion.

What words shall we use when we write about God? When you write about Muslims, Allah is often used when it is uncalled for. It is the same word as Christians use, it just means God but in Arabic. (R 9)

The debate led to guidelines that the editor formulated and mailed to the news staff. Without detailed recommendations, you cannot follow up on how well reporters or departments live up to the goals, he argued and added that managers must be prepared to fight to fulfil the goals.

At the managerial level ethnic diversity is extremely sparse. Media researcher Edward Pease and his research group found that having a minority executive in a decision-making capacity could make a significant difference in how American news organizations dealt with diversity issues (Pease, Smith & Subervi 2001: 6). Even if there are reporters who have foreign backgrounds, the gatekeepers are still male, white journalists, one critic said (respondent # 7). A general view among the participants is that the reporting practices are hard to change.

It's tremendously tough because the conventions are so fixed. You have re-porters who have been in the newsroom for 45 years and you have editors who have been working for a long time and who the staff respect. /.../ I don't think it's impossible. You have to identify the key persons, those with the most power, and try to persuade them. (R 5)

Respondent # 1 felt that Swedish reporters feared asking questions that made them look ignorant or prejudiced. At the same time, they neglected their duties when they automatically let a reporter from an immigrant background cover migration issues, she argued.

Go ahead, take care of this problem so that we don't have to deal with it. That's what they imply. (R 1)

Representation

Nearly all of the journalists who work for radio and television companies have received racist mail and/or threats from the audience because of their foreign backgrounds or their accent.

There were many listeners that didn't like me and complained a great deal. /.../ A lot of letters were really mean. /.../ It was strange that people could be that angry. Especially since I hadn't said something stupid. I am not a fool who says racist or stupid things about the elderly or other people. I just made my news stories and then tried to present them in a good way, I really tried. Now my accent is perhaps a bit better. But then I didn't know which syllable to stress in words. It was a bit strange that people could get so furious about that. I wasn't accustomed to such letters so I cried and was pretty shook up. (R 4)

Respondent # 5 said:

Anyone with a foreign name gets this kind of mail. /.../ It made me very sad. Why should I receive mail like this? I am just doing my job.

Added another:

I receive a huge amount of threats just because I look the way I do. /.../ I have received death threats, poop has been sent to me – it can be really tough at times. /.../ The first threat was when I got a small piece of white paper where someone had drawn a swastika and had written on an old typewriter: "you bloody negro, go back to Africa" or something like that. At that time I didn't take it seriously and I just shrugged my shoulders (R 7).

But later threats have been more serious and personal. "It sounds awful, but I have actually gotten used to it" (R 7).

Despite the threats, none of them want to give up their careers as journalists. But there is another side of what their faces and/or their names represent. Especially the younger journalists view themselves as representatives of other people with a migrant background, and this involves a special sense of respon-sibility. Respondent # 14 described himself as an ambassador:

Somewhere in the back of my head I have the idea that I don't just represent myself as an individual, but my whole group, my whole community. My aim, right from the start, was to show that we are more than *blattar*, we are human beings, we are multifaceted, and we enjoy a lot of different things.

Respondent # 8 felt that he made a statement by being visible.

I want to reach many people and want those who have migrant backgrounds to feel included. There is an extra dimension to what my face and name signal and that is important for [company's name]. So in that respect I feel responsible, because nobody tells me to do it. /.../ Viewers with an Arabic background, for instance, can identify themselves in a different way. And then I hope that others, the Swedes, think that I am doing a good job.

This visibility has helped him to gain confidence and recognition among im-migrant groups. Several other participants have received positive reactions from their audience and their readers. One (R 5) remarked:

I am full of pride for what my face represents /.../ People with migrant backgrounds write to me and they feel proud, young people contact me and wonder how I entered journalism. Those things make me very happy, because then in some way it has worked to have me there. /.../ To be a role model just by appearing on TV, doing the job that I love – that is just amazing.

Respondent # 13 was very emotional about the positive reactions.

People come up to me all the time and say: "I don't know you, but I know who you are and I just want to say that the heart swells in my chest when I see your name in the newspaper." I almost start to cry when I think about it. To me it is absolutely fantastic if it means something for my community that I can contribute to giving the news coverage an extra nuance.

Three Approaches to Diversity

In this section I will present the motivations behind three media companies' concerns about diversity issues and their attitudes towards business diversity goals. Is the emphasis on better business, better journalism or both? The case studies represent different types of companies that operate within the Stockholm media market and include interviews with managers of three Swedish news organizations, namely *Södra Sidan*, *Sveriges Radio* and *TV4*.

Södra Sidan

The newspaper *Södra Sidan* [On the South Side] started in 2006 and is published by Medborgarpress Stockholm AB. It is a small bi-monthly free sheet distributed to all households in several southern suburbs of Stockholm, with a reported circulation of 54,000 and a staff of four. It was launched out of the discontent with the misrepresentation of minority groups in mainstream media. It can be described as a primarily mission-driven paper emphasizing the social responsibility function of journalism, claiming an active role for journalism, and putting public journalism into practice.

The founder of *Södra Sidan,* Rouzbeh Djalaie and the co-editor Petter Beckman, want to pursue alternative journalistic practices in order to reach new audiences by addressing counter-issues, that is, news issues not found in the agendas of the mainstream media. The paper focuses on the relationships between different ethnic groups in the host country and on issues of communicative rights in multi-ethnic societies. It was born partly out of Rouzbeh Djalaie's personal experiences as an inhabitant of one of the southern suburbs of Stockholm and his frustration with the mainstream media representations of his neighbourhood. It has no diversity program, but the entire operation can be regarded as such.

In much of the general media reporting the suburban areas are often connected to social problems, crime and violence. Rouzbeh Djalaie explained:

> You read *Dagens Nyheter*[4] or some other large newspaper and feel a bit set aside. This is not my world, it's somebody else's world. You see, I'm not included in their picture of the public and when I exist it's only when something dreadful has happened. /.../ One might think that the reporting has improved but in the end nothing much has happened.

To his mind, this kind of negative reporting is intrinsic to the shared news values of mainstream journalism. This view is supported by media researcher Simon Cottle (2000; 2007). Cottle has shown that the identification of a shared professional ideology of objectivity and the often internalized acceptance of shared news values reinforce a tendency towards the standardized nature of news. As Shohat and Stam (1994) have argued there is a powerful blend of media commercial interests and the taken-for-granted cultural assumptions of media professionals that promote the reproduction of dominant cultural and political norms. This 'professionalism' can be seen as influential to the problematic nature of journalists' reporting on multicultural issues. In the reporting journalists follow known patterns, Djalaie added:

> Most journalists assume that this is an area full of problems that society must solve, not that the people living here are fully capable of finding ways out on their own. /.../ If *Dagens Nyheter* reports something about Tensta, then the team can't spend an entire day there.[5] So they have to identify the key persons to talk to and those with features that fit into their own worldview.

Södra Sidan has a highly targeted audience, and Djalaie's primary concern is not to change the general media representation of the suburbs, but to instead give inhabitants of the local community the possibilities of describing their own daily lives, creating a forum for discussion and thereby contributing to a better society. According to Djalaie, this can't be achieved as long as you cling to traditional reporting codes for journalists or to established news values. Therefore the differences in working methods are what most separate *Södra Sidan* from mainstream media. His description of *Södra Sidan* is that of a solution-oriented paper, in contrast to most news medias' focus on problems. Among other things, *Södra Sidan* has organized meetings on important local public issues.

> It is very much about being able to join in the public debate, about being listened to and being taken seriously /.../ This is not an ordinary newspaper. You could say that it's a form of social project /.../ When we meet people

we talk about how problems can be tackled. And sometimes we take the initiative of creating solutions.

More than anything it is about time, he concluded.

> I can be in the town square for two hours and just chat with people, it doesn't even have to result in an article. /.../ I don't approach people with a specific question that I want people to answer yes or no to.

The editors are in close contact with the inhabitants and the paper has a readership panel that meets once a month. Djalaie stressed the value of finding out how well the paper meets the needs of the readers and of getting responses to their journalistic product. But the panel is also a platform for market research. Djalaie believes that news organizations need to create a different sort of relationship with the public, one that re-examines the journalists' role to sources and to readers, and changes conventions about what is news and how it is covered.

> This type of journalism works, not only in areas where there are social problems, but everywhere.

Sveriges Radio

Sveriges Radio (SR) is the largest public service radio company in Sweden and is financed by a compulsory licence fee. Since commercial radio broadcasting channels first began operating in the early 90s public service radio's share of daily listeners of has steadily declined from 70 percent to less than 50 percent of the population. In 2007 a major reorganization of SR was implemented. The change included staff cuts and reductions in budgets. The shift also had an impact on SR's diversity policy, involving a shift from niche programmes, i.e. *Brytpunkten* [Breaking Point] to a general diversity within all programming. Commercial competitors have placed pressure on the company's profile and critics remark that public broadcasting more and more resembles commercial media.

The underlying principles of the broadcasting licence are formulated in the Radio and Television Act. The act stipulates certain fundamental rules regarding the assertion of democratic values and the principle of equality. Moreover, SR's broadcasting licence requires the company to provide a diverse array of programming reflecting the various cultures present in Sweden. The company's diversity policy states that Sweden is a multicultural society. Therefore, overall programming aims at appealing to all Swedes, wherever they live and regardless of their age, gender, and cultural background. The policy also states that diversity should be a natural part of all of the company's programming. Diversity should be seen as including ethnicity, disability, age, faith, sexuality, class, political affiliation and regional differences. SR does not support hand-selecting their staff. Job advertisements must be formulated so as to attract persons of different ethnic origins and SR's policy for cultural diversity is to be mentioned.

Anne Sseruwagi is former editor-in-chief of Sweden's International Radio and now holds a position which among other things includes the monitoring of diversity issues in SR's organization. Her impression is that the attitudes towards diversity within media institutions have changed considerably in the past few years.

> For a number of years we have been following a systematic diversity strategy and to my mind SR has been fairly successful. /.../ I believe you can notice it when you listen to our programs. Diversity has become more of a natural part of our programming and is not stressed in the way it used to be. Nowadays diversity is more often embedded into the processes of programme making and nobody makes a big thing about it.

The company's general diversity strategy is detailed in a number of diversity plans and directives. They are part of the company's planning cycle and are taken into account throughout the entire hierarchy. All channels and editorial departments have diversity plans of their own, Sseruwagi explained. The plans include monitoring of journalistic diversity goals.

> Many desks monitor diversity from a gender perspective. It is easy to keep track of men and women but how do you handle other types of diversity? It's not self-evident how to monitor disability or ethnicity.

Diversity promotes the journalistic product, Sseruwagi stated, and mentioned the role of news managers.

> Managers need to be aware of the importance of diversity and they must put pressure on the staff, otherwise diversity is easily forgotten/.../ If you don't fulfil the diversity goals it should have consequences, no increase in wages, for instance.

In a situation where the public service companies are challenged and put under pressure by their commercial competitors, *SR's* diversity strategy can prove to be of vital importance to the company, Sseruwagi claimed.

> We need to be role models in this field. It's imperative that we reach a variety of listeners and that we are able to equalize access to information, and in that way maintain a democratic function.

Sseruwagi also pointed to the difficulties of increasing or even maintaining the diversity of the editorial staff. She also pointed out the lack of diversity at the managerial level as a serious dilemma.

> We must downsize. Therefore it's even more important that the few recruitments that we make are part of the company's strategic considerations /.../ The persons that we hire today are the company's future key persons.

TV4

TV4, Sweden's largest commercial channel, started in 1990 and is owned by Bonniers, the major domestic media company. It has the second largest daily reach after the public service TV channel SVT 1 (Harrie 2009: 106). It's news programme Nyheterna was the most viewed of all TV-news in 2009 (*Årsrapport 2009*). The company's diversity plan of 2006 states that:

> Diversity is the mixture of all the ways we differ from each other. /.../ To respect, value and look after the assets of backgrounds, perspectives and ideas is a source of creativity (*TV4 Mångfaldsplan* 2006).

The diversity plan establishes that TV4 is a workplace with and for people with all kinds of backgrounds. It stresses that all employees have "an obligation to help create a working environment free from discrimination". One goal is that 20 percent of the staff should have immigrant backgrounds by the year 2008, corresponding to the average share of Sweden's population by that time. This goal, however, has not been reached.

The task of the news department is to produce national news throughout the day, or as the company puts it:

> The news of TV4 should be the viewers' main option and provide a comprehensive account of the major news events in Sweden and the world. We will also follow the viewer's perspectives and concerns of their everyday lives (Nyheternas policy).

Anne Lagercrantz, head of news, considered diversity as "a major issue".

> I strive for diversity, or at least to reflect the rest of the population. Because my newsroom doesn't do that. They are white, middle-aged, middle class, live in villas or live in Södermalm[6] – of course it is a huge problem.

She stated that it is it vital that her staff represents a variety of backgrounds, not only in terms of ethnicity but also social backgrounds and age. The uniformity of the newsroom and the tight deadlines are hindrances to achieve the goal expressed in the news policy.

> In a homogeneous newsroom you know what is rewarded and /.../ in the tremendous time pressure we easily recognize a good news story. But we need to broaden what we consider a news worthy story. We need to see them and we need to find them. And if we all have the same backgrounds we can't do that.

Diversity in staffing and news content is an issue of trustworthiness to the company. But in addition to that, Anne Lagercrantz recognized the commercial value of diversity. The point is simple; the TV4 news must be relevant to people with a variety of backgrounds.

> The solution for the company is to have an editorial awareness, to be goal-oriented and to stress that diversity is important.

She advocates the use of 'diversity mathematics' to keep track of the diversity in content and staffing, and adds: "The measuring of numbers is a blunt tool but it gives a rough understanding of the situation." For a number of years Anne Lagercrantz has been engaged in promoting the situation of women in the editorial offices. She sees several similarities between the efforts to enhance gender equality and her engagement in diversity.

> I think we see exactly the same mechanisms with diversity as with gender. To me it's dead easy. We reward likeness, that what we recognize. /.../ The challenge is to break these barriers.

Conclusion

To sum up, to all three organizations diversity has both a journalistic and a market value. All three need to attract readers/listeners among migrant groups from both a moral and a market perspective. Journalistic improvements and financial necessity seem to be the motives behind enhancing diversity in the organizations, but in different proportions.

The demographic changes of Sweden raise questions about the relationship between media and citizens. *Södra Sidan's* target group doesn't coincide with the metropolitan papers' and versa. The concern of *Sveriges Radio* is, however, to reach everybody. The company is required to serve the public interest; diversity is embedded in the function of public service. TV4 is a commercial channel but when Anna Lagercrantz formulates its mission, "to be close to all people's everyday", it is in wordings very close to the public service ideal.

One could argue that Rouzbeh Djalaie's view of the reader in fact is part of his self-image as a journalist and his role in society. To him, citizen activism can help produce media that are more responsive to the needs of citizens in a diverse democratic society. Communicating with members of the audience is what journalism is all about, to Djalaie. This is a view that generally is not included in the professional identity of journalists in Sweden. It is argued that the discussion and therefore the problematization of responsibilities of news media organizations in Sweden regarding diversity potentially affect the core values of the occupational ideology of journalism. But journalism is a slow-moving and tradition-bound profession.

The situation of journalists with foreign backgrounds raises the question of power relations on the editorial staff. It is possible to suggest parallels with the strategies by which women deal with male-dominated newsrooms. According to Liesbet van Zoonen, they can either choose to be "one of the girls" or "one of the boys". To become one of the boys, women need to adjust to the unwritten laws, norms and expectations that exist in a masculine environment in order to be accepted as an equal and a "real journalist" (van Zoonen 1998). Everett Stonequist's thoughts on marginalization (Stonequist 1937/1965) can easily be linked to the strategies that journalists with foreign backgrounds make use of to cope with their situation in the newsrooms. According to Stonequist the marginal man belongs at the same time to two (or more) cultures and experiencing exclusion, in both the new and the old culture. In these worlds one is often "dominant" over the other. This dual membership will lead to confusion, internal conflict and ambivalence of the individual. "He will, in fact, be a kind of dual personality" (Stonequist 1937/1965: 4). Several of the interviewees indicate that adapting to current standards is needed to gain acceptance and to be able to advance in the organization. They express the dilemma and even conflict between the expectations to be someone "different", introducing alternative news beats and yet to be "normal", adhering to mainstream newsroom practises. More aggressive market strategies aiming at reaching larger audiences also enforce assimilationist tendencies.

Often newsroom diversity programs have focused on hiring to create diverse content. Numbers alone are not the entire story. To change the situation an increased recruitment of journalists of minority backgrounds will not be enough, nor will well-intentioned diversity policies. Newsroom cultures include a variety of codes that a journalist with a foreign background and with the determination to gain acceptance in the workplace do not question. They are confronted with several factors that make it difficult or impossible to get news beats concerning minority or migration issues accepted. Several of the journalists that I interviewed said that they refrained from proposing such news stories. Clint Wilson comments that established perspectives in media prevent change towards cultural pluralism in the content. He takes the situation of black journalists who worked in "white" editorial offices in the U.S. as an example: "Their survival on the job depends upon how well they conform to newsroom policy expectations and how they 'fit in' with fellow workers" (Wilson 2000: 97).

Clint Wilson and Félix Gutiérrez identify five developmental phases in the news about ethnic minorities: (1) exclusionary, (2) threatening issue, (3) confrontation, (4) stereotypical selection and (5) integrated coverage (Wilson & Gutiérrez 1985: 135 ff). Twenty-five years later, the last stage is in large part a vision not yet realized. It is characterized by a media coverage based on a "we" which includes all citizens. To accomplish that objective, news professionals need to redefine news values and the definition of "in" and "out" groups. This provides a clear challenge for newsrooms to transform standardized professional practices and newsroom cultures.

The findings of *The News and Race Models of Excellence Project* indicate a correlation between management, diversity efforts in hiring and content, newsroom attitudes on diversity and the actual content of their news products (Pease, Smith & Subervi 2001). Charles Westin and his research group, who analyzed diversity practices in six Swedish companies, reason that diversity is harder to bring about in authoritarian and rigid organizations. Westin believes that a dynamic and democratic leadership is of central importance for positive consequences of diversity to emerge and to promote an open atmosphere in the workplace (Westin 2001: 183-184). This coincides with what media researcher Ingrid Östlund (1994) found was characteristic of creative newsrooms. One could assume that more innovative newsrooms would be more open to pluralism and more likely to invest in more diverse kinds of reporting practices and recruitment. The current situation is clearly unsatisfying. Understanding the organizational structures and cultures can also help in understanding why change does not take place.

Notes

1. An earlier version of this chapter has been published in conflict & communication online, Vol. 8, No. 2, 2009, http://www.cco.regener-online.de/2009_2/pdf/hulten.pdf. It is here republished in a revised form with the kind permission of the publisher of that journal, professor Wilhelm Kempf.
2. An additional interview has been conducted with Anne Lagercrantz, head of news at TV4. See the section Three approaches to diversity.
3. Areas with large immigrant populations.
4. *Dagens Nyheter* is Swedens's second largest daily newspaper and is published in Stockholm.
5. Southern suburb of Stockholm.
6. Trendy area of Stockholm.

References

ASNE (2009) American Society of Newspaper Editors, U.S. newsroom employment declines, www.asne.org/article_view/smid/370/articleid/12.aspx, retrieved August 2010.

Awad Cherit, I. (2008) Cultural diversity in the news media: A democratic or a commercial need? *Javnost – the Public*, 15(4): 55-72.

Berggren, J. (2002) Enklast när alla är lika, www.quickresponse.nu/artiklar/2002/maj/enklast-nar-alla-ar-lika/, retrieved August, 2010.

Cottle, S. (1997) *Television and ethnic minorities: Producers' perspectives : A study of BBC in-house, independent and cable TV producers*. Aldershot: Avebury.

Cottle, S. (ed.) (2000) *Ethnic minorities and the media: Changing cultural boundaries*. Buckingham: Open University Press.

Cottle, S. (2000) 'A rock and a hard place: Making ethnic minority television', in Cottle, S. (ed.) *Ethnic minorities and the media*. Buckingham, Philadelphia: Open University Press, 100-117.

Cottle, S. (2007) Ethnography and news production: New(s) developments in the field. *Sociology Compass* 1 (1), 1-16. www.blackwell-compass.com/subject/sociology/article_view?article_id=soco_articles_bpl002, retrieved June, 2009.

Deuze, M. (2002) *Journalists in the Netherlands an analysis of the people, the issues and the (inter-) national environment*. Amsterdam: Aksant Academic Publishers.

Discrimination Act, SFS 2008:567, www.ud.se/sb/d/108/a/115903, retrieved August 2010.

Freedman, D. (2008) *The politics of media policy*. Cambridge: Polity Press.

Harrie, E. (2009) *The Nordic media market 2009: Denmark, Finland, Iceland, Norway, Sweden: Media companies and business activities*. Göteborg: Nordicom. Electronic resource, www.nordicom.gu.se, Publikationer [Publications].

Horsti, K. & Hultén, G. (forthcoming) Directing diversity: Managing cultural diversity media policies in Finnish and Swedish public service broadcasting, article accepted for publication in *International Journal of Cultural Studies*.

Journalists at Work (2002) Journalism Training Forum. Skillset, www.skillset.org/uploads/pdf/asset_262.pdf?1, retreived June, 2009.

Kretzschmar, S. (2007) 'Diverse journalists in a diverse Europe? Impulses for a discussion on media and integration', in Sarikakis, K. (ed.) *Media and cultural policy in the European Union*. Amsterdam: Rodopi.

Lentin, A. & Titley. G. (2008) 'More Benetton than barricades? The politics of diversity in Europe', in Titley, G. & Lentin, A. (eds) *The politics of diversity in Europe*. Strasbourg: Council of Europe.

Löfgren Nilsson, M. (2007) 'Journalistiken – ett könsmärkt fält?' [Journalism – a gender-marked field?] in Asp, K. (ed.) *Den svenska journalistkåren* [The Swedish Journalist]. Göteborg: JMG.

Malik, S. (2002) *Representing Black Britain: A history of Black and Asian images on British television*. London: Sage.

Mc Cracken G.D. (1988) *The long interview*. Newbury Park, Calif.: Sage.

Nyheternas policy (2006) [The policy of the news]. Unpublished document, TV4, Stockholm.

Pease, E.C., Smith, E. & Subervi, F. (2001) The news and race models of excellence project – overview connecting newsroom attitudes toward ethnicity and news content. Maynard Institute for Journalism Education, www.mije.org/files/industrystudies/news_and_race2.pdf, retrieved June, 2009.

Sarikakis, K. (2007) 'Mediating social cohesion: Media and cultural policy in the European Union and Canada', in Sarikakis, K. (ed.) *Media and cultural policy in the European Union*. Amsterdam: Rodopi.

Shohat, E. & Stam, R. (1994) *Unthinking Eurocentrism: Multiculturalism and the media*. London: Routledge.

Statistics Sweden (2009) Sveriges befolkning, kommunala jämförelsetal, 31 december 2009 [Sweden's population. Comparative municipality figures, December 31, 2009], www.scb.se/Pages/ProductTables____25795.aspx, retrieved August 2010.)

Stonequist, E.V. (1937/1965) *The marginal man: A study in personality and culture conflict*. New York: Russell & Russell.

TV4 Mångfaldsplan (2006) [TV4 Diversity Plan]. Stockholm: TV4.

van Zoonen, L. (1998) 'One of the girls? The changing gender of journalism', in Carter, C., Branston, G. & Allan, S. (eds) *News, gender, and power*. London: Routledge.

Westin, C. (ed.) (2001) *Mångfald som vision och praktik. Utvärdering av sex företag och organisationer* [Diversity as theory and practice: Evaluation of six companies and organizations]. Norrköping: Integrationsverket.

Wilson, C.C. & Gutiérrez, F. (1985) *Minorities and media: Diversity and the end of mass communication*. Newbury Park: Sage.

Wilson, C. (2000) 'The paradox of African American Journalists', in Cottle, S. (ed.) *Ethnic minorities and the media*. Buckingham, Philadelphia: Open University Press.

Årsrapport 2009 [Annual Report 2009], www.mms.se/rapporter/tv-tittandet/ar.asp. retrieved August, 2010.

Östlund, I. (1994) *Kreativa redaktioner. Om konsten att bygga en kreativ organisation* [Creative newsrooms: On the art of building a creative organization]. Sundsvall: Redaktionsbyrån.

Examining Ethnicity in German Newsrooms

Heike Graf

In this chapter, I use a difference-theoretical approach in order to examine how ethnicity is observed in German newsrooms. This is an approach based on observation theories (e.g. Spencer-Brown 1969, von Foerster 1984, Luhmann 1997). The notion of 'observer' and 'observation' as used here greatly differs from standard language use, and means, according to observation theories, that it is by noting a difference that one becomes aware of things. In other words, one can only observe something if it is different. In this chapter, observing means drawing distinctions and describing them (Graf 2010: 94-99).

Based on interview utterances, I want to explore how ethnicity functions in the context of journalistic production, and how it gains importance within specific contexts. I use the term 'ethnicity' to denote an aspect of one's relationship to a group of people with whom one shares a cultural heritage, and whose culture is defined as different from that of other groups. One's membership in an ethnic group need not depend on attributed racial characteristics, or on nationality. When one discusses people with migrant backgrounds, cultural differences are observed as distinctive and become socially relevant, and social relationships acquire an ethnic dimension (see also introduction and Jönhill's chapter discussing the notion of ethnicity in this volume). In my analysis, I use the system theoretical concept of the distinction between inclusion and exclusion, in order to analyze the interview utterances. I will start with some theoretical remarks, followed by the description of the empirical material and the analysis of the interviews, which are structured around themes of recruitment, the coverage of topics, issues of language, careers, and experienced impact on reporting.

The Theoretical Approach: Distinction Inclusion/Exclusion

In order to analyze how ethnicity functions in media-production environments, I relate ethnicity to the distinction of inclusion/exclusion. I do not choose the distinction discrimination/equality, because this distinction is used in a moralizing manner (good/bad); it includes too many normative statements. To illustrate this: Generally, most people are excluded from media organizations (similar to other organizations), which is neither a good nor a bad thing. But if we state that most people are discriminated against within media organizations, we would judge it as negative. Or another example: If an informant says that he is excluded from the job because of turn-taking, on the one hand this might be bad for him, but on the other hand this might be good in regard to respecting the rules of the organization. This distinction of exclusion/inclusion allows different observer perspectives and, therefore, more options and combinations in the analysis of the material. In contrast, employing a normative distinction (good/bad) would restrict the complexity of the interviews from the very beginning, as the intention would be to discuss only distinctions that are observed as wrongfully drawn (see also Hellman 2008).

The distinction inclusion/exclusion, however, is a cognitive rather than a normative one. It generally denotes a person's general participation, or non-participation, in the communication that takes place within media organizations. Or as Niklas Luhmann defines it, inclusion is a distinction whose inner side indicates the social consideration of persons and its outer side is not indicated. This means that we can only speak of inclusion when exclusion is possible. Only if we observe that there are persons or groups who are not included or integrated, can we then explore conditions for integration (Luhmann 1997: 620, 621). That was precisely the case when we defined our research aim: We observed that journalists with migrant backgrounds are rarely included, or in other words, 'underrepresented' in newsrooms.

According to Stichweh (2005), the distinction inclusion/exclusion is a hierarchical rather than a binary, 'either-or' opposition. One of these sides can be a generic term. If we take an example from our topic, one can describe the European program "More colour in the media" as mentioned in chapter 1, as a measure to help to include excluded journalists with migrant backgrounds within media organizations. My informants also provide several examples, which I will discuss below, of how inclusion can accompany exclusion and vice versa, and how this constitutes a dynamic process.

As stated by Stichweh (2006: 136) there are two general mechanisms that include individuals: the mechanism of situation, which names or addresses persons, and the mechanism that forms structures through expectations. When the individual is not being addressed, nothing is expected of that person. I can make this point clearer by using the example of the National Integration Plan mentioned in chapter 1. This plan utilizes the situation mechanism: Journalists of migrant background are addressed and are to be integrated, or included, in media organizations. It also uses the structure-forming mechanism: Expectations about individuals are expressed. It is stated, and expected, that editorial staff members who have migrant backgrounds, and thus have first-hand knowledge of immigration issues, can report competently on integration issues (Der Nationale Integrationsplan 2007: 159-160, see also Graf 2010: 98).

In this context, a person's frames of references, information resources, and life experiences are expected to have an important impact on his or her journalistic work. Strictly speaking, a migrant background almost automatically connotes expert knowledge of intercultural matters. This expectation can lead to forms both of inclusion and also of exclusion, should the person not live up to these expectations. The emphazised difference (that is, that migrant journalists are experts on migrant issues) might be situational and temporary, and would, in that case, not contribute to the development of lasting inequalities. But if effects of differences accumulate, lasting inequalities can arise (Stichweh 2005: 171).

The Design of the Study

The study is based on semi-structured face-to-face interviews (with the exception of one telephone interview), each lasting approximately one hour. The selection of interviewees was done according to the snowball principle: interviewees were chosen on the basis of personal recommendations. It was not easy to get journalists interested in taking part, and some never answered my request or cancelled the interview at the last minute. Using recommendations was helpful to me in getting them interested and putting them under some kind of 'obligation'.

Nevertheless, the group of my interviewees is a good mixture of age, gender, first/second-generation immigrants, permanently employed/freelancers, and different cultural backgrounds. A total of twenty-one journalists with migrant backgrounds, ten women and eleven men, between 25 and 55 years old (with an average age of 38) were interviewed in Berlin during May, September and October 2007, and April and November 2008. Nine of these are employed on permanent contracts; the remainder are on fixed-term contracts or are freelancers. Half of them work within the press media. Only one informant has a management position (editor-in-chief) at a radio station. Nine were born and partially trained in a foreign European country. They are first-generation immigrants. The other interviewees are second-generation immigrants; they were born and raised in Germany. Most of those who are employed on permanent contracts in German mainstream media are first-generation immigrants. All but three obtained degrees in journalism, or some other academic field, in their home countries. It is perhaps surprising that it is the first-generation immigrants who have obtained permanent employment contracts, despite the fact that some of them are not fully proficient in German. This is because, in Berlin in particular, conditions have existed that make it easier for those with a migrant background to obtain permanent employment as an editor. As mentioned in chapter 1, the public broadcasting service SFB launched a radio program "Radio Multikulti", targeting Berlin residents from different cultures. Until late 2008, the radio offered immigrant journalists excellent opportunities to obtain permanent contracts because they were also needed to create bilingual programmes, both in their mother tongues and in German.

Ten of my interviewees have a Turkish background, and three a Russian background. The others have Middle-Eastern, North-and South European, North-African, Latin-American, and Asian backgrounds. The largest immigrant community in Berlin is Turkish. Its history dates from the 1960s, when the first migrant workers came to Germany. Berlin's Russian community is more recent; it coalesced during the 1990s.

The interviews are structured around two themes. The first concerns recruitment and career opportunities. The second, more general theme, is that of working conditions. In this chapter, I will concentrate on recruitment, the coverage of topics and issues of language and careers, and finally, on the question of the impact of their reporting from my interviewees' point of view. The aim of my study is, as mentioned above, to determine which functions ethnicity is ascribed in relation to the various themes addressed in the interviews.

Inclusion in Media Organizations: Employment

Inclusion in media organizations occurs through different kinds of employment. Media organizations are based on membership. Not everyone can become a member of a journalistic organization. Organizations generally serve to exclude the majority of people; otherwise they would not be organizations (Luhmann 2006). The organization must therefore draw distinctions among the applicants on some basis. In Germany, there are several formal requirements for membership in media organizations, such as the successful completion of an academic or professional education and an excellent command of the German language. Membership is regulated through various contracts. Nowadays, the contracts are more varied, and there are several forms of membership. A journalist may work on a permanent contract, as a freelancer, or may even get employment as a "fester Freier", that is, as a freelancer committed to work for some fixed period of time, such as a year. Journalism is a field, which has spearheaded the development towards an ever-growing proportion of the workforce being employed on a temporary or part-time basis.

The degree to which immigrant journalists are included in media organizations and the role played by ethnicity in the hiring process is also related to the respective media organizations and their requirements. A radio station that focuses on multicultural issues is more inclined toward recruiting media workers with migrant backgrounds.

When discussing the employment situation, my interviewees' observations can be divided into three categories: 1) a migrant background is an advantage, 2) a migrant background is a disadvantage, and 3) a migrant background is not decisive for employment opportunities. I want to concentrate on the first two groups in order to further examine the distinctions my interviewees make when they describe their experiences based on their ethnicity.

For most of the full-time employees I interviewed, ethnic origin had played a positive and/or advantageous role. The primary reason for this is that media organizations seek to promote ethnic diversity in their newsrooms (see chapter 1). The interplay between ethnic background and professional experiences was decisive during the recruitment process. Apparently, being of non-German origin was, when combined with past work experience, an advantage for the candidates. This is confirmed by the story told by German TV's first co-anchor-woman with a migrant background. As of April 2007, Dunja Hayali, who is of Iraqi origin, co-anchors the prime-time news show on the public broadcasting network ZDF. She is the first co-anchor-person with migrant background. According to an article published on the *Deutsche Welle* website, it was no secret that the broadcasting network ZDF had been looking for a presenter with a migrant background. The article quotes Hayali as saying:

> Of course my qualifications were the most important criterion, but there's no denying my immigrant background was an added plus in bagging the job. (Phalnikar 2007)

ZDF was looking for a presenter who was of obvious immigrant origin, and who could play the role of integrating German immigrants. For that role, a blonde woman with blue eyes would not do. Hayali spoke of a "migration bonus". Her migrant biography has become a news item and she has given more than 50 media interviews. At first, she was irritated by the attention, but over time she began to see herself as a sort of a trademark that she could brand (Hayali 2007). The enormous attention that she received displays the media's belief that an event is newsworthy if it strikes our attention by being distinctive. The fact that Hayali's story was considered newsworthy illuminates a context: presenters with migrant backgrounds are generally absent from the information and news programmes of mainstream television.

Searching for a "visible" immigrant presenter seems to be a common strategy among those seeking to increase the number of employed journalists with migrant backgrounds. This strategy may, however, cause irritation when no distinction between cultures is drawn. One informant tells a story about a TV station that was looking for a presenter for a program discussing German-Polish issues. The program's target audience consisted of people living on the border of Germany. The editors asked a journalist with a different background (neither Polish nor German) to fill the position. The journalist in question was very surprised at the offer. He finally declined because he could not identify himself with the task of reporting on German-Polish matters, and feared that he might jeopardize his future career if he entered into this field. The offer gave rise to some consternation, and he began wondering whether Germans think all foreigners look alike. Clearly the editors' primary objective was to employ a 'visible' migrant journalist. They apparently did not care from whence he or she came, for a woman with a Kurdish background eventually got the job. It seems that the program editors wanted to avoid having a presenter with 'typical' German features – blond hair and blue eyes. For the editors, a visible ethnic difference was relevant. For the Kurdish journalist, having a non-Polish background was obviously not a sufficient reason to turn down the job.

To be recruited as a 'visible' migrant on TV can also be experienced as meaning that 'appearance takes precedence over qualifications'. One journalist gives a drastic description of how he experiences his employment situation:

> I am the token Turk at [name of the TV station]. I was employed against the will of my section head. It came entirely from above. (Man, TV, R5)

Here, the informant claims the distinction of being a "token" – a person who was awarded his position because of his ethnic background rather than his qualifications. The claim that even his direct superior, with whom he has to work most of the time, opposed his employment makes his statement more forceful. This decision from above – that is, from the gatekeeper who decides on the recruitment of new staff – did not meet with unanimous approval on the floor. The informant later adds that he has not completed his academic or professional training (although he does have journalistic experience) and therefore does not meet all the formal job requirements. But due to organizational decisions aimed at furthering the participation of journalists with migrant backgrounds, he was ranked higher than an applicant with a non-migrant biography. His employers expected his knowledge of the Turkish community to compensate for his lack of formal education; he will, they feel, have a special competence which the organization requires. The TV station needs a presenter who can also address Turkish viewers, and a decision came from above to employ this particular person. For this journalist, ethnic background has become an advantage.

The distinction between being a 'token' journalist and a 'normal', competent journalist is brought up in several interviews. The emphasis on the 'token' role, which often leads to a distinction between being competent and being incompetent, can also stress the notion of a disadvantaged ethnic background. I want to illustrate my point with the following quote:

> When I was employed, it was of course my fear that I would fill a foreigner quota. I did not want to do that, actually. For that reason I asked the bosses: Look, very honestly, was I employed because of the foreigner quota? No, they said, it was really because of your professional qualifications. (Woman, radio, R8)

This informant had expected to be given a 'token' role, but was told that the opposite was the case. She was told that her qualifications, not her ethnic background, had earned her the position. Unlike the informants mentioned above, she meets all the formal requirements for the job, but she associates foreign origin with having less competence. She hopes that the others do not have this association, and is inclined to believe in the executive editors' answer, despite having experienced some ups and downs in her career. During the interview, it becomes clear that she connects other observations on the difference between competence and incompetence to issues of ethnicity. She gives another example, from her time as a trainee:

> It was like that at the meetings, when it came to assignments: I put my hands up three times, and no-one else did that. Even so, I did not get the job even if no-one else was interested in it.[...]
>
> *HG:* Was this because of your migrant background?
>
> Of course. Yes, of course. More than anything, yes. (Woman, radio, R 8)

During her internship, she thought that the following assignment would provide an excellent training opportunity. The assignment concerned a popular tourist sight, nothing special or difficult; if she made mistakes, there would be no serious consequences. This being the case, it was a good training topic. In this situation, however, her biography appeared to be a barrier. She had come to Germany as an adult, and so had not experienced growing up in the country; she had not learnt about its culture from the cradle. She speaks German with a slight accent. As a non-native, she observed she was not qualified to report on a local tourist attraction in radio. Marking ethnicity in relation to cultural knowledge of the majority culture, and, therefore, in contrast to competence, hints at an organizational culture that legitimizes inequality. The unspoken expectation may be: 'you do not belong to the titular society, you do not know all the 'secrets' and, ultimately, you are not fully qualified to report on that society.' Here, ethnicity functions as an excluding mechanism, one that serves to prevent a particular group of people from addressing certain topics.

Another female interviewee gives an additional example of an exclusionary mechanism based on ethnicity. She denies the existence of the "migration bonus" that Hayali refers to in her own case. This woman, who has been in the media business for more than fifteen years, explains that while there may be exceptional cases like Hayali's, in general, little has changed:

> When I started in TV, I was told that I had better leave [...]. 'We prefer blondes'. Of course they did not say it to my face. That happened only once. During the casting – off the record – someone recommended that I become an author, behind the camera. The time is not yet ripe for such exotic 'cases' as me. (Woman, TV/ radio, R6)

This journalist feels that she is being labelled as someone who does not fit in because of her appearance. She is too "exotic" to conform to the visual norm. This is to her disadvantage. A print journalist of Asian origin tells a similar story. During his internship at several media organizations, the teacher had tried to talk him out of attempting a career as a TV presenter, citing his Asian origin as the reason. TV producers expect a presenter who conforms to the established visual standard of a presenter. This is a typical mechanism for exclusion with respect to features as appearance. This exclusion seems to be more than situational and temporary. It is a general exclusion, one which leaves the excluded with only two options: to assume a role behind the camera, or as a relatively 'invisible' person in radio or print media. Here, lasting inequalities have arisen. Inequalities can be transient. Norms can change, but it takes time. The desire not to surprise may also explain the dismissal of the exotic. Only that which is different is perceptible and gains attention. A presenter's difference is supposed to be negligible, for noticeable differences may, for instance, be perceived as negative, or may distract the viewer's attention from the programme presented. The recruitment of Hayali as a co-anchorwoman, however, attracted a good deal of attention to the news programme, which I do not believe harmed the programme.

To summarize, the main distinctions in regard to employment, assignment, and migrant background are, on the one hand, the function of a different background as an "plus", one which gives advantages; and, on the other, the function of a different background as a "minus", as something that is seen as a disadvantage. In other words, a migrant background is either perceived as giving competence or as causing incompetence. This means that the main distinction is the dichotomy of competence/incompetence. In cases when an interviewee's migrant biography has been perceived as causing a lack of competence, he or she more often articulates the experience of inequalities. In case of the "token" role discussion, we see that ethnicity is an advantage and inclusion (getting the job) but in a excluding manner by being less formally qualified than the other colleagues and therefore disadvantaged. For this journalist, exclusion becomes obvious when talking about career possibilities, as I will show later.

The next section is concerned with the topics that my interviewees cover in their journalistic work. Here as well, the interviewees refer to expectations that confront them because of their migrant backgrounds. By mapping out their varying expectations, one can uncover several mechanisms of inclusion and exclusion.

Coverage of Topics

Generally, the employment of journalists with migrant backgrounds is linked to specific expectations. It does not matter whether they are recruited because of their different ethnic backgrounds or not. As mentioned above, the interviewees all observe that they are expected to be experts on their respective cultures. As one press editor relates:

> I was not explicitly recruited because of my ethnic background, but implicitly it did play a role. If there is a certain topic that relates to my background, I am always addressed: 'You are [Nationality], won't you infiltrate that group and report on it?' It is like belonging to a secret society. One can speak the language and therefore it is assumed that one has access to all the people who speak that same language. (Man, press editor, R10)

Having a certain ethnic background means 'automatically' having access to and an understanding of one's own ethnic group. The reporter observes that the people in his work environment perceive various ethnic groups as homogeneous and as easily accessible to those who speak their languages. His colleagues do not realize that ethnic groups also consist of individuals, and that contacting its members requires more than mastery of the language. In other words: When it comes to topics related to a person's own ethnic group, ethnicity is often seen as intrinsic to competence. How can a person respond to this expectation? The interviews reveal two common patterns: the person may confirm the expectation and act accordingly, or he or she may fail to do so. If the latter, the person must develop strategies to survive the disappointment that this causes. The above-mentioned press editor cannot fulfil expectations. He is forced to reveal the limits of his intercultural competence to his colleagues. In his case, this had no consequences; it did not cause lasting inequalities, for he had not been recruited explicitly because of his background. He covers a wide range of other topics in his work.

Those media workers who are first-generation immigrants and who speak accented German are more recognizably immigrants. Hence, they find it more difficult to thwart this kind of expectation. This means that they are given fewer opportunities to cover topics that are not directly related to immigration. In this context, some informants draw a distinction between the past and the present (by implicitly referring to the ongoing political discourse on integration), and between the newcomer and the established journalist. Those informants with longer experience of journalistic work in Germany are most likely to make this temporal distinction. As one newsman puts it:

> In the early 90s, when I began working as a journalist, the expectation was: you are [nationality], please treat this topic. I did not accept it. I always tried to get topics that I liked. I did not succeed, for the staff did not believe that I also could deal with other than [nation] topics. After having been turned down 30 times, you eventually do what is expected of you. (Man, radio, R1).

The journalist refers to the beginning of his career, when he was forced to conform to commonly-held expectations in order to survive as a journalist. In the interview, he expresses the belief that media organizations' expectations may have changed somewhat since then. Now that he has established a reputation and has become section head, he feels that, as a well-known name, he has the freedom to select topics: "If you have become an 'institution', you are unassailable, and feel capable of covering other topics" (man, radio, R1). If one wishes to cover other than those 'normally' expected topics, it is essential that one makes a name for oneself. Breaking the pattern of reporting exclusively on ethnic issues is a struggle against expectations – one which can be won.

The journalist who covers regions unrelated to his or her own background can face problems when trying to sell the story to the newsroom. To clarify this point: Reporting on ethnic issues does not mean being an expert on all ethnic issues or regions. As a journalist with a migrant background, you are supposed to be an authority solely based on your own ethnicity. If you do not have the ethnic background needed to treat a topic, and are not officially assigned to do so, you are excluded from taking it on. This is an exclusion mechanism that limits the respective journalists' opportunities to work with new topics. A newsman tells his story:

> Lately I have also been interested in America, because I was there for two months. But now I really see that I have far fewer chances of getting the topic accepted because of my East European background. There are other expectations of me. I say: 'I was there for two months and spoke to different interesting people', and they say: 'Well, every one else was there already, and for two months, too' […[So, I suggested a fabulous topic and got no response, not even a refusal. They totally ignored me. Only one, the [name of the radio station] finally sent me a reason: 'We have a correspondent there, and he does it'. (Man, radio/TV, R3)

On the one hand, this journalist feels excluded because of his different ethnic background, which is neither German nor American. On the other hand, he is also being excluded because he does not hold the position required: he is not an assigned correspondent. The latter is a structural exclusion mechanism; that is, not holding the required position, a mechanism that goes for all journalists. In this case, the particular region might also be a reason for his exclusion. In news coverage, the (North) American region is of very great importance, and several reporters are usually assigned to the area. There seems to be no need for additional reporters.

The coverage of topics is not always associated with unfulfilled expectations. It can also lead to their fulfilment. It is often claimed that the migrant reporter can take on the role of an insider. An interviewee refers to her accumulated and actual knowledge, as well as to the contacts she has within her own ethnic group:

> I know the weak points of my community, [...] or which topics are tricky. I know the rights and also the problems of the migrants from my own experience. I already know how to treat the topic. [...] I can handle it better than my German colleague. (Woman, radio, R4)

When she compares herself to her German colleagues, she makes the distinction between one's own and not one's own experience in relation to knowledge. Having more experience of different cultures in one's own life implies having a greater awareness of different modes of intercultural communication. In her statement, the journalist repeats the general assumption that underlies the National Integration Plan, i.e. that those with migrant backgrounds and cultural experiences are better equipped to handle this type of topic than those who lack a commensurate background. Some, but not all, interviewees make this distinction. One male informant finds that his background makes it difficult for him to remain unbiased when reporting on a specific ethnic conflict. He therefore cannot guarantee balanced reporting:

> My interest does not lie in immigration policy or the [...] conflict [...] I am not able to comment on this conflict. I am too partial because of my family. (Man, press, R 21)

For this journalist, personal experiences have deprived him of distance to a specific issue, which is a hindrance to good journalism. Being too close, or too emotionally involved, may have a negative influence on reporting. He does not have the expert knowledge (and does not want to acquire it), and therefore does not want to cover this field. Personal experiences do not necessarily give expert knowledge.

The choice between confirming or disappointing expectations is also influenced by insecure conditions within the job market. A freelance journalist makes her choice clear when she describes the situation within the job market:

> To be a freelance journalist with a migrant background is not at all bad.
> If I offer a story to an editorial staff about an integration topic that fits my
> knowledge about Turkey, I sell it immediately. It is automatically assumed
> that I have higher intercultural competence. (Ataman 2007)

When it comes to treating certain topics, having a migrant background pays off. Here, a reference to the market economy is made, which is important in covering topics of this kind. In the same context, another journalist laconically speaks of a "[..] unique selling point. It is a question of making use of German expectations" (man, press editor, R 10). He notes that branding is more important than expert knowledge. The market economy has taken priority over expertise. Irrespective of whether ethnicity makes the person an expert or not, he or she will use it as a means of getting ahead; what counts are commonly-held expectations. If you, as a freelancer, live up to this common expectation, you have an advantage when it comes to being included in journalistic work, whether it is selling topics or seeking employment.

To sum up: My informants' responses show that they have to deal with the common assumption that they are experts on the ethnic groups to which they belong. This can greatly reduce the individual journalist's scope of possible of topics. If you have, and can make use of, the 'right' background – i.e. if you live up to expectations – you generally have an advantage when seeking assignments and jobs. If you do not choose to exploit your ethnic background, you have to explain your choice. The freedom to do non-ethnic topics is often seen as the outcome of a long struggle. These topics, which my interviewees prefer, are the result of a complex conglomerate of expectations and disappointments. 'Normal' expectations are described above, but they seem to be more changeable than static. The experienced expectations vary according to the individual. Those who feel recognized as having expertise on other topics find it easier to avoid 'typical' ethnic ones. The context together with individual motivations influence how best to deal with various expectations. Expectations are temporal, and can change if repeatedly frustrated.

Language Matters: Dealing with Accented Speech

As mentioned above, the profession formally demands an excellent command of the German language. In this context, the grounds for accepting accents are discussed in the interviews. Here, my interviewees have noted that people of different ethnic origins are treated in a normative manner. Some accents are more acceptable than others. Someone who belongs to a prestigious ethnic group, for example, receives a "sympathy bonus" which "is not valid, however, for Turkish or Russian colleagues" (woman, radio, R2). Belonging to a high-prestige ethnic group gives you linguistic leeway, for you are likely to encounter an accepting attitude. This is not the case for those who speak with, for example, a Russian accent:

> The reputation of the Russians is not as good as that of French or American people. It is cooler to be an American. (Woman, radio, R8).

Subtle excluding mechanisms depend on distinctions between high-prestige and low-prestige cultures. These distinctions, in other words, generate inequalities when they are based on normative (good/bad) assumptions. The above quote shows that Russians are less welcome than, for instance, Americans and that an accent that reveals a Russian background may lead to disadvantages and therefore exclusions from assignments. There may also exist advantages – mainly in connection with specific topics – as I will show below.

Speaking with accent is quite often seen as a hindrance to advancement. A female, first-generation immigrant who speaks German with a slight accent tells me she was astonished by the reactions she encountered:

> If an individual with an accent says, 'well, I work in German media and can be heard on radio", it raises a few eyebrows. All are surprised and that slows me down (Woman, radio, R8).

She perceives the reaction as something negative. It makes her feel bad and also stands in the way of her promotion. She feels that her accent costs her recognition as a genuine journalist, someone competent enough to make career advances. This is a matter not of mastering the language, but of the distinction between speaking with or without an accent. Some media organizations define people who speak with an accent as falling short of professional requirements. The journalist quoted above, for instance, is employed on assignments in special radio programmes, but does not believe in a career in TV media organizations. She explains this by referring to unspoken norms in German media, which exclude people with accents:

> To be a visible migrant journalist is one thing, to be an audible migrant journalist is, however, something entirely different. [...] There will never be an anchorwoman with an accent. (Woman, radio, R8)

In German media, the accent issue is comparable to the dialect issue. During the first era of (Western) German television broadcasting, standard German was the norm. But when the third (regional) programme was launched in the late 1960s, dialects were no longer banned from the screen. Nonetheless, standard German remains the rule for several central, nationwide news programmes. The language issue is a problem mainly for first-generation immigrant journalists, and is often cited as a 'minus' when it comes to landing assignments that are not directly related to the applicants' particular ethnic background. Journalists with a migrant background, who came to Germany as an adult, and who want to cover non-ethnic topics, must cope with the exclusion that afflicts those who do not master standard German. Once again, the issue is the distinction between "speaking with an accent/without an accent", rather than "comprehensible/incomprehensible accent". I am referring here to accents that in no way impede understanding. Nevertheless, incomprehensibility is often used as an argument for prohibiting accented German on TV and radio.

There is one exception to the unspoken ban on accents. Accents may be permissible when directly linked to a given topic. If the journalist is covering events taking place in Russia, a Russian accent connotes authenticity. The accent enforces the message. To paraphrase Ataman, above: Those who originate from the country being covered are automatically assumed to have expert knowledge. Accents have to fulfil a function; they have to be related to the specific topic and/or context. If a journalist with an accent reports on issues concerned with his or her home country, accented German is acceptable. If a given programme focuses on, for instance, multicultural urban life, it is also accepted that one or several of its journalists speak with an accent. But an accent is less accepted if the journalist in question is reporting on a topic that has no relation to his or her origin and is outside the context of special multicultural programmes. This runs the risk of precluding journalists with accents from taking on most of the assignments available in radio and TV broadcasting. This, at least, is the situation today.

But having a non-German mother tongue can also be an advantage in written language. It may provide a means by which one's written German can be improved:

> I think that if one works with languages, and has lived abroad for a long time, one has a greater chance of enriching them.[...] I still sometimes write commentaries interspersed with [Nationality] and [Nationality] idioms and proverbs. And when I translate them into German, or experiment with them, it makes my German language style more interesting. (Woman, radio, R2)

Speaking several languages fluently is also seen as an advantage. Commentaries, which are very much based on working with language and on choosing convincing phrases and idioms, can gain stylistic richness if they include ingredients from different languages; these can function as spices in a dish.

They can, for instance, attract more attention, which is essential both to the media, where competition is tough, and to the journalist. However, another informant would disagree with the woman quoted above. He claims that he never will be a poetic "Edelfeder" (literally "noble pen") (man, press editor, R 18), for, although he grew up in Germany, his parents' foreign origins meant that he did not learn German from his mother as a 'mother tongue'. He will, he fears, never acquire a supreme grasp of the German language. Being proficient in writing has a price and is a result of hard work, as a newspaperwoman expresses drastically: "I even learned orthography in the loo. [...] One has to work much harder" (woman, press, R13).

To sum up: Language issues focus mainly on a bi- or multi-lingual person's opportunities, and difficulties, when it comes to handling the German language. Being fluent in several languages may enrich one's journalistic language, but it may also reduce one's language skills. Speaking with the 'wrong' accent halts careers, or at least provides an obstacle to one's own development. Lasting exclusion mechanisms occur, in particular, when experiencing an accent ban, as well as a general, normative demarcation between cultures.

Career

According to Luhmann, the term career is not limited to denoting the fulfilment of ambitions, moving ahead, or being a success (Luhmann 2006: 102). There are careers that suffer reverses or come to a halt. Luhmann argues that there are pauses in every career; these are interpreted as having either a positive or a negative impact on the individual's development. My informants reflect on these types of breaks; breaks that are closely connected with the topics and language issues discussed in the previous section. More precisely, when the informants focus on career setbacks, they tend to relate them to specific organizational constraints or even to structural peculiarities. Seeking explanations for setbacks in one's career fulfils an important function: it makes it possible to handle the ups and downs.

The various interviewees disagree on the role different cultural backgrounds play in creating career setbacks. Some claim that this plays a minor role; others maintain that it is a determining factor. The latter is claimed by a first generation immigrant journalist, who does not see any chance of promotion because of cultural and ideological clashes. According to this journalist, success goes hand in hand with assimilation, which the journalist in question is not willing to accept, as the following quote shows:

I have already resigned myself to not having a splendid career as a result of my non-German origin. Every single attempt to start a career would involve my accepting ideological conditions that I am not willing to accept. It is different, however, for my younger colleagues, those who are born and grew up in Germany. They have better promotion prospects. It is because they are rather ready to bow to the demands from their colleagues, and that they are already shaped by the German education system. (Man, press/radio, R 16).

The quote implies ideologically and culturally closed media organizations that are not open to different perspectives, and that are only interested in reproducing their own values and perspectives. Having the 'wrong' ethnic and cultural origin is seen as an impassable obstacle in one's path. In contrast, the following quote from another first generation immigrant journalist shows, that ethnicity is not the only explanation for the interviewee's lack of promotion:

When the [name of the broadcasting station] refused several times to send me [to name of the city] as a correspondent, I thought I was unsuitable because I had too little distance to the topics, due to my ethnic background. At the time I thought so. But now I do not believe in that explanation. It has to do with the internal career ladder, and it was not my turn. [...] That kept me busy for a time, because it was a pity. If it was because of my background, it would have meant that I never could do that, or that I have to wait until they have forgotten that I am a [nationality]. (Man, radio/TV, R3)

In this quote, the informant reflects on whose 'fault' it is that he did not get the job. Eventually, the informant stops attributing the setback to himself – that is, his own lack of competence. Instead, he starts blaming the organization. This move towards blaming the organization's formal structure strengthens his desire to continue his journalistic career. It is pragmatic. Because he cannot change his background, he can only hope that his background will be forgotten. His distinction shifts its focus, from competence to pecking-order or turn-taking. This makes it possible for him to hope that he will be considered for the position in the future.

Similarly, a female journalist attributes setbacks in her own career to informal communication problems caused by a superior who prevented her from receiving training within the TV organization. Also in this case the organization's formal structure is one cause behind the setbacks.

I could not get ahead in TV, and this was 99.9 % due to the boss. The colleagues got the order from him not to promote me. This I was told years later, over a glass of wine. There were two aspects that came together: being a woman – the boss had certain problems with women – and being a foreigner. I would have loved to work in TV. But it was not my fault that it did not work. (Woman, radio, R8)

Being both a woman and an immigrant is seen as a barrier to advancement. The superior's motives belong to the *incommunicablia,* which the people involved know about but do not communicate. The informant explicitly attributes the setback in her career to her superior's decision. The latter seems to base his decision on biological characteristics and on ethnicity. This type of explanation for setbacks implicitly blames the individual. For this journalist, the doors to the TV studio are locked. Here, the above-mentioned accumulated effect occurs; as a result, the journalist lacks experience in working in TV and cannot not show samples of her internship within TV. The fact that she has no documented TV experience, in turn, leaves her with little chance of getting a job in TV broadcasting, and may result in a lasting exclusion from that segment of the journalistic field.

Here, we have an example of exclusion that is caused by the system's structural peculiarities, such as special roles and position assignments (Stichweh 2005: 173). In this case, a particular person has the position of playing a gatekeeper role and therefore has influence over careers as well as over the quoted interviewee's career. On the one side, special persons (e.g. superiors, bosses, heads of departments) get disproportionate respect and influence on persons, and, on the other side, one is also willing to be influenced or to accept the decision (Stichweh 2005: 174). In this case it leads to exclusion, and in another case e.g. of the "token Turk" to inclusion, because a gatekeeper from "above" has given the decision to employ the person (see R 5).

Another female journalist attributes setbacks in her career to an organizational culture, which is observed as being hierarchical and less tolerant of critical comments and questioning:

> I would not blame my migrant background for everything. I am a fighter and not everyone likes that. I often comment things, I discuss, I want to have things clarified, and I absolutely do not acknowledge hierarchies, if I feel that is nonsense. Therefore, it certainly has something to do with my personality. (Woman, press, R13)

The combination of being of foreign origin and having a questioning mind seems to be a disadvantage for the newspaperwoman when it comes to position advancement. She has her own opinion, and is not malleable, which is, according to her, not desirable within the organization. In the interview she blames the organization for not being grateful and for not supporting a person who "has increased the esteem of the newspaper" (woman, press, R13) by offering new perspectives, thanks to her different ethnic background.

Another story about career setbacks links these directly to ethnicity, in a statement that relates ethnicity to confidence. In the following quote, the journalist describes an organization culture which is characterized by a lack of confidence in placing immigrant media workers in leading positions:

Presently, my career has come to somewhat of a halt. It is always said that
more immigrants should work in the media. The situation is like this: there
is more demand for people in front of the cameras than in executive positions. We have not come so far yet. But I hope I will experience that. [...].
That people have enough confidence that somebody with twenty-five years
of experience in journalism or fifteen years of management experience can
also move on to a higher position. (Man, radio, R1)

This man's experience is that the trend of recruiting journalists with migrant
backgrounds extends only to lower-level positions of the hierarchy, and to
'visible' immigrant news presenters. Despite his many years of professional
experience, this journalist cannot advance as a result of Germans' lack of confidence in immigrant journalists, which, in turn, prevents them from giving more
responsibility to experienced immigrant journalists. The inability to advance
one's career is related to the organizational context, which resists changes.
The journalist can communicate his desire to obtain a higher position, but he
doubts that he will be successful, because the organizational environment is
generally experienced as not being ready for change as yet.

Career pauses and opportunities are not exclusively related to the issue of
ethnicity. When individuals are generally satisfied with their career, ethnicity
probably does not play a decisive role. There are, for example, pauses that
are caused by general organization requirements such as training issues. In
the words of a presenter:

I have already advanced a lot in my career. It is not easy to become a presenter
on TV. But if I want to join the first league in a public service organization,
I have to possess a university degree. I don't. (Man, TV, R 5)

This man attributes his career successes to himself, and the impossibility of
further advancement to both himself and the organization. In other words, he
does not have the required competence, and he will not advance in his career
until changes occur. He may graduate, he may move to another organization,
or the organization may change its requirements.

Those who have already achieved a higher position express greater satisfac-
tion with their career. Pauses would be easier to handle for those in executive
positions and, according to one female journalist's statement, ethnicity does
not affect her chances of getting ahead:

I feel quite safe in my job. Even if my radio station disappears I will remain
employed in the broadcasting company in some capacity. I am also well
known, know many people, and could imagine finding a job as an editor
elsewhere in the company. (Woman, radio, R2)

In general, my informants do not connect their career successes to the issue of ethnicity. If they do so, they consider ethnicity as a "plus" in the employment situation, and an asset when it comes to getting assignments. But when it comes to setbacks in their career, ethnicity plays a more dominant role. Ethnicity is seen as an obstacle. This obstacle may be harder to overcome for a woman, who is surrounded by a staff that is almost exclusively male – in Germany, only 37 percent of all journalists are women (Weischenberg et al. 2006: 45). Ethnicity is also seen as a barrier to career advancement. Having a migrant background means inspiring less confidence from the organization, and that may halt a career. According to these cases, the organizational culture is perceived as excluding media workers with migrant backgrounds, due to their 'different' appearance, their accent (as described above, in the section on accents), or their origin. People with these differences observe an organization that is informed by the idea of a homogenous society. This observation often refers to a common organizational structure that gives persons in leading positions the right to decide over careers and assignments. If these persons are perceived as narrow-minded or prejudiced, my interviewees feel disadvantaged. But my interviewees expect the organization, including their leading persons, to change, reflecting changes in society at large. They perceive a distinction between the present and the future, which both raises their expectations about what lies in the future and affects their present decision-making.

Does a Migrant Background Make a Difference?

This section deals with how my informants experience their impact on media reporting based on their backgrounds. In research, we can often find a structuralist approach which claims that structural constraints of the media organization are decisive for the media product, that the individual media worker has little or no impact on the media product, and therefore is consequently seen as a small piece of the machinery (Breed 1955, Shoemaker et al. 1996, Shoemaker 1991). Other scholars, however, have shown that the personal and professional judgments of the individual journalist influence the selection and coverage of news (Tuchman 1972, Gans 1980). In line with this latter approach, Patterson et al. (1996) and Donsbach (2004) claim in a more recent study that there are the subjective beliefs and predispositions that influence the journalist's perception and therefore the media product. We can also follow Weischenberg's model of influence factors within journalism in order to find arguments for that approach (Weischenberg 1994: 431). He compares journalism with an onion consisting of different concentric layers, where he places the media worker with his/her predispositions formed by biography, and profession expressed as political and social point of view, and self-image etc. at the centre or core of journalism.

It is the media worker, who eventually constructs the media product – not in a vacuum– but influenced by society, media organization, and information including the type of coverage.

In line with this model, my interviewees describe their own judgments as decisive when selecting news and addressing migrant issues. Their answers refer to their professional self-images and touch on mainly two fields of work: An entire series of responses is about efforts to change media coverage by striking a different perspective in order to work against negative and stereotypical reporting, with the aim of promoting tolerance in and integration of society, as the various quotes show:

> Well, I want to change the coverage style of migrants. Sometimes the reports in the German media are very biased, which upsets me. (Woman, radio, R 4)

> My concern is writing more complex stories [...] We cannot reduce it to a Turk problem. (Woman, press, R 15)

> I see many things differently than my German colleagues do. They have a very Christian, Occidental or Western perspective on everything, without judging it negatively. (Man, press R16)

> Many second and third generation immigrants say today: 'I want go back and I am proud to be [Nationality] and my heimat is there'. That is because of the discrimination they have experienced here. They hope that it is at least better in their country of origin. Therefore, I would like to encourage them to stay here by airing success stories. (Woman, press, R 9)

They feel responsible for contributing to topics which have received insufficient attention in the media and are important to a multicultural society.

Another series of utterances is about the role they play within the media organization. They describe themselves as door openers to migrant communities as an editor claims: "I have an extensive contact net that my colleagues only stand to gain from" (woman, press R13). They not only deliver useful contacts when investigating a story, but might also influence thinking on these issues among the colleagues in the newsroom. Their peers can learn from journalists with migrant backgrounds, and can become more sensitive to ethnic issues and perspectives, as the same editor has observed:

> Since I have this focus on migrant communities, I contribute to a reflection on this issue within the editorial staff [...]. Meanwhile, it also has an impact on my colleagues. (Woman, press, R 13)

A great number of responses concern the role models my interviewees experience. It begins already in the newsroom, and the fact of being the only one with a migrant background. This results in taking on some kind of responsibility, e.g. representing an entire culture and acting as bridge between cultures:

> In the morning most of the chief editors I work for drive out of their basement garage or of their gardens into the basement garage of their publishing houses. And in the evening they go back home. They do not know any Kreuzberg, have not even eaten kebab. Probably I am the only Turk they know. (Woman, press, R 15)

It is not only within the organization that they feel they are on some kind of 'mission': They also feel this when it comes to the public. A TV presenter gives an example of his positive impact on migrants when he is onscreen:

> Yesterday, I got a call from a friend [...]. I have not heard from him for more than 10 years. He said: 'I saw you on TV. My parents always watch your news show.' And I realized what I want, I also want to address the people who have immigrated. Here, I have an important function. (Man, TV, R 5)

Addressing an audience with migrant backgrounds is important for him in order to work towards getting immigrants included in society. In speaking about this concern, he implicitly invokes the other side of the issue: As the quoted press editor above shows, people with migrant backgrounds are insufficiently addressed and represented in the media, and if so, mostly in a negative light (e.g. Meissner et al. 2001, Ruhrmann et al. 2000). Therefore, another media worker stresses his symbolic presence in the media, in light of his successful career:

> In the meantime, I have the moral obligation, as somebody who has succeeded, to be a good example. [...] The people see me and hear my stories and cannot believe then, [...] that I come from an illiterate family. (Woman, press, R15)

By showing positive individual stories of social inclusion, this woman wants to offer good examples to identify with and to break the pattern of negative coverage of immigrants. This is not only addressed to immigrants but also to the entire society and, therefore, could help in tearing down the wall between natives and immigrants. As another journalist puts it:

> I also want to give Germans the possibility to get to know us. In some cases, they do not dare to get in touch with us. (Woman, press, R 9)

According to her, the German people lack knowledge about the life of the various immigrant groups. They live separately from the immigrants, and have only a few possibilities of coming into contact with immigrants. But the journalist can bridge the knowledge gap. In line with the other interviewees, she sees herself as a 'mobilizer' – in contrast to the more neutral role of a 'disseminator'– and wants to promote cultural encounters in the society.

My interviewees observe themselves as active contributors to cultural diversity in society, and feel free to do so. Often they describe themselves as pioneers, as media workers who develop new approaches and contribute to new viewpoints. Obstacles for diverse newsrooms and media coverage are seen as a structural problem, as the 'wrong' people have leading positions, meaning people who are not aware of the challenges of a diverse society. For example, it is observed that a chief editor who is married to a immigrant woman is more open to migrant issues than a person without contact to migrants (woman, press R13), which has an impact on the climate of the entire organization, and therefore, an impact on media reporting. The correlation between pro-diversity attitudes in the newsroom and equitable media coverage related to diversity is also stressed by Pease et al. (2001). The researchers find that:

> it does seem clear that the degree to which news managers can communicate their vision regarding diversity to the newsroom, and the degree to which the journalists and other employees buy into that vision, heavily influence whether news coverage will include the full diversity of the communities journalists serve (2001: 9).

The open-mindedness towards these issues varies quite a bit among media workers, and this influences the climate in the newsroom and therefore elbowroom for the journalist. If one cannot decide over how to report, and the scope is too limited, the journalist has the chance of refusing stereotypical stories, as a freelance journalist relates:

> I say no to some stories because the media always are too biased. For example, in 2005, when a woman was shot to death by her brother. [...] I got a lot of requests from almost all of the newspapers. Consistently, I refused all of them, because the media always wanted sensational stories. And that did not correspond to my idea of enlightenment and that simply was too dangerous to me, writing a perfectly investigated story, with the media then making a typical story out of it. I am always annoyed at that. (Woman, press, R 15)

The media organization has lost the possibility of an alternative media coverage, and the freelance journalist herself has not contributed to the reproduction of stereotypes. The notion of refusing unwanted assignments is an often articulated 'last resort' when my interviewees feel they are losing control over their products. That goes above all for freelancers. But if you are an employed editor, you have a greater influence already from the beginning: "You write the article by yourself and can make your own cultural references" (woman, press R 20).

Summing up, the degree of impact on reporting about migrant issues depends on the working climate, that is, on staff who are open or not to different viewpoints, on the position the journalist holds and last but not least, on the journalist him/herself based on one's self-image including the degree of involvement and responsibility for these issues. My interviewees tend to be a type of journalist who is very confident about his or her role in society. They are more inclined to make a difference, that is, to address integration issues and to promote reflection and cultural encounters in society. On the one hand, the results can depend on the interview situation. I informed my potential interviewees in advance about the theme of the research project, and those who were willing to be interviewed were often already interested in these issues themselves, and were therefore more reflective. On the other hand, the answers correspond to other studies (see also Camauër in this volume, and e.g. a recent study by Nishikawa et al. 2009), as well as a representative study conducted in the Netherlands by Deuze (2005). The author concludes that one's ethnicity has an impact on the professional self-perception of journalists with migrant backgrounds, and advocates a proactive social role for media and a critical awareness of the pitfalls of stereotyping minorities (Deuze 2002: 125).

Conclusions

My material, as described above, consists of in-depth interviews and, therefore, on observations communicated in an interview situation. Observation is selective. What is selected depends on the observer (the interviewee) related to the interview situation and to the topics discussed in the interview. In other words, different individuals may observe the same object differently. Here, it is not an issue of identifying the real content of an observation. Rather, the ambition is to understand the narratives' self-constitution. We know from Saussure that when we use language we make use of signs, and that these signs do not give us access to the real world. Rather, they demonstrate the differences we make in the observations we communicate. The word 'migrant' is not the migrant *per se*. Nor does it represent a migrant. But it differs from other words, such as 'native', 'foreigner', 'traveller', 'stranger' – that is to say, it is a word that denotes difference. The fact that interview answers are linked to the observer, rather than to a representation of the real 'world' of journalistic production, may appear to question the value of conducting the interviews, insofar as we are seeking knowledge about media organizations. But each observation refers to a 'self' as well as an 'other' (Luhmann 1997). Therefore, we can only say something about the other-reference if we place the observation in relation to the self-reference of the informant.

I want to sum up the distinctions my informants make in observing their working conditions. They vary a good deal, since they are connected to the individuals and their observed experiences as communicated within the interview situation. Nevertheless, I see four main patterns in their descriptions of recruitment, working conditions, and career possibilities, and their impact on media reporting. Migrant background is seen as:

1. An advantage and part of one's competence

2. An advantage yet implying a lack of competence

3. A disadvantage and implying a lack of competence

4. Not making any difference (see also Graf 2010: 99).

The first pattern refers to examples where migrant background is seen as an "added plus" and often connotes quite specific competence in intercultural issues, which is an advantage. The second pattern summarizes the "token" discussion: migrant background has become an advantage in order to get the job, but is also observed to imply a lack of corresponding competence. Here, ethnicity is explicitly including (getting the job) and also implicitly excluding from e.g. career possibilities by being less formally qualified. The third pattern refers to exclusion mechanisms at the working place regarding appearance, accented speech, a lack of confidence etc., which hint at an organizational culture that legitimizes inequalities. The fourth pattern has emerged in connection with all of the discussed topics, and is sometimes explicitly or implicitly expressed. For example, when an interviewee is generally satisfied with his/her career, meaning that migrant background is observed as part of competence, ethnicity does not make a difference. There are, e.g., pauses that are attributed to general organizational requirements such as training issues or internal career ladders.

Generally, ethnicity can be described as generating difference in my interviewees' meaning-construction processes. The ethnicity-related difference between being sufficiently or insufficiently competent is important when describing recruitment and job conditions. In a manner of speaking, ethnicity generates difference when it comes to qualifications. Ethnicity can be intrinsic to competence, and can even be seen as "plus"; and/or it can be part of incompetence, and perceived as a "minus". Having a different ethnic background can be an advantage to the media worker if he or she can fulfil common expectations. It is a disadvantage when these expectations are disappointed.

I can distinguish between two groups of migrant journalists, and see here similarities to Dominic Boyer's study on East German journalists after 1989

(Boyer 2005: 197): the one group is the "sponsored" migrant journalist who has to show off his/her competence in migrant issues and the other the "tolerated" migrant journalist who assists the media company, but without chance of advancement.

Interviewees who have reason to feel a lack of competence because of their origin, and belong to the latter group, pay more attention to the issue of ethnic background when they discuss job conditions and career opportunities. As a result, career pauses and setbacks are often seen as related to ethnic origin. In this context, ethnicity functions as a mechanism for legitimizing inequalities. Those who see their migrant origin as a 'plus', or as intrinsic to their competence, generally describe their experiences as positive. They attribute career setbacks to general market and job conditions rather than to ethnic origin.

These distinctions have also to do with a specific environment. What can we say about the selected distinctions, which are related to the newsroom environment? The newsroom culture is observed as being characterized by expectations, which may restrict journalists with migrant backgrounds to certain narrow topics – those related to migration and integration issues, and migrant topics more or less open to alternative media coverage. If a journalist is fluent in another language, it is automatically expected that he or she will easily penetrate that language community. Such expectations are sustained on several levels. On the government level, they are inherent in the National Integration Plan; on another level, by migrant journalists who claim, on the basis of their origins, to be experts on these questions. Such expectations can be to a journalist's advantage or disadvantage. If one fulfils expectations, one is at an advantage. If one fails to meet them, one is disadvantaged and may be excluded from jobs and assignments. One can struggle against them, attempt to prove oneself capable, and thus work to change expectations. This takes time, and requires persistence and courage on the part of the individual journalist.

In the cases where differences become normative, we can see special mechanisms for including and excluding coming into play in the media organizations. Not all foreign cultures have the same value. Some cultures are more readily accepted than others; certain accents are more acceptable than others. There are high- and low-prestige cultures. Or, to put it in other words, these distinctions generate inequalities insofar as they are based on normative (good/bad) assumptions, which are used, in turn, to exclude people from jobs. The same goes for norms and standards. When a visible difference – for instance, an "exotic" appearance – does not fit the norm, inequalities can arise, and have, in fact, arisen.

In the fall of 2007, a conference on migration and media was held in Berlin. Media workers, actors, politicians, and researchers with and without migrant backgrounds participated. The essence of the utterances of media workers with migrant backgrounds was: "We want to be 'normal', and we do not want to be asked where we come from" (Draussen 2007). They did not wish to be token journalists or to be singled out on the basis of their ethnic background. Instead, they wished to be treated simply as competent media workers doing their job. Such statements reflect the rarity, in this context, of media workers with different backgrounds. As long as they make up a tiny minority of those who work behind and before the news cameras, microphones and newspaper desks, they will remain distinctive. To my mind, the problem is not primarily related to being distinctive but to the ways in which differences are treated, including the connection of differences with certain types of distinctions. If a different ethnic background is simply read as being less competent, and this leads to fewer or no job opportunities, then multicultural society faces a serious problem.

References

Ataman, F. (2007) 'Du bekommst bestimmt einen Job' [You will definitely get a job]. *Journalistik Journal.* http://journalistik-journal.lookingintomedia.com/?p=59. Retrieved December 15, 2007.

Boyer, D. (2005) *Spirit and system: media, intellectuals, and the dialectic in modern German culture,* Chicago: The University of Chicago Press.

Breed, W. (1955) 'Social control in the newsroom', *Social Forces,* 33(4): 326-335.

Der Nationale Integrationsplan. Neue Wege – neue Chancen [The National Integration Plan. New path – new chances] (2007) www.bundesregierung.de/Content/DE/Archiv16/Artikel/2007/07/Anlage/2007-07-12-nationaler-integrationsplan,property=publicationFile.pdf, Retrieved May, 20.

Deuze, M. (2005) 'What is journalism?: Professional identity and ideology of journalists reconsidered', *Journalism,* 6: 442-463.

Donsbach, W. (2004) 'Psychology of news decision: Factors behind journalists' professional behaviour, *Journalism,* 5: 131-157.

Draussen? Drinnen? Dazwischen? Migration und Medien: eine offene Beziehung [Out-side, in-side, in-between? Migration and media: a open relationship], Bundespresseamt Berlin: 29.-30.11. 2007.

Graf, H. (2010) 'Interviewing media workers', *Mediekultur. Journal of media and communication research,* Denmark, 49: 94-107.

Gans, H.J. (1980) *Deciding what's news.* New York: Vintage Books/Random House.

Hayali, D. (2007) on conference: 'Draussen? Drinnen? Dazwischen?. Migration und Medien: eine offene Beziehung'. [Out-side, in-side, in-between? Migration and media: a open relationship], Bundespresseamt Berlin: 29.-30.11. 2007.

Hellman, D. (2008) *When is discrimination wrong?,* Havard: University Press.

Luhmann, N. (1997) *Die Gesellschaft der Gesellschaft* [The society of the society]. Bd.1, Frankfurt a. Main: Suhrkamp.

Luhmann, N. (2006) *Organisation und Entscheidung* [Organization and decision]. Wiesbaden: VS Verlag.

Meissner, B., Ruhrmann, G. (eds) (2001) *Das Ausländerbild in den Thüringer Tageszeitungen 1995-1999. Eine quantitative und qualitative Inhaltsanalyse* [The image of foreigners in the Press of Thuringia. A quantitative and qualitative content analysis]. Erfurt.

Nishikawa, K. et al. (2009) 'Interviewing the interviewers: Journalistic norms and racial diversity in the newsroom', *Howard Journal of Communications,* 20(3): 242-259.

Nohrstedt, S.A., Camauër, L. (eds) (2006) *Mediernas Vi och Dom. Mediernas betydelse för den strukturella diskrimineringen* [Media's we and them. Media's relevance for structural discrimination], SOU: 2006:21, Stockholm: Justitiedepartementet.

Patterson, T.E., Donsbach, W. (1996) 'News decisions. Journalists as partisan actors', *Political Communication*, 13: 455-68.

Pease, E., Smith, E., Subervi, F. (2001) *The news and race models of excellence project – connecting newsroom attitudes toward ethnicity and news content*, St. Petersburg: Poynter Institute for Media Studies.

Phalnikar, S. (2007) New face on German tv highlights dearth of minority presenters, www.dw-world.de/dw/article/0,,2456173,00.html, Retrieved April 20, 2008.

Ruhrmann, G., Demren, S. (eds) (2000) 'Wie Medien über Migranten berichten' [How media report on migrants], in Schatz, H., Holtz-Bach, C., Nieland, J.-U. (eds) *Migranten und Medien. Neue Herausforderungen an die Integrationsfunktion von Presse und Rundfunk* [Migrants and media. New challenges for the integration function of press, radio and TV], Wiesbaden: Westdeutscher Verlag.

Shoemaker, P.J. (1991) *Gatekeeping*. Newbury Park: Sage Publications.

Shoemaker, P.J., Reese, S.D. (1996) *Mediating the message: theories of influences on mass media content*. 2. ed., New York: Longman.

Spencer-Brown, G. (1969) *Laws of form*, London: George Allen and Unwin Ltd.

Stichweh, R. (2005) *Inklusion und Exklusion. Studien zur Gesellschaftstheorie* [Inclusion and exclusion. Studies on theory of the society]. Bielefeld: transcript.

Tuchman, G. (1972) 'Objectivity as strategic ritual. An examination of mewsmen's notions of objectivity', *American Journal of Sociology*, 77(4): 660-679.

Von Foerster, H. (1984[1960]) *Observing systems*. 2. ed. Seaside, Calif.: Intersystems Publications.

Weischenberg, S., Malik, M., Scholl, A. (eds) (2006) *Die Souffleure der Mediengesellschaft. Report über die Journalisten in Deutschland* [The prompters of the media society. Report on journalists in Germany], Konstanz: UVK Verlagsgesellschaft.

Weischenberg, S. (1994) 'Journalismus als soziales System' [Journalism as social system] in, Merten, K., Schmidt, S.J., Weischenberg, S. (eds). *Die Wirklichkeit der Medien: Eine Einführung in die Kommunikationswissenschaft* [Media's reality. An introduction to communication studies], Opladen: Westdeutscher Verl.

Making a (small) Difference?

Swedish Media Workers' Views on the Contributions of their Ethnic Minority Colleagues

Leonor Camauër

In our contemporary world, the media play a crucial role in shaping relations between countries and ethnic groups, both nationally and transnationally. In the scholarly world, a large body of research shows that the media represent ethnic minority groups in highly negative, problematic, and stereotypical ways (see below). But *how* do these poor representations relate to the ethnic make-up of newsrooms? Does any such connection exist at all? Some scholars view this connection as a matter of course:

> The ethnic demography of the newsroom cannot be divorced from the ethnic balance of media content ... Issues of media performance cannot be separated from the issues of recruitment and retention of staff. (Downing & Husband 2005: 152)

Other researchers, however, are more cautious. In a study focusing on the frequency and character of appearances of ethnic minority members across different media genres, Edström and Nordberg (2005) found that the various genres perform quite unevenly in this respect. News and debate were found to perform poorly (and thus to contribute to the reproduction of discrimination), while genres such as the family page, in-depth portrayals, and satire showed a higher degree of inclusion of minority members. While acknowledging the centrality of the news genre (not least because of its norm-building character), the authors do not believe that it is here that change will be achieved first (Edström & Nordberg 2005).

Edström and Nordberg relate the underrepresentation of minority members in media output to the low degree of participation of journalists with an ethnic minority background in the Swedish media market, which also results in limiting the possibilities of the recruitment of managers and directors with the same background. The authors warn us, however, against positing too strong a connection between media output and the presence of minority journalists in the newsrooms, a connection often made in the literature on media, representation, and ethnicity (Edström & Nordberg 2005: 293 and 312). They argue that a comparison with a similar problematic, the link between the representation of women and the increased presence of female journalists in newsrooms, shows that

> it is nevertheless the worlds of men which dominate the news reporting and women are clearly under-represented in the news output. It thus seems that there is a kind of glass ceiling for female participation, which is supported by both male and female journalists and builds upon the media logic and journalistic culture rather than any gender belongings. In a similar way it can be assumed that an increased ethnic diversity in the newsrooms can influence the output – but it is not self-evident that it will do so. (Edström & Nordberg 2005: 312, my translation)

Campion (2005) has addressed the same problematic in her interview study with over one hundred media workers in the British broadcasting industry (including public service, independent companies, and freelancers). In short, she notes that progress from a diversity perspective has been slow and that "There have been many false dawns. Pioneering initiatives ... all have come and gone without any lasting impact on mainstream program output" (Campion 2005: 4, see also Hultén in this volume). Among the factors behind this slow progress, Campion notes the mismatch between diversity rhetoric and concrete action, and the overly homogeneous make-up of the group of senior managers: "the mix of senior people ... has barely changed at all in twenty years" (2005: 4), to which one has to add "the lack of diversity at the senior level of every single public service broadcasting organization in Britain" (Campion 2005: 14). Due to this homogeneity, she goes on, senior managers were viewed as having no personal motivation for increasing the cultural diversity of the output.

Another important point raised by the study is the lack of effective accountability mechanisms: "There is no penalty, no consequence for failure to address the issue. Nobody loses their job or gets their salary docked for ignoring whole sections of the audience" (Campion 2005: 14). The above findings could be interpreted as showing that ethnic diversity in the newsrooms does not matter. But they can also be read as suggesting that diversity *alone* is incapable of achieving change as long as other institutional factors remain unaltered.

While research in the field of media and/in the multiethnic society, in the Nordic as well as other western countries, has for a long time heavily focused on issues of representation of immigrants, ethnic groups and racism (see Brune 2004, Cottle 2000, and Horsti 2008 for reviews of this field), the area of news production has been considerably less investigated. In Sweden, for instance, Djerf-Pierre (2007) discusses, among other things, the ethnic make-up of journalists as an occupational group, and Djerf-Pierre and Levin (2005) and Camauër

(2006) investigate the situation of journalists with an ethnic minority background in Swedish media. A review of the field has noted that "in Sweden there is a lack of research on the ethnic make-up of the media, e.g. of the newsrooms. Perhaps the most important is to investigate the consequences of a supposed under-representation, and the changes that a radical make-up change would involve" (SOU 2005: 56, p. 161, my translation).

This article presents findings of an interview study which aims at exploring how 12 Swedish media workers view the connection between ethnic diversity in their newsrooms and a more diverse output. More specifically, it focuses on three main questions:

1.   How do media workers with a Swedish background, based on their own experience, perceive the contributions of colleagues with other ethnic backgrounds to the newsrooms' overall work in terms of the novelty and the specificity of these contributions?

2.   To what extent and based on what arguments do media workers with a Swedish background consider that ethnic diversity in the newsrooms is necessary?

3.   What are the features of the professional routines and institutional conditions which in the perception of the media workers with a Swedish background hinder the employment, retention, and strong performance of colleagues of other ethnic backgrounds?

Determining who has a 'Swedish', or a 'foreign', or 'ethnic minority' background is always problematic, as people's subjective feeling of belonging may not always correspond to facts such as where they were born. Although it may not be the optimal solution, in this chapter I use 'Swedish background' in the same sense as Statistics Sweden does, i.e. for designating persons born in Sweden with at least one parent born in Sweden, and the same goes for 'Swedish media workers'.

The article is structured as follows. After a brief discussion of 'ethnicity' in relation to the concepts of 'majority' and 'minority', I give a characterization of the social make-up of newsrooms in Sweden/Stockholm. Then I discuss the theoretical-analytical framework of newsrooms as communities of practice. This is followed by an account of the specificities of the empirical study and the presentation of the findings, which is structured into five main themes. The findings are finally further reflected upon in the conclusion.

Ethnicity, the Majority, and Minorities

In line with constructionist understandings, I see ethnicity as historically embedded and socially constructed. Eriksen argues that ethnicity, rather than something that individuals or groups have, is to be seen as "aspects of relations between groups which regard themselves – and are regarded by others – as culturally distinctive" (1998/93: 13, my translation). Importantly, and contrary to widely spread beliefs, it is not cultural differences per se which are the main definer of ethnicity, but the extent to which people see them as significant and then act according to this perception (Barth 1994/69; Eriksen 1998/93: 212).

'Majority' and 'minority' are "relative and relational" concepts (Eriksen 1998/93: 152, my translation). Majorities and minorities are certainly not homogeneous, and considered diachronically, their make-up and character changes as the children and grand children of migrants become incorporated to them or assume different in-between positions. I suggest, however, that at specific points in time, it is possible to speak of majorities and minorities, no matter how much internal variation they may encompass and however blurred their boundaries may be.

Several authors point to the fact that 'ethnicity' is typically related to minorities (Eriksen 1998/93: 12) or evokes associations with migrants or outsiders to the dominant culture (Ålund 2002: 3). There is thus an assumption that ethnicity is not applicable to majority groups (Arnstberg 2008: 18, Ålund 2002). Eriksen argues, however, that despite this assumption "majorities and dominant groups are equally 'ethnic' as minorities" (Eriksen 1998/93: 13, my translation).

In distinguishing between media workers 'with a Swedish background' and those with 'other ethnic backgrounds' or 'ethnic minority backgrounds', I do not mean to attribute these groups any essential, homogeneous ethnic identity. Nor am I suggesting that they occupy more or less privileged epistemological positions from which one group or the other would be more or less capable to know and interpret inter-ethnic relations, minorities, and Swedish society. I rather suggest that the participation of ethnic minority members in newsrooms' work is important, partly as a matter of equal access to any sector of the labor market, partly because I assume that (at least some) members of minorities may contribute with something different and novel to the newsrooms. This assumption, however, is not derived from any supposed essential identity but from their social position *as* members of minorities.

The Context

An encompassing background on the ethnic diversity of newsrooms in Sweden and Stockholm, the related legislation, and media companies' policies and diversity efforts is provided in Hultén and Graf (in this volume). I therefore limit myself here to a brief summary of the ethnic make-up of the newsrooms and a few additional remarks.

There is an even distribution of journalists across gender lines in Sweden at present, and this parallels the population as a whole. However, there are significant imbalances both within the occupational group as such and between the latter and the entire population when it comes to class and country of origin/foreign background (Djerf-Pierre 2007).

A survey from 2005 found that 7 percent of the journalists in Sweden had a foreign background (Djerf-Pierre 2007: 28). Hultén and Graf indicate that some 6 percent of the journalists in Sweden were foreign-born in 2008 (as compared to 14 percent in the whole population), and for the Stockholm region they estimate the number of foreign-born journalists at some 800, which represents some 6 percent of the approximately 12,500 working in Stockholm. The share of the same group in the Stockholm population is 21 percent (Hultén & Graf in this volume).

As regards class, the 2005 survey found that the working class was significantly underrepresented, and that people from 'white collar' and 'higher white collar' had a share of 55 percent of the occupational group as a whole, as compared to a share of 25 percent of the total population (see Djerf-Pierre 2007: 22).

At a more general structural level, media companies are operating in an increasingly competitive climate. As publications and channels proliferate and audiences become more and more fragmented, public service broadcasters have to face the competition of satellite and cable channels, newspapers have competition from the free sheets, and all 'old' media now competes with Internet-distributed media. At the European level, Chakravartty and Sarikakis note that the deregulation of the broadcasting sector has been followed by "a reregulation in favour of the private media" (2006: 100), and Hadenius, Weibull, and Wadbring believe that the media systems of the Nordic countries seem to be departing from their prior social responsibility ideology and evolving toward a sheer market model (2008: 47).

One of the features that characterizes today's processes of news production is especially relevant in the context of this study. Companies are increasingly relying on lower numbers of permanent employees, while the share of the work force recruited as substitutes and through manpower firms becomes higher. The new, flexible media companies place higher skill requirements on their employees, and employ less people in the newsrooms (Nygren 2008: 61-63).

Newsrooms as Communities of Practice

The concept of 'community of practice' (Lave & Wenger 1991) has fruitfully been applied by John Downing and Charles Husband to the study of media production processes from the perspective of ethnic diversity (Downing & Husband 2005, Husband 2005). Broadly speaking, this concept affords an overarching framework for a combined analysis of socially situated, everyday working life production practices and the production and reproduction of social structures.

A community of practice is defined as "a set of relations among persons, activity, and world, over time and in relation with other tangential and overlapping communities of practice" (Lave & Wenger 1991: 98). Communities of media practice are involved in both producing media products and in reproducing themselves as such through the introduction and socialization of newcomers. Through participation in these communities, members develop individual and collective identities and acquire not only professional skills, but also, and more importantly, a set of values, all of which form the subjective axis of communities of practice (Downing & Husband 2005, Husband 2005). The other central axis of these communities, the institutional one, "is made up of the interaction of resources, power, space and time in a specific setting" (Burkitt et al. 2001: 37). Thus, depending on institutionally specific affordances and constraints of the environment, each community will develop its own everyday working routines and unique work place culture, and each will be subject to specific pressures (Husband 2005). These two dimensions are constantly shaping each other, and the explicit focus on their articulation constitutes the crucial merit of the communities of practice as an analytical framework (Downing & Husband 2005).

An example of the advantages of attending to this articulation can be seen in an analytical distinction made by Burkitt and his associates in a study of communities of nursing practice in the UK. The study concluded that "nurses construct their identity in relation to *both an imagined community and an actual community of practice*" (Burkitt et al. 2001: 28, emphasis in original). Borrowing Anderson's (1981) influential concept, the authors explain that in constructing their identities, nurses relate to an 'imagined community' which is held together by a set of crucial values (e.g. giving holistic care), "but which remains imagined in that it is never actually constituted in space and time" (Burkitt et al. 2001: 28). In contrast, the actual community of practice is constructed in everyday working life and interaction. However, since each community of practice is deeply embedded in economic, political and social contexts, there were cases in which, due to various institutional constraints, members felt that they could not realize the central values of the imagined community (Burkitt et al. 2001: 28, 32). In such cases, "core values become a distant ideal, so that everyday working practices are experienced as unsatisfactory" (Burkitt et al. 2001: 32). The authors, however, view the tension between the values and ideals of the imagined community and the realities of the practice of the actual community as both necessary and productive, however problematic and even painful this tension might be to community members. This is because the values and ideals of the imagined communities were found to provide the nurses with a platform from which they could criticize the extant health care system and envision how care work could be done. From this vantage point, the imagined community's values and ideals can be seen as a sort of resource for resistance (Burkitt et al. 2001: 32). This distinction between actual and imagined communities has proven to be fruitful for the analysis of my interview material.

The Interview Study

The method used in the study was the semi-structured individual interview. Two main criteria guided the selection of the twelve interviewees. First, they should be news media workers with a Swedish background and with experience of working with media workers with an ethnic minority background, as colleagues and/or managers. Second, the interviewees, as a group, should show as much variation as possible with regard to gender, age, number of years in the profession, and type of media where they worked/had worked (print, radio, or television and private or public service sector).

The selection of the twelve respondents was made through a combination of approaching potential interviewees whom I already knew filled the mentioned criteria, and snow- balling. They were all guaranteed anonymity in order for them to feel that they could speak more freely. For this reason, they are presented here as a group.

Of the twelve interviewees six were men and six were women. Five were between 30 and 45, and seven between 50 and 65 years old. The length of their professional experience varied as follows: three had five to ten years, three had 15 to 20 years and six had 25 to 40 years of experience in the media field.

When the interviews were conducted (November 2008 to June 2009), all respondents were/had been reporters and all but four held/had held managerial positions at different levels. Five of the twelve worked in print media (one of whom had moved to a position outside the media field proper while still working with media issues), two on radio and five on television. Six of the twelve worked/had worked exclusively in the private sector, two exclusively in the public service sector, and four were/had been in both. Two of the twelve interviewees had retired but continued working on a freelance basis. Most of them, though, had previous experience from different media and media sectors.

With two exceptions, the interviews were conducted in the respondents' work places (the remaining two took place in a library and a home). Nine of the interviews were between 40 and 55 minutes long, the three others were around 90 minutes long. The interviews were transcribed in their entirety and the quotes given below have been slightly edited after being translated to English (part of them by translator Kaj Jordison, part of them by me).

The transcripts were submitted to a thematic analysis through which a number of themes and subthemes were identified. When accounting for results of qualitative research, one usually faces a dilemma: how to indicate how dominant or rare themes appearing in the interview material are, without giving misleading quantifications. This is because although it is important that the readers be given a sense of the spread of specific themes and the views expressed by the interviewees in relation to them, an emphasis on figures or proportions may lead readers in the wrong direction because the samples of interviewees in qualitative research are not representative in any statistical sense. Rather than frequencies, qualitative research strives to locate structures of meaning in the empirical material. In qualitative interview studies, all of the structures emerging from the material are important, no matter how widely spread they are across the material as a whole, because they are all a part of the overall structure of meaning found in the transcripts. An account of results which suppresses structures only occasionally appearing in the material would not be telling the whole story.

In the present study, a middle ground solution has been adopted to solve this dilemma: themes and views appearing in nine to twelve interviews have been labeled as *dominant patterns,* themes found in six to eight interviews as *frequent* patterns, themes emerging in three to five interviews as *less frequent patterns*, and finally, themes discerned in one to two interviews as *rare patterns*.

The sensitive character of ethnicity issues in whatever context begs the question of the epistemological status of the knowledge derived from the interviews. To put it bluntly, were the interviewees being political correct, not least since I am myself foreign-born? My straight forward answer is that while I cannot state that they were not, I did not find inconsistencies in the transcripts which could suggest instances of political correctness.

In presenting my findings below, rather than accounting for the totality of respondents' views on the subject at hand, I focus on exploring the themes that relate to the specific questions of this study. The results of the study are structured into five main themes: the specific contributions, the contributions questioned and qualified, the arguments for increased ethnic diversity in the newsrooms, and the professional routines and institutional conditions (as factors hindering ethnic diversity in the newsrooms).

The Specific Contributions

The interviewees were asked whether they, based on the experience of their own interplay (as managers and/or colleagues) with minority media workers, believed that the latter contributed something novel, different, or specific to the overall newsroom work.

Several subthemes emerged from the material: the different range of networks, the different set of perspectives and frameworks of reference, the different experiences, and the benefits of minority media workers' participation in the newsroom conversation.

The Different Range of Networks

There was wide agreement among the interviewees as to this specific substantive contribution of media workers with an ethnic minority background. The acknowledgement of it constitutes a dominant pattern found in the interview material.

According to the respondents, the different networks of the minority media workers make it possible to widen the scope of the news coverage and the range of social groups covered:

> And other contact networks, which means that we get access to new groups, which allows us to produce new news. (R 4)

> Yes, last Monday, for instance, I wrote a story on labor migration, and then it was through [name of colleague with a minority background] that I got in contact with a man who knew a man who was undocumented. His story was, of course, important for me and, besides, this is a group [the undocumented] which is difficult to reach directly … I think this happens all the time, that you help one another with sources. (R 4)

> They didn't just have knowledge and experiences that we didn't have but also … to be admitted into [places] where we normally are not let into, that is also interesting … So this was something that sort of happened several times. (R 3)

> I believe that it [the presence of media workers with an ethnic minority background] has given the newsroom … more contacts in settings in which we, as typical Swedes … We haven't got such contacts, as you know … We have got much more diversity into the programs this way. (R 7)

The Different Set of Perspectives and Frameworks of Reference

The novelty and specificity of the minority media workers' contributions was also construed in terms of their ability to bring into newsroom work a different set of perspectives, ideas, frameworks of reference, angles of approach, and even different kinds of knowledge. This ability was also widely mentioned, and constitutes a dominant pattern in the interview material:

> Well, [they] have other experiences and thereby a different perspective on things. 'Have you thought [of this]? Haven't you thought [of that]?' … That's

157

why they are valuable as co-workers, because they come with a different perspective. (R 9)

I would probably say that they contribute with other approaches, other ways of seeing things ... other ideas, perhaps. (R 11)

Yes, you know, no doubt they contribute with knowledge of other cultures and other ways of thinking and suchlike ... we are white average Swedes, we haven't always got special knowledge of how other people think ... Why don't we think like this instead? (R 11)

The Different Experiences

Although less widely mentioned, the ethnic minority media workers' different range of experiences, as compared with those of their Swedish colleagues, was also viewed as a specific contribution. The different experiences as a specific contribution appeared as a frequent pattern. While only briefly mentioned by respondents 3, 4 and 5, it was discussed more extensively by other interviewees:

Within journalism we have become some kind of a white mass ... This is the way it works ... because everything goes so fast there, you rush to what you understand, what you know. And to [the places] where you know you'll find people you can talk to. This is what I feel, that it is so important to obtain [into the newsroom] experiences from everyone ... I mean, there are an awful lot of immigrants in Sweden, and here we are and haven't a clue. (R 7)

Yes, and naturally they come with their special experiences and that's why they are so important for the media. There is now a very conscious endeavor in [name of newspaper] to try and recruit people with other ethnic backgrounds, since it is good to have people with different experiences when you are to depict society. (R 9)

One of the people that I've worked with has only recently obtained a residence permit in Sweden, others have lived their whole lives in Sweden. I mean, it's a very big difference between background and experiences ... If you've been in the asylum process and then make a documentary about the asylum process, you definitely possess knowledge that no one else has, and perhaps it's not about foreign background but rather that you've been through the asylum process ... an experience that not all foreign journalists in Sweden have either. (R 2)

Minority media workers' different experiences are thus contrasted to Swedish journalists' lack of experience of specific social environments and groups, and are seen as a valuable resource for achieving the journalistic mission of representing all areas of society. However, the very connection between 'different experiences' and having an ethnic minority background was thrown into question by several interviewees (see below).

The Benefits of Minority Media Workers' Participation in the Newsroom Conversation

This subtheme appears as a less frequent pattern. Here the contributions are construed as not only influencing the ethnic minority media workers' own journalistic products, but also as having positive consequences for their colleagues and the news production process itself. Respondent 4 related the significance of these internal discussions to the journalistic mission of "catching what happens in society and making it relevant and interesting". Other respondents put it this way:

> Co-workers with immigrant backgrounds have played a significant part there, as prompters ... as a reminder for the others ... yes, sure, I see, there's also that perspective. So it's not only their work but also how they affect the whole group's way of thinking ... by comments at a lunch table and such things, you sit and talk and yeah, sure. (R 9)

> The advantage of having people with mixed backgrounds and mixed experiences is that you, perhaps one of the most important stages in journalism is the newsroom conversation, that you formulate your questions and decide on how you will go about things in the working party. So having an editorial staff with for instance a Muslim background or whatever, it's not only that it makes it easier to ask the right questions when you are in the field, but above all, that you can decide the right issue, the angle [of a story], in a dialogue, in a conversation where you go further and where you see new things. And where you understand how things are connected by just twisting and turning them from different starting points. (R 1)

Contributions Questioned and Qualified

Within this theme, the perceived contributions of ethnic minority media workers were questioned and qualified. The theme comprises three subthemes: questioning of the contributions: professionalism more important than ethnic background; qualification of the contributions: no necessary connection between contribution and ethnic background; and qualification of the contributions: contributions countered by newsroom routines. In the latter two, one finds a qualification of the contributions and their ability to make a difference in the final journalistic product.

Questioning of the Contributions: Professionalism More Important than Ethnic Background

The subtheme questioning of the contributions appears as a rare pattern, expressed as a negative response to the question of whether the respondent thought that the minority media workers contributed something novel or specific to the collective production work. This response did not acknowledge any specific or novel contribution: "They were recruited for their professional skills and not for their ethnic or other background" (R 6).

Qualification of the Contributions: No Necessary Connection Between Contribution and Ethnic Background

This qualification (a frequent pattern) destabilizes the connection between contributions and ethnic background per se. More concretely, it includes the expression of doubts by respondents 1, 2, 4, 5, 8, and 12 as to the generality of the contributions, i.e. it was emphasized that not all minority media workers were making these contributions all of the time. Respondent 8 stated for instance that "people with a foreign background *may* contribute with somewhat different perspectives" (my emphasis), and that minority media workers may be interested in diversity issues to different extents. Another respondent put it this way:

> You see, it's twofold, I don't actually think that it [the ethnic background per se] makes a difference journalistically ... In some cases, though, I think you contribute with other contacts, and other inputs, but it doesn't have to be like that, it doesn't have to be like that at all, but in some cases it's as if you contribute with a different perspective and other contacts, but that, of course, is quite a big difference. (R 2)

When asked about the potentially novel or specific contributions of ethnic minority media workers to the newsroom work, Respondent 1 answered that they probably make these contributions, and added:

> It is very difficult to separate the foreign background in particular from, for instance, having grown up in [a specific suburban environment] ... Foreign background per se does not imply a specific experience. Experience, one's own experience of immigration, of being a refugee, is indeed a highly relevant competence that is added ... The foreign or the ethnic is as you can understand absolutely impossible to distinguish and to say that it would constitute a specific quality.

...

> If one despite one's foreign background grew up in an academic middle class family, for instance, then the prospect of bringing an awful lot of new ideas [into the newsroom] is lower. (R 1)

With different degrees of explicitness, the three last quoted respondents thus detach contributions from ethnic background per se. In addition, respondents 1 and 2 make a distinction between ethnic background per se and the experience of certain social environments and groups, which they see as poorly covered by mainstream media. It is this experience, which minority media workers may or may not possess, that they regard as a journalistic asset.

Qualification of the Contributions: Contributions Countered by Newsroom Routines

This subtheme (a less frequent pattern) refers to the ability of the contributions to achieve a change, to make a real difference to the journalistic product, which was related to certain newsroom routines and the everyday work of today's journalism.

> And then it's not always the case that they [the minority media workers] gain a hearing for their ideas, and that's why I also think it's important that there are supervisors who can implement the whole thing. (R 5)

> I believe that there is a powerful normalizing process, in fact everything becomes kind of the same in a newsroom. (R 4)

> On the whole it's a question of production capacity, the newsroom of [newspaper] is so short-staffed, is so slim-lined that you cannot work there if you can't write fast ... So, of course, those who have a mainstream approach get rewarded, since you pretty much have to be competent in the way that's expected. It's difficult to be accepted if you have a very deviating way of working ... so in this way more immigrant journalists do not, it does not imply a change for the newsrooms. (R 9)

> We have purposely tried to employ temps with a different ethnic origin ... And thought that this would at least give us broader contact networks, other ideas and so on, but it appears all too often, in my view, that these temps ... they, of course, want to do their best ... and they adjust to the newsroom culture we have here ... from time immemorial and try to imitate those who work here already ... but there are many exceptions, there are indeed, that's why I say that they certainly contribute, but perhaps not quite as much as we had hoped. (R 11)

The construction of the ethnic minority media workers' contributions which the respondents, based on the experience of their own interplay with the former, make in the interviews is far from monolithic and robust. The ethnic minority media worker emerges as a subject who may make a number of factual and highly valued contributions, but who does not always and not necessarily do this. Ethnicity is viewed by some respondents as a potential source of the contributions that s/he may make, but not as a sufficient cause of these. Her or his ability to make an enduring and robust contribution is seen by some of the respondents as hampered by a series of routines within the actual communities of practice and the more general constraints of the media institutions (these routines and constraints are discussed in the sections below).

Also, in expressing their sense and qualifications of the specific contributions of ethnic minority media workers, the respondents constructed their *actual community of practice* as one which is made up of "typical", "white average Swedes", who for the most part lack contacts with other ethnic groups and access to their environments, as well as a knowledge of other groups' ways of thinking. These traits of the communities of practice were typically taken for granted, and the view that even media workers with a Swedish background may have these contacts and knowledge appeared as a rare pattern, which suggests an implicit understanding of what can be expected from majority and minority members, respectively. This community was also seen as locked into standardized working procedures and styles of writing, as well as the routine thinking derived from the criteria of news evaluation which prevails in overly homogeneous groups.

One can thus see that the distinctness of the contributions of ethnic minority media workers (their different networks, perspectives, experiences, etc.) that had been stressed in previous public debates is qualified in important respects by the interviewees. However, all of the respondents advocated the need to increase the number of ethnic minority media workers in their communities of practice. In the next section, I turn to how they argued for this.

The Arguments for Increased Ethnic Diversity in the Newsrooms

All interviewees stated that they were favorable to making their newsrooms more ethnically diverse, using arguments in which the (expected, but not always factual) contributions played an important role, even though they were further twisted and turned, and were also subsumed under more general journalistic and social values. The main argument (a dominant pattern in the interview material) was *the imperative of adequately and fully representing society*. A second argument emerging from the interview material (as a less frequent pattern) was: *increased ethnic diversity results in a better journalistic product*.

The main argument for increasing ethnic diversity in the newsrooms was formulated as a core value of the *imagined community of news production practice*: the journalistic imperative (worded, for instance, as a "duty", a "task" or a "mission") of adequately and fully (textually) representing or portraying society, Sweden, or the world.

The main argument would be that it [increased ethnic diversity in the newsroom] is necessary in order to be able to produce a relevant journalism in a society which is multicultural and marked by many different sorts of experiences in the recipient segment. Doing relevant and successful journalism is a matter of discovering the issues and the angles ... which actually hit the mark in regard to the interests of the expected receivers ... This is considerably more difficult to do when you have an old-fashioned, homogeneous all-Swedish newsroom. So you have to make sure that the newsroom in its experiences and frames of reference is in some way in contact with the Sweden you have around you. (R 1)

The basic argument is, I suppose, that if you want to portray a society, it is an advantage if you have representatives from different sectors of this society, both men and women, both young and old, both immigrants and native Swedes. (R 9)

Our mission is to mirror society and its development, and then you must of course also mirror it as an occupational group, you have to be a miniature society with all the sectors a society has if you are to mirror it in a good way. (R 10)

One could say that there is a democratic aspect to it, in some way it is our duty to give as complete a portrayal of the world and Sweden as possible. And we cannot do this if we haven't got a newsroom which is fairly representative, and by that I mean diversity in all respects, not just ethnic, but gender of course ... class... (R 11)

I use 'adequately' representing society here as an (analytical) overall designation for a series of necessary output qualities such as the variation of sources, perspectives, and angles that the respondents mentioned in their answers.

In the arguments for making the actual communities of practice more diverse, the respondents referred, more or less explicitly, to the increasingly multicultural character of society and the size of immigrant groups. And, related to this, the bulk of the argument was that all sectors of society, i.e. not only ethnic minority groups, must be represented in the newsrooms in order for these to fulfill the goal of fully and adequately portraying society in their journalistic output. It is worth mentioning here that Swedish journalists as an entire occupational group clearly align themselves with the principle of fair social representation: one finding of the encompassing statistical study *Den svenska journalistkåren* [The Swedish Journalists] was that some 90 percent of that group considered that "it is very or rather important that the make-up of the profession mirrors the population's make-up" (Djerf-Pierre 2007: 18, my translation). In arguing for an increased numerical/proportional representation of ethnic minority media workers, respondents did not posit that the former would 'represent' their respective groups in the sense of 'speaking for' them or furthering their interests. They rather suggested that the presence of minority journalists entailed a potential enlargement of the spectrum of knowledge, perspectives and experiences that would be available in newsrooms (cf. my discussion on the qualification of the contributions above).

The analysis thus shows that this support for the sheer proportional representation of social groups in the newsrooms does not tell the whole story: underlying the respondents' argument was also the notion that this democratic, fair representation of all groups has a potential bearing for the ability of their actual communities of practice to (textually) represent society in an adequate way. A few respondents used the mirror metaphor in their answers, while most others expressed a notion of (textual) representation which emphasized a multiplicity and variety of perspectives rather than a one-to-one correspondence with reality.

In discussing the second argument, increased ethnic diversity results in a better journalistic product, the respondents brought up, as can be seen in the quotes below and in the quote of respondent 1 above, the benefits of increased diversity for the journalistic product itself: better news stories, enhanced breadth, and new, fresh issues and angles. Importantly, interviewees also emphasized the enhanced relevance of the media products for the ethnic minority sectors of their audiences *as* part and parcel of the journalistic quality. And, although the weight placed on this relevance can at least in part derive from market calculations, it could be argued that the ethnic minority sectors of the audience are in any case treated like every other market sector.

> The crucial part is that it [the increased ethnic diversity in the newsroom] can contribute ... to the journalistic breadth. New angles. In short, that it results in a better newspaper ... It should enrich the journalistic product and of course the social life in a newsroom ... By extension it makes a paper more important to its readers. (R 5)

> It's important that the news gets better and that it, above all, interests more people. And besides, I think that diversity generates an interest of its own ... but it doesn't have to depend solely on what these people will contribute with as individuals. (R 8)

I think that the strongest argument by far ... in a way we have an obligation to represent Sweden as it appears ... And then with what you contribute, but each person contributes with his/her own thing ... but I think that if you mirror Sweden as it appears ... you would, in a way, still get further. But that people, the audience, feel at home, since it surely must be [a medium] that works for everyone and not just for those who belong to a certain segment of society. So that's what I would view as the best argument, and what people bring with them could be considered a bonus, it kind of varies from person to person and case to case. (R 2)

The core value of the imagined community of news production practice that was emphasized in the discussion of this second argument was *journalistic quality*, which in the respondents' utterances appeared as including both qualities of the textual product (e.g. breadth, freshness, novelty) and the ability of the product to be viewed as relevant by ethnic minority audiences.

The specificity and factuality of ethnic minority media workers' contributions to the actual communities of practice, which I dealt with in section 'Contributions questioned and qualified' above, were further reflected upon within the discussion of the arguments for increased diversity. For a few interviewees, the mention of the contributions constituted an important part of their line of argument, in combination with one or both of the arguments mentioned above. A few others, in contrast, either qualified or distanced themselves from the contributions *as* an adequate argument. Respondent 8 (see quote above), for instance, stated that the importance of diversity in the newsroom was not necessarily tied to specific individual contributions. Respondent 2 (see quote above) regarded the contributions as highly dependent on individuals' traits and abilities, and therefore as problematic to be assessed in group terms. For respondent 1 (see first quote of this section) it was the particular set of experiences and frames of reference that media workers of whatever ethnic belonging (including the Swedish) bring with them to the newsrooms, rather than ethnic belonging per se, which was important. Both respondents 1 and 12 criticized the contribution argument which has been advanced in e.g. public and media debate, as such, for being "superficial" and "shaped by simplistic thinking" (R 1) and on what one could label as strategic-professional grounds:

[The contributions] are not the best reason for recruiting. Because I believe that they should be recruited for their own merits ... Because if we only recruit them *because* they have contacts ... then they will be used only for this ... I mean that we must step over this threshold, that they come from over there and therefore they must cover only what they are familiar with. No other reporter works this way. In other words, there is still a sort of exoticism surrounding this [idea] that we should take them in because they have other perspectives. Sure, it will be OK to begin with, but one cannot leave it at that, because then they will only be assigned to cover immigrant issues. (R 12)

According to the two arguments found in the interview material, increased ethnic diversity in the newsrooms is necessary for producing a journalism which is able to represent (both in the make-up of the working place and textually), in consonance with, and relevant to, contemporary multicultural Sweden. The dominant argument for increased diversity, the imperative of fully and adequately representing society in media output, expresses a core value of the respondents' imagined community of news production practice. The argument draws support from the principle of fair social representation in the profession, a principle which was mentioned by respondents and also enjoys wide support from the journalistic occupational group as a whole. More diffusely, the argument is underpinned by the assumption that a more symmetric representation of social groups in the newsrooms has consequences for their ability to adequately and fully portray society.

The second argument, that increased ethnic diversity results in a better journalistic product, relates to another core value of the respondents' imagined community of practice, journalistic quality, which was specified in terms of textual qualities and their related capability of making the journalistic product relevant to a diverse audience.

The occurrence and specificity of the contributions of ethnic minority media workers were implicitly assumed by, and subsumed under both arguments. In the discussion of the arguments, as well as in the examples given in the previous section, the contributions as such by specific individuals in particular cases were not denied. However, they were explicitly and recurrently qualified by several respondents, and the qualifications concerned rather their ability to make a difference in the overall workings of the actual communities of practice, and the adequacy of using them as an argument for increased diversity, or of making too strong a connection between them and ethnicity per se.

Professional Routines

In discussing the everyday workings of their actual communities of practice, respondents dealt with a series of tensions between daily routines and the core values of the imagined community of practice. Two main factors were viewed as hampering diversity in both newsroom work and the journalistic outcome: time shortages and the standardization of reporting practices.

Time Shortages

The time shortages resulting from staff downsizing, budget cuts, etc. is an institutional constraint which was regarded by respondents as having great influence on reporting routines. This subtheme appears in the material as a frequent pattern.

Respondents saw time shortages as severely curtailing reporters' possibilities of going out to the suburbs to interview people and make reportages, since they also were expected to monitor the telegrams coming from news agencies during their watch. The lack of time also made it difficult for media workers to participate in meetings and seminars where diversity was brought up (R 2).

The intense working pace and the short time assigned to different production tasks also caused journalists to "rush to ... what you know. And to [the places] where you know you'll find people you can talk to" (R 7), and resulted in increasingly standardized journalistic products: "you have to write quickly ... so mainstream styles are rewarded" (R 9).

According to respondent 3, time shortages also play a role when it comes to the willingness of editors and managers to admit trainees into different sections of a larger newsroom, since doing so implies that the editor must take time to supervise them and appoint other reporters to mentor them.

The Standardization of Reporting Practices

The standardization of both newsroom work and the journalistic product as such appears as a less frequent pattern. Newsroom work was viewed as already so "chiseled" by managers (R 5), or as so patterned by newsrooms' "normalizing process" (R 4), that there was no maneuvering room left (R 5) which resulted in everything becoming the same (R 4). Respondent 9 believed that mainstream styles of journalistic work were rewarded due to the lack of time that characterizes today's newsroom work (see the preceding section). Another respondent related the size of the organization and the task of producing news around the clock to the pervasiveness of the standardization of routines:

> [Programme title] is the news machine which turns around the clock and is continuously producing ... [it is] rather traditional, it keeps on puffing and changes very slowly, I suppose, and not so daringly ... 'this is the way we have always worked' ... But we are trying to change this, we have internal processes ... everyone has participated in seminars about these issues and things have happened, we have changed our ways of working both with regard to routines and this can also be seen ... in our output.

The hindrance is rather this newsroom culture which lies within the walls in some way, 'this is the way we do [Programme title]' ... This is, I suppose, the way it is in such a large working place in some way, it is fixed. We are very happy when we see things which differ from this. (R 11)

Respondent 1 brought up more explicitly the routine thinking derived from prevalent news value assessments and overly homogeneous groups:

The worst and most damaging of all things within normal, pre-diversity jour-nalism is that there you have a bunch of people sitting on a couch ... and being all too similar, one has been socialized into a certain way of thinking about news evaluation, everyone has quite a similar social background, most have lived all their lives in Sweden, and therefore, obviously ... the mental activity becomes bad. You believe that you arrive at a good subject through discussion, but what happens in fact is that you are just reproducing things that everyone takes for granted, and it is not until you put together your group in another way that something happens, that you have the chance to do what you are supposed to do, namely to be curious, open and ready to change, so to speak, to see possibilities and perspectives. (R 1)

The above examples show how time shortages and standardization are sensed as challenges to practices oriented towards realizing the core value of fully and adequately representing society. For instance, not having time to search for new sources implies a continued reliance on routine sources, and the short time available for writing news stories increases the risk of keeping to the same old angles, issues, and styles. The tensions between core values and actual practices were negotiated by some respondents in various ways: they stated that they tapped into the networks of colleagues with another ethnic background, benefited from the newsroom discussions and the different perspectives that the latter brought to these, and a few of them either moved to another medium or managed to obtain separate funding which allowed them to temporarily leave everyday newsroom work and devote time to specific projects where they could put their ideas into practice.

Institutional Conditions

As actual communities of practice, the newsrooms are embedded in broader institutions, the media companies, whose overarching conditions, e.g. size, mission, profile, managerial style, and employment philosophy all affect in various ways the daily workings of the newsroom.

Two subthemes stood out within the overall theme dealing with the general institutional conditions of their companies that respondents regarded as hindrances to ethnic diversity in the newsrooms: the recruitment of media workers of another ethnic background and economic constraints.

The subtheme *recruitment of media workers of another ethnic background* appears as a dominant pattern. According to the interviewees, because of budget cuts the media companies have few or no permanent positions at all to offer, employment freezes are standard, and they only appoint substitutes, especially during the summer months (R 5, 7 and 8).

For a number of years, media workers of whatever background have had the possibility of obtaining a permanent position after having worked as substitutes for three years in the same company (R 11). This is in accordance with the Security of Employment Act (LAS), that all employers in Sweden are bound to follow.

Thus, the main chance for media workers to enter the market is to obtain a substitute position, perform well, give a good impression to their managers and either be called again the next time the company needs a substitute, or hold the substitute position for the magical three years. This benefits those who have already managed to get their foot into the market, but constitutes a problem for those who have not. As respondent 8 put it, the companies "recruit among other substitutes who have worked in similar [companies]". The reliance on recommendations and managers' previous knowledge of the applicants is also related to the chronic time shortages afflicting newsrooms:

> So on the one hand it would take more time to interview those who sought summer temporary work ... They often know who they would like to hire, people that they'd seen before and then recognized, safe bets, so to speak ... so of course it meant extra work if they were to interview a lot of new people who they neither recognized nor had any relation to. (R 3)

Some companies advertise their positions (R 11), while others do not: "we advertise seldom, it is rather informal" (R 8). And even when the companies advertise, they also tend to rely on "recommendations" of people who know the applicants from before when making appointment decisions:

> A company such as [name of company], which is an attractive employer, it's rather difficult, as soon as we advertise ... we receive an awful lot of applications, several hundred applications ... And because of that it's all too easy to go on recommendations. If you then mostly have white Swedes, it's hard to get recommendations [for ethnic minority media workers], considering we don't have that kind of contact network, so to speak. (R 10)

Both respondent 10 and 11 report that their companies use/used to clearly indicate in their ads that they strived for "gender equality and diversity" (R 10), or "a broad competence" and diversity as regards "knowledge of other languages and experiences" (R 11). The latter also noted that they used to have their ads "in other newspapers, such as *Metro* [a free sheet]" (R 11) as a way of broadening their recruitment basis.

However, this wording in the ads seem to weight lightly when the companies rely on recommendations or the managers' impressions/previous knowledge of the applicants as they make their appointment decisions.

Media companies are increasingly moving towards an overall staff structure with few permanent employees and many freelancers, consultants and fixed term contracts: "You want to have as small a permanent [work force] core as possible" (R 10). This respondent sees the current labor legislation as a hindrance to the recruitment of ethnic minority media workers, and regards appointments for lengthy projects as a potential solution.

Another company has begun using the services of a manpower firm to recruit substitutes in order not to be bound to follow LAS (R 11). This firm selects and sends a number of CVs to the media company:

> But in practice we make the choice, these are the ones we consider interesting. Many of them have already previously worked here as substitutes, and will gain access that way instead. But it has led to a state where we couldn't actively search for new talents, as we don't know where to find them. They haven't approached us and asked if there are any jobs ... so we have continued using our old substitutes to a great extent. Which has been a drawback since this issue of diversity then, we have had to put it aside a bit this year. Then there are several here, with a different ethnic background, working this summer anyway. (R 11)

Several respondents stressed the possession of high journalistic skills and previously demonstrated good performance. For respondent 10, this has become increasingly important because of the low degree of mobility in the company: since almost no one quits and there are few permanent positions to offer, those who are employed must have "the best competence" (R 10). For respondent 6, the main criteria to follow was good previous performance (rather than letting ethnic background influence recruitment decisions) since "we have to do as much as possible in so short time as possible". Another respondent located the problem in the shortage of competent journalists:

> I believe that one problem is that we're rather short of very good journalists with non-Swedish backgrounds, we're short of very good journalists on the whole, many are being educated but ... I don't think that there are any im-

mediate prejudices, no, [such as] we can't recruit that person because he or she isn't an ethnic Swede. (R 9)

Respondent 12 referred to a particular case in which a newsroom declined to keep a reporter whom they had previously appointed on a non-permanent basis. This interviewee does not quite believe the reasons which were given, and thinks that the managers mistrusted the ability of the reporter to cover certain events in an objective way because of the reporter's ethnic background. This respondent sees the decision of the managers as an expression of a type of cultural scale which ranks and attributes different degrees of credibility to people coming from different parts of the world.

This was the only example of mistrust in the ability of ethnic minority media workers to be objective which appeared in the interview material.

Thus, structural features of the media companies, the current labor legislation, the budget cuts, and applicants' lack of previous work experience and high journalistic skills all appear as factors which the respondents perceive as contributing to the current standstill in the recruitment of media workers with an ethnic minority background.

A potential way out of the recruitment standstill, especially as regards ethnic minority media workers without previous work experience, was sketched by one respondent, who emphasized the need of flexibility with regard to the work experience requirement and the widening of the range of journalism schools which are given priority at the moment of selecting students on practice placements:

> To go for young, interested people and maybe accept someone with less experience, give them an internship, to lower the thresholds if you go for people who are talented, but might lack experience ... be some kind of nursery, and think a bit differently when recruiting. It isn't that there aren't any people with immigrant background in the institutes of journalism ... if one then chooses ... [a university college] and not the university, then you're also more likely to get someone in with immigrant background. (R 8)

The subtheme *economic constraints* appears explicitly as a less frequent pattern. However, the companies' economic situation and budget cuts underlie both the structural changes and the more specific employment decisions and newsroom routines that the respondents brought up, no matter the degree of explicitness to which 'economics' is dealt with in the interview material. One respondent referred to the precarious economic situation of the company as a sort of chronic state: "We have had a bad economic situation forever, actually. So there has never been any money for anything" (R 9).

For respondent 5, the precarious current economic situation of media companies, especially newspaper companies, affects their ability to be more diverse:

Right now, unfortunately, we have to deal with the economic boundaries, and because of that it is probably only the large companies which will be able to sufficiently go in for really implementing their diversity policies. (R 5)

The employment of ethnic minority journalists was to a great extent seen as a matter of cost, which it clearly (although not exclusively) is, and alternatives such as prioritizing their appointment within the framework of current budgets, or the argument that they also could bring a profit in the form of an expanded market, did not appear in the context of this discussion.

Fixed economic bounds and the de-prioritization of diversity goals influenced decisions on diversity projects. A respondent who worked with several projects in a company reported that one of these was funded by an external actor. But when this interviewee wanted to go on working to increase diversity in the newsroom, the managers did not want to invest company money in this:

I didn't want to do another project because I didn't think it should be a project any longer, but rather that they had to employ people [media workers with a minority background] now on a temporary post ... because the departmental managers said 'we'd love to accept immigrants, but we don't want to hire them or pay them any money, if we get some extra money to do so, it'll be alright' ... and I thought that that was wrong. (R 3)

The respondents singled out two main institutional conditions hindering the achievement of increased diversity in the newsrooms: recruitment and economic constraints. Budget cuts, staff downsizing, the current labor legislation, the usual reliance on managers' recommendations of applicants regarded as 'sure bets' (as a way of saving the time it would take to interview new applicants), and lack of high journalistic skills appeared as factors perceived as contributing to the current standstill in the recruitment of media workers of another ethnic background.

The thrust towards hiring people whom managers know and whom they know they have worked well with before is nothing new in the media world. In an analysis of the American television industry, this phenomenon, "hiring people you are familiar with and trust" (Downing & Husband 2005: 163) is labeled by the authors as 'cronyism' and regarded as contributing a considerable share to the reproduction of the ethnic asymmetry of the industry. For employers, cronyism works as a sort of guarantee that the appointed professionals will work well and effectively, which is badly needed in the context of a fiercely competitive industrial environment (Downing & Husband 2005). Although cronyism negatively affects several different social groups, e.g. young media workers (of whatever ethnicity) lacking professional experience, it is clear that ethnic minority media workers will especially suffer from it.

The economic constraints were viewed as pervasive and as hindering the recruitment of ethnic minority media workers and preventing companies from implementing their diversity policies and investing in specific diversity initiatives. For the most part these perceived hindrances were rather taken for granted than scrutinized, which begs the question as to the extent to which the respondents were reproducing an overall institutional discourse when explaining the reasons for the recruitment standstill and the slow progress of diversity efforts.

The tensions between the core values of the imagined community of practice and the factual institutional constraints were mostly negotiated by respondents in relatively abstract terms. They noted, for instance, the growing awareness of the need for more diversity among company managers, as well as the increasing acknowledgement of the contributions of ethnic minority media workers. The respondents saw, though, a problem in the lack of continuity in the companies' diversity efforts (see Camauër forthcoming for a more detailed discussion of this theme).

Conclusion

Based on the experience of their interaction with media workers of a different ethnic background, the Swedish journalists and managers interviewed in this study identified a number of specific contributions made by the former to the overall newsroom work: their different range of networks, frameworks of reference and experiences, and the benefits of minority media workers' participation in the newsroom conversation. The contributions were recognized and highly valued, but rather than reified, they were qualified by respondents on two main grounds. On the one hand, ethnicity per se was sensed as a potential, but not sufficient, cause of the contributions, i.e., they stated that ethnic minority media workers do not always and/or not necessarily contribute this way, and that in many cases the possession of specific experiences plays a more decisive role. On the other hand, the ability of the contributions to make a difference in newsroom work was perceived as being hampered by the pervasive routines and working conditions of the actual communities of practice (e.g. time shortages, ingrained news evaluation criteria, and standardized styles of framing and writing stories). On the whole, time shortages, the standardization of newsroom work, and more general institutional factors such as employment philosophies, recruitment practices, and economic constraints were singled out by respondents as hindering increased diversity in the newsrooms.

In spite of these qualifications of the contributions, all respondents advocated an increased ethnic diversity in the newsrooms. In doing so, they drew on two arguments: on the one hand, most respondents expressed a sense of a "mission" or a "duty" to fully and adequately represent society, Sweden, or the world. They thus both related to a crucial value of their imagined community of practice and aligned themselves with the tenet of symmetric representation of all social groups in the journalistic profession, a tenet which, as we know from previous research (Djerf-Pierre 2007), is widely supported by journalists. On the other hand, a few respondents sensed that increased ethnic diversity in the newsrooms results in a better journalistic product. Underlying both arguments was an implicit assumption concerning the (qualified) occurrence and specificity of ethnic minority media workers' contributions.

The above-summarized findings suggest a series of contradictions at a deeper level. For instance, if the professional routines are so deeply anchored, they could on the one hand serve as an argument for hiring more media workers with an ethnic minority background (e.g. the latter can provide the contacts and different perspectives that Swedish journalists do not have the time to acquire and develop). On the other hand, though, *because* they are so profoundly ingrained, these same routines are attributed the power to erase the distinctness of the contributions of ethnic minority media workers, which in turn means that employing more of them would not yield any change.

In a similar manner, respondents appeared to be aware of the hindrances to increased diversity that ingrained professional routines and institutional constraints constitute, while at the same time taking them for granted. The analysis of the interviews shows that on the whole, they saw few ways out from the status quo. This can be seen by considering how respondents handled the experienced tensions between crucial journalistic values (the imagined community of practice) and factual institutional conditions (the actual community), in practice and discursively. In practice, contradictions were solved through either tapping into the resources provided by their ethnic minority colleagues, temporarily escaping into special projects, or by moving to media outside the mainstream. The problem here is that as long as the number of media workers of other ethnic backgrounds remains low, the available resources to tap into will be equally scarce. The two other solutions, working with specific diversity projects or leaving mainstream media, suggest that in respondents' views nothing can be done to improve the situation in mainstream media.

At the discursive level, tensions were dealt with mostly in abstract ways, for instance by referring to managers' growing awareness of the benefits of ethnic diversity in the newsrooms. At the same time, however, the lack of continuity of the companies' diversity work was seen as one of the causes of the slow progress achieved over time.

Respondents characterized their newsrooms as mainly populated by "typical", or "white average Swedes". Although this was seen as a problem, media workers with a Swedish background were with a few exceptions implicitly construed as lacking the necessary knowledge, networks, and insights into ethnic minority groups for achieving a more diverse journalism. This contributes to normalizing a sort of peculiar exception to the expectations that otherwise are placed on media workers in general: that they will have or acquire the necessary contacts and knowledge for fulfilling their routine tasks, no matter the subject they are assigned to cover.

Broadly speaking, my findings as to the perceived hindrances for diversity in both newsrooms and journalistic output are in consonance with results of a recent survey of Swedish media companies (see Appendix in this volume). They also resonate with the point made by Campion (2005) on the lack of continuity of companies' diversity efforts as several respondents stressed that the commitment to diversity work varied greatly among senior managers and over time.

Previous research has identified a number of components of effective and robust policies and efforts against racism and for more diversity in the media. Downing & Husband stress the significance of "explicit, unambiguous and measurable" (2005: 180) aims for media workers' practice, "institutionally supported positive rewards for relevant improvement, and negative sanctions for failure" (2005: 182), a point also made by Campion (2005), and a realistic allocation of resources. Without the latter, diversity work "has all the sincerity of children making promises with their fingers crossed" (Downing & Husband 2005: 181). These components are for the most part absent from the diversity policies (whether in writing or not) of the Stockholm media companies that the respondents of this study worked for.

A majority of the diversity managers of Swedish news media companies who participated in the survey conducted within the framework of this project were of the view that diversity efforts have a beneficial impact on companies' business and good will (see Appendix in this volume). Translated into more crude political economy terms, this points to what Titley calls "the commodity value of difference in consumer societies" (2009: 160).

In a situation where diversity policies are overly general and usually lack mechanisms for accountability, and where the implementation of the policies remains intermittent (see Camauër forthcoming) and limited by the companies' actually existing economic constraints, competitive pressures and employment philosophies, together with the newsrooms' pervasive professional routines, one can only assume that the commodity value of both policies and efforts will remain high, while the ways of getting around currently existing barriers to ever-increased diversity are still to be imagined.

References

Anderson, B. (2006/1983) *Imagined communities: Reflections on the origin and spread of nationalism.* London: Verso.

Arnstberg, K.O. (2008) *Sverige och invandringen* [Sweden and immigration]. Lund: Studentlitteratur.

Barth, F. (1994/69) 'Introduction', in Barth, F. (ed.) *Ethnic groups and boundaries: The social organization of culture difference.* Oslo: Pensumtjenstene/ Universitetsforlaget.

Brune, Y. (2004) *Nyheter från gränsen. Tre studier i journalistik om "invandrare", flyktingar och rasistiskt våld* [News from the border. Three studies on journalism on "immigrants", refugees and racial violence]. Göteborg: Institutionen för journalistik och masskommunikation, Göteborgs universitet.

Burkitt, I. et al. (2001) *Nurse education and communities of practice.* London: The English National Board for Nursing, Midwifery and Health Visiting.

Camauër, L. (2006) 'Mediearbetare med utländsk bakgrund och majoritetsmediers diskriminerings-mekanismer' [Media workers with a minority background and the discrimination mechanisms of majority media], in Camauër, L. & Nohrstedt, S.A. (eds.) *Mediernas vi och dom. Mediernas betydelse för den strukturella diskrimineringen* [The media's us and them. The role of the media in structural discrimination]. SOU 2006:21.

Camauër, L. (forthcoming) 'Drumming, drumming, drumming. Diversity work in Swedish newsrooms', in Eide, E. & Nikunen, K. (eds.) *Media in motion: Cultural complexity and migration in the Nordic region.* Farnham: Ashgate.

Campion, M.J. (2005) *Look who's talking: Cultural diversity, public service broadcasting and the national conversation.* Oxford: Nuffield College, www.nuff.ox.ac.uk/guardian/lookwhostalking.pdf, retrieved 2010 01 09.

Chakravartty, P. & Sarikakis, K. (2006) *Media policy and globalization.* Edinburgh: Edinburgh University Press.

Cottle, S. (2000) 'Introduction. Media research and ethnic minorities: mapping the field', in Cottle, S. (ed.) *Ethnic minorities and the media.* Buckingham: Open University Press.

Djerf-Pierre, M. (2007) 'Journalisternas sociala bakgrund' [Journalists' social background], in Asp, K. (ed.) *Den svenska journalistkåren* [The Swedish journalists]. Göteborg: Institutionen för journalistik och masskommunikation, Göteborgs universitet.

Djerf-Pierre, M. & Levin, A. (2005) 'Mediefältets janusansikte: medieeliten, journalisterna och mångfalden' [The Janus face of the media field: the media élite, the journalists and diversity], in *Makten och mångfalden. Eliter och etnicitet i Sverige* [Power and diversity. Elites and ethnicity in Sweden]. Rapport från Integrationspolitiska maktutredningens forskningsprogram. Ds 2005:12. Stockholm: Justitiedepartmentet.

Downing, J. & Husband, C. (2005) *Representing 'race': Racisms, ethnicities and media.* London: Sage.

Edström, M. & Nordberg, K. (2005) 'Det villkorade medierummet. En diskussion om genrer, makt och mångfald' [The conditioned media room. A discussion on genres, power and diversity], in *Makten och mångfalden. Eliter och etnicitet i Sverige* [Power and diversity. Elites and ethnicity in Sweden]. Rapport från Integrationspolitiska maktutredningens forskningsprogram. Ds 2005: 12. Stockholm: Justitiedepartementet.

Eriksen, T.H. (1998/93) *Etnicitet och nationalism* [Ethnicity and nationalism]. Nora: Nya Doxa.

Hadenius, S., Weibull, L. & Wadbring, I. (2008) *Massmedier. Press, radio och tv i den digitala tidsåldern* [Mass media. Press, radio and tv in the digital age]. Stockholm: Ekerlids Förlag.

Horsti, K. (2008) 'Overview of Nordic media research on immigration and ethnic relations: From text analysis to the study of production, uses and reception', *Nordicom Review* 2: 275-293.

Husband, C. (2005) 'Minority ethnic media as communities of practice: professionalism and identity politics in interaction', *Journal of Ethnic and Migration Studies* 31(3): 461-479.

Lave, J. & Wenger, E. (1991) *Situated learning: Legitimate peripheral participation.* Cambridge: Cambridge University Press.

Nygren, G. (2008) *Nyhetsfabriken. Journalistiska yrkesroller i en förändrad medievärld* [The news factory: Journalistic professional roles in a changed media world]. Lund: Studentlitteratur.

SOU 2005:56. *Det blågula glashuset – strukturell diskriminering i Sverige* [The blue-yellow glass house – structural discrimination in Sweden]. Swedish Government Official Report on discrimination on grounds of ethnic and religious belonging.

Titley, G. (2009) 'Pleasing the crisis: Anxiety and recited multiculturalism in the European communicative space', in Salovaara-Moring, I. (ed.) *Manufacturing Europe: Spaces of democracy, diversity and communication*. Göteborg: Nordicom.

Ålund, A. (2002) *The spectre of ethnicity*. Norrköping: MERGE.

Appendix

Swedish Media Companies on Diversity Survey, June 2008

Project: "Lines of Diversity: Multicultural Perspectives on Journalistic Production"

Södertörn University

Summary

- The concept of diversity is very strongly associated with ethnic background and gender.

- Almost 9 out of 10 of the approached news medias state that it is important or very important to actively work with diversity issues and that the company benefits from diversity work.

- About half of the media companies have a diversity plan set down in writing, but the proportion varies between different media types.

- About 7 out of 10 news medias believe that the diversity work improves the company's competitiveness and gives it a good reputation.

- Media companies with a diversity plan consider that diversity creates a better working climate and journalistic result to a higher degree, as well as making it easier to meet the audience's needs.

- The factors that the media companies state obstruct the diversity work most are economic reasons, employment freeze, and difficulties in recruiting.

- Half of the news companies report that 5 percent or less of the employees have a foreign background. Of these, 16 percent state that they have no employees with a foreign background.

Sample and Method

Target group: People responsible for diversity issues in small, medium and major News Media Companies with a geographical distribution in Sweden

Selection: Register from InfoData/Basun Interview method: Telephone interviews Period of investigation: May 22 - June 9, 2008 Completed interviews: 103 Percentage of answers: 64 percent

What does the concept of diversity mean to you?

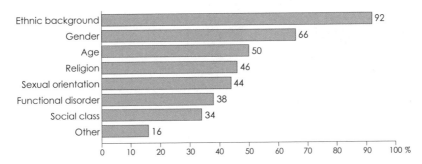

The concept of diversity is above all linked to ethnicity and gender and to a lesser degree to age, religion, sexual orientation, functional disorder and social class.

What does the concept of diversity mean to you? (Other answers)

- To mirror diversity in society
- To address all different listeners
- To talk about things that occur in many different groups
- Various types of businesses
- Democracy
- Various experiences
- To be able to choose between two newspapers, for example

How important do you consider it to be to actively work with diversity issues in media companies?

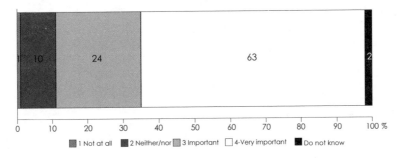

Almost 9 out of 10 of the approached news medias state that it is important or very important to actively work with diversity issues.

Has your company a written plan for how one should work on diversity?

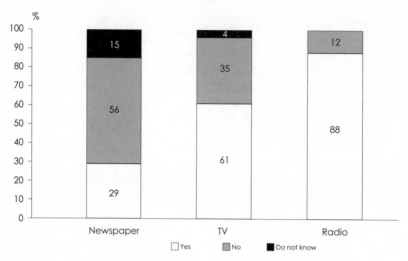

Newspapers have a diversity plan set down in writing to a much lesser degree than TV and radio. Newspapers also value the benefits of diversity work less than radio and TV

Is the diversity plan a part of the gender equality plan?

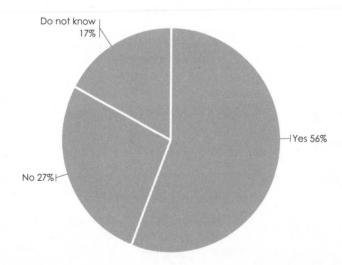

Of all the companies, 52 percent have a diversity plan set down in writing. Of these the diversity plan is included in the gender equality plan in about half, or 56 percent, of the cases.

To what degree do you consider that the company could benefit from diversity work?

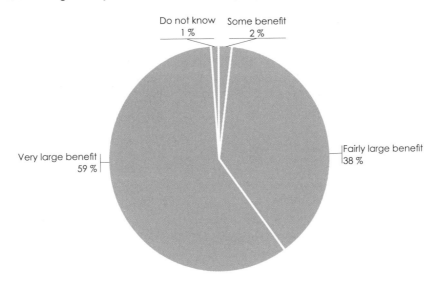

Almost 6 out of 10 news medias state that the company could benefit greatly from diversity work and almost 4 out of 10 consider that the benefit is considerable.

Ratio that completely agrees that diversity promotes/improves:

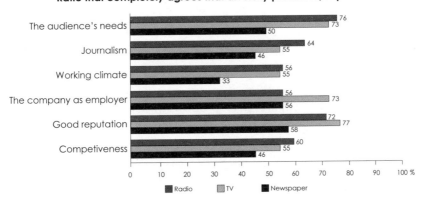

The newspaper companies generally value diversity work less than radio and TV.

To what degree do you consider that the management allocates resources to pursue diversity work?

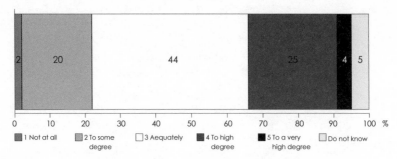

Almost every third company experiences that the management allocates resources to diversity work to a high or a very high degree.

Do you experience any obstacles in pursuing diversity work at your company?

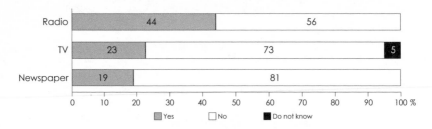

The radio companies experience that there are obstacles in pursuing diversity work to a higher degree than other companies.

Do you experience any obstacles in pursuing diversity work at your company? (What obstacles? Open answers)

- Economic obstacles. Recruitment freeze.
- An almost non-existent staff turnover, homogenous working teams.
- Difficulties in recruiting people.
- A clear strategy is needed; it might exist centrally, but not locally with us.
- Old structures and hierarchies that do not let new people in.
- Our own attitudes.
- The people in key positions might not be sufficiently aware, in other words, we ourselves could be an obstacle.

Do you experience that there are any disadvantages with diversity work?

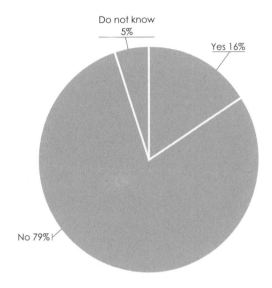

Of the approached companies, 8 out of 10 consider that there are no disadvantages with diversity work. The most common comment among those who consider that there are disadvantages is that it is time-consuming and resource-demanding.

What position do you hold?

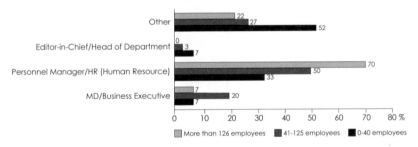

The person responsible for diversity issues at the media companies is also responsible for staff and HR related issues in most cases, with the exception of the small companies. The diversity responsibility at these companies can, for instance, lie in the hands of the news director, channel manager, or financial controller.

How many of the office employees do you estimate have a foreign background, i.e., are foreign-born or have two foreign-born parents?

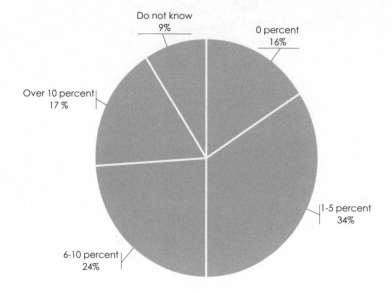

Half of the news companies report that 5 percent or less of their staff has a foreign background. A quarter estimated the share to be between 6 and 10 percent. Almost 2 out of 10 stated the share to be more than 10 percent. Every tenth company did not know.

Questionnaire

Questionnaire to News Media Companies on diversity May 2008

Hello, my name is NN and I am calling from the research institute Proves Research. I would like to talk to the person responsible for staff and HR issues at your company.

At the moment, we are conducting a survey on diversity within media companies by the order of a research project at Sodertörn University on newsroom diversity in Swedish news medias.

To be on the safe side, I would like to emphasize that I am not selling anything, but wonder if you could be so kind and answer a few easy questions, which will take about 4 minutes. Your answers are, of course, anonymous and you will receive a report with the results of the survey when it has been completed. Would that be ok?

(1) Yes, proceed

(2) No, unable to do it at the moment, book a new time and finish

(3) No, do no t want to participate - finish

1. **What does the concept of diversity mean to you? SPONTANEOUS ANSWERS, multiple answers can be marked**

(1) Gender

(2) Ethnic background

(3) Age

(4) Sexual orientation

(5) Religion

(6) Social class

(7) Functional disorder

(8) Other responses, namely:_____ To be coded

(9) Do not know

2. **How important do you consider it to be to actively work on diversity issues in media companies?**
    Mark on a scale from 1-5, where 1 = Not at all important, and 5 = Very important on all levels and for all employees

(1) Not at all important

(2)

(3) Neither/nor

(4)

(5) Very important

(6) Do not know

3. **Has your company a written plan for how one should work on diversity?**

(1) Yes

(2) No

(3) Do not know

4. **Is the diversity plan a part of the gender equality plan?**

(1) Yes

(2) No

(3) Do not know

5. **To what degree do you consider that the company could benefit from diversity work? Mark on a scale from 1-5, where 1 = No real benefit, and 5 = great benefit**

(1) No real benefit

(2) Some (fairly small) benefit

(3) Fairly large benefit

(4) Very large benefit

(5) Do not know

6. MATRIX
   I will now read 6 statements about how you might think that diversity work could affect your company.
   For each and every question, mark on a scale divided into five degrees how much you agree, ranging from 1= Do not agree at all, to 5= Agree completely

1. Diversity work can improve the companies competitiveness   12345 (6=Do not know/cannot judge)

2. Diversity work gives the company a good reputation   12345 (6=Do not know/cannot judge)

3. Diversity work strengthens the company as an attractive employer   12345 (6=Do not know/cannot judge)

4. Diversity work contributes to creating a better working climate   12345 (6=Do not know/cannot judge)

5. Diversity work contributes to better journalistic results   12345 (6=Do not know/cannot judge)

6. Diversity work contributes to a better understanding of the audience's needs   12345 (6=Do not know/cannot judge)

7. **To what degree do you experience that the management allocates resources to pursue diversity work?**

(1) Not at all

(2)

(3) Adequately

(4)

(5) Very high degree

(6) Do not know

(2) No

(3) Do not know

8. **Do you experience any obstacles in pursuing diversity work at your company?**

(1) Yes

(2) No

(3) Do not know

Filter Q8:1
7. **What kind of obstacles?**

Open answer. To be coded

9. **Do you experience that there are any disadvantages with diversity work?**

(1) Yes

(2) No

(3) Do not know

Filter Q9:1
9. **What disadvantages?**

Open answer. To be coded

10. How many of the office employees do you estimate have a foreign background, e.g., are foreign-born or have two foreign-born parents?

Open answer. To be coded (shown in % together with the approximate number of employees, as well as a definition of the place of work, e.g. **"20 % out of approx. 30 people employed at the newsroom"**)

11. What position do you hold?

(1) MD/Business Executive

(2) Personnel Manager/HR (Human Resource)

(3) Editor-in-Chief/ Head of Department

(4) Other, namely:_____ Open answer. To be coded

12. Can we get back to you by e-mail if we need any complementary information?

(1) Yes

(2) No

(3) Do not know

Filter Q12:1

13. What is your e-mail address?

Open answer

Thank you for your participation!

For further information on the research project, contact lecturer Heike Graf, project leader, (heike. graf@sh.se) or lecturer Gunilla Hultén (gunilla.hulten@sh.se) at Södertorn University.

The Authors

LEONOR CAMAUÈR is Associate Professor at the School of Humanities, Education and Social Sciences, Örebro University, SE-701 82 Örebro (leonor.camauer@oru.se). Her research interests include minority media production, the inclusion of minorities in main stream media production, the discursive construction of 'cultural difference' in main stream media output, and the Swedish cartoon controversy. She is currently involved in an EU funded research program which investigates television use by Arabic-speakers in seven European countries. She was also one of the initiators of the Nordic Research Network Media, Migration and Society.

HEIKE GRAF is Associate Professor at the School of Culture and Communication, Södertörn University, SE-141 89 Huddinge (heike.graf@sh.se). Her recent research has included research on intercultural communication, as well as newsrooms studies according to ethnic diversity. Among her publications is a study on mainstream media's coverage of minority media (*How do mainstream media communicate minority media?*, 2009).

GUNILLA HULTÉN is Research Fellow at the Department of Journalism, Media and Communication, Stockholm University, Box 27 861, SE-115 93 Stockholm (hulten@jmk.su.se) and Assistant Professor of Journalism at Södertörn University, SE-141 89 Huddinge. Her current research involves diversity and newsroom cultures, and diversity media policy making in Swedish public service broadcasting companies.

JAN INGE JÖNHILL is Associate Professor of Sociology at the School of Humanities, Education and Social Sciences, Örebro University, SE-701 82 Örebro (jan.i.jonhill@oru.se), and researcher at the School of Culture and Communication, Södertörn University. In his dissertation and other publications in the 1990s he has introduced sociological systems theory (as developed by Niklas Luhmann) in Sweden. His recent research includes issues of ethnic and national diversity and diversity management in media and communication from a perspective of systems theory and organizational sociology. His recent publications include a book on inclusion and exclusion as a general distinction in society and on issues of diversity (*Inclusion and Exclusion. A Distinction that makes a Distinction in the Multi-cultural Society*, forthcoming 2011; will be published in Swedish at Liber Publishers, Malmö).